D1037520

Neuroscience and the Soul

The Human Person in Philosophy, Science, and Theology

Edited by

Thomas M. Crisp, Steven L. Porter & Gregg A. Ten Elshof

William B. Eerdmans Publishing Company
Grand Rapids, Michigan

Wm. B. Eerdmans Publishing Co.
2140 Oak Industrial Drive N.E., Grand Rapids, Michigan 49505
www.eerdmans.com

Published 2016
Printed in the United States of America

22 21 20 19 18 17   2 3 4 5 6 7

ISBN 978-0-8028-7450-4

Library of Congress Cataloging-in-Publication Data

Names: Crisp, Thomas M., editor. | Porter, Steven L., 1970– editor. | Ten Elshof, Gregg, 1970– editor.

Title: Neuroscience and the soul : the human person in philosophy, science, and theology / edited by Thomas M. Crisp, Steven L. Porter & Gregg A. Ten Elshof.

Description: Grand Rapids, Michigan : William B. Eerdmans Publishing Company, [2016] | Includes bibliographical references.

Identifiers: LCCN 2016024697 | ISBN 9780802874504 (pbk. : alk. paper)

Subjects: LCSH: Mind and body—Religious aspects—Christianity. | Theological anthropology—Christianity. | Human beings. | Persons. | Neurosciences. | Soul.

Classification: LCC BT741.3 .N48 2016 | DDC 128/.1—dc23
LC record available at https://lccn.loc.gov/2016024697

Contents

PART 2
Recent Debate about the Bearing of Contemporary Brain Sciences on the Mind-Body Problem

PART 3
Recent Debate in Theology about the Mind-Body Problem

Introduction

It is utterly common among religious and non-religious people alike to think of the human person as having two parts: a material part, the body, and a spiritual or non-material part, the soul. The body is corruptible, decays, and eventually dies, but the souls lives on, enabling personal survival beyond the death of the body. Religious and philosophical traditions differ among themselves about the post-mortem career of the soul: some say it will be reunited with a body in an eschatological resurrection, others that it will dissolve into everlasting unity with the Divine, others that it will be reincarnated many times, others holding different views yet. There is considerable diversity in how we think about the soul and its destiny, but that we have souls, spiritual or non-material parts of us that are distinct from our bodies and capable of surviving the death of our bodies, is a perennial and widespread human conviction.

It has become commonplace among educated denizens of the contemporary scene, however, to think that traditional belief in the soul has been debunked by the discoveries of modern neuroscience and related fields. Partly motivated by advances in the brain sciences but for other reasons as well, Christian thinkers in increasing numbers have been exploring and defending alternative ways of thinking about the human person, ways of thinking that do not involve belief in immaterial souls. Other Christian thinkers, many of them prominent and able scholars apprised of the deliverances of the brain sciences, maintain that traditional belief on these topics is as warranted as ever, and have developed a variety of arguments to show as much.

During the fall and spring semesters of the 2012–2013 academic year, the Biola University Center for Christian Thought gathered an interdisciplinary group of philosophers, theologians, and scientists from around the country to discuss these topics. Our goal was to facilitate a conversation among leading representatives of divergent perspectives on the question of how to think about the soul.

Some were traditional "substantive dualists" (believers in the traditional body-soul dichotomy), others were "Christian physicalists" (adherents of traditional Christianity who hold that we humans are entirely made up of material stuff and have no non-material soul or spirit), and some held other views besides. We hosted weekly, often lively, discussions at our Center's "roundtable" and concluded the year with a conference at Biola University in May of 2013. This volume comprises several essays from that conference (and several that were recruited to the project later).

Our goal in collecting these essays together is twofold. First, we think they will be of interest and of help to specialists on these topics. The dialogical format of the volume sheds light on nuances of the discussion not easily revealed by other formats of presentation. Secondly, we hope to give the non-specialist a window into the debates going on among Christian thinkers about these topics. There are able scholars on various sides of the issue and vigorous discussions happening in the pages of academic books and journals. It is difficult, though, for the outsider to get anything but a cursory sense of the nature of the back-and-forth of this debate without wading thoroughly into the literature. One can read what this or that specialist has written for or against traditional belief in the soul, but one must then be prepared to delve into the literature to find what competent critics have said in response and what the specialist in question has said in reply.

This volume aims to remedy that difficulty, and is different than any other volume in the literature we are aware of, in that it samples recent work among leading philosophers and theologians on the existence of the soul—some arguing for, others arguing against—and then puts those scholars into conversation with leading critics of their views. The goal is to give thoughtful non-specialists a high-level introduction to what leading Christian thinkers are saying for and against the existence of the soul, how they are interacting with the deliverances of recent brain science, and how they are responding to one another. All essays were commissioned for the volume[1] and represent state-of-the-art treatment of the topic.

Chapter 1, "Do My Quarks Enjoy Beethoven?," by philosopher William Hasker, is an exploration of a doctrine he calls *material composition*, the the-

1. Though two of the essays, Swinburne's and Kärkkäinen's, are versions of earlier essays.

sis that human beings and other sentient organisms consist of physical stuff and nothing else. At the heart of the essay is a discussion and defense of the so-called "unity-of-consciousness" argument against material composition, defended in various versions over the years by Descartes, Leibniz, Kant, and more recently, Daniel Barnett, Eric LaRock, and in previous writings, Hasker himself. Roughly stated, the argument purports that the subject of conscious mental experience—the self or center-of-consciousness *having* the experience—cannot be a composite material object like a brain or a human organism. Our conscious experiences come to us as highly *unified*: the various colors spread across one's visual field at any given time come to one as part of a single, comprehensive, visual experience, and not as so many separate experiences. It is clear on reflection, though, say friends of the unity-of-consciousness argument, that this unity cannot be accounted for by the properties or interrelatedness of the various parts of one's brain or body. For how would it work? Is having a conscious experience a matter of the parts of one's brain having *parts* of that conscious experience? That can't be, for several things having their own conscious experience don't add up to a single thing's having one, unified conscious experience. Hasker explores other possibilities, arguing that each is equally far-fetched and thus that the material composition thesis cannot account for the unity-of-consciousness experience. Whatever you—the subject of *your* conscious experiences—are, you are not materially composed, and indeed, not a composite object of any kind: you are an ontologically simple thing. A clear implication, says Hasker, is substance dualism.

In Chapter 2, "Materially-Composed Persons and the Unity of Consciousness: A Reply to Hasker," philosopher Timothy O'Connor defends one of the possibilities explored and rejected in Hasker's chapter, that conscious experience is a property had by materially composed human persons, but is such that no "part" of the experience is had by any part of those persons, nor is it itself had by any of their parts. Chapter 3, Hasker's "Rejoinder to O'Connor" contains his reply.

Chapter 4, "Why Top-Down Causation Does Not Provide Adequate Support for Mental Causation," by philosopher J. P. Moreland, presents an argument against the existence of what has come to be known as "top-down" causation. It is sometimes suggested that nature is replete with examples of *emergent* properties—properties possessed by complex, composite objects which are utterly different in kind than the properties and relations characterizing the micro-objects that compose those objects, and that nature is also replete with cases in which possession of such emergent properties by larger objects causally influences the behavior of the micro-objects composing those larger objects. Proponents of physicalism with respect to human persons (*physicalism*, henceforth: the idea, again, that we humans are made up entirely of physical stuff) will sometimes point to such cases of "top-down" causation as illustrative of how it is that possession of conscious, mental properties by complex, higher-level organisms causally influences the behavior of the microparticles comprising those organisms. It is a must for any remotely plausible theory of the mental and the physical that it be capable of accommodating the existence of causal interaction between the mental lives of persons and the matter comprising their bodies, as it's surely about as obvious as it gets that our conscious mental experiences are causally relevant to the behavior of our bodies. It would be a serious theoretical cost of physicalism indeed if it could not accommodate this datum. Moreland argues in this chapter that it cannot, that nature is *not* replete with examples of the kind of causal interaction between emergent properties and matter allegedly on display in the interaction between emergent mental properties and matter, and that top-down causation of the sort postulated by many physicalists is not possible. Substance dualist accounts of the relationship of the mental to the physical aren't saddled with this problem, and, suggests Moreland, are the best option for understanding that relationship.

In Chapter 5, "Emergence and Causal Powers: A Reply to Moreland," neuropsychologist Jason Runyan takes issue with each of Moreland's main claims, arguing that, contra Moreland, there is no good reason for skepticism about the existence of widespread top-down causation in nature, and that there are plausible versions of physicalism that don't fall prey to Moreland's argument against the possibility of top-down causation. Moreland responds in Chapter 6.

In Chapter 7, "The Impossibility of Proving That Human Behavior Is Determined," philosopher Richard Swinburne interacts with recent experiments which have been taken by many in the brain sciences to suggest that human actions are caused not by our intentions to perform those actions, but by events in our brain occurring prior to the formation of those intentions. If this were so, if it were never the case that raising one's hand, say, was caused by one's intention to raise one's hand, but always by goings on in one's brain prior to one's ever having formed the intention to raise one's hand, it would follow that the relationship between our bodily behavior and our conscious mental lives is not at all what it seems and that a radical rethinking of traditional views about the relationship between mind and body is in order. Swinburne urges in this chapter, though, that it is extremely unlikely that we could come to have good epistemic reason for accepting any theory on which all of one's intentional actions are caused by brain events prior to the formation of one's intentions, because, says Swinburne, "our very criteria for a well-justified scientific theory make it almost impossible for a theory of this kind to be well justified." Since it seems clearly to be the case that our intentions to behave in this or that way sometimes cause us to behave in this or that way, in a manner uncaused by previous causes, and since it follows from his argument that there cannot be counterevidence to this, then by what Swinburne calls the Principle of Credulity—roughly, that one should believe that things are as they seem to be absent counterevidence—it follows that, contra the claims of certain contemporary brain researchers, we should continue to believe that our intentions sometimes cause our behavior, uncaused to do so by previous brain events.

In Chapter 8, "On the Import of the Impossibility," philosopher Daniel Speak responds with skepticism to a crucial premise of Swinburne's argument, the claim that it seems clear to us that our intentions sometimes cause our behavior in a manner *uncaused to do so by previous brain events.* Speak grants that we often experience ourselves as free to act differently than we in fact act, but wonders whether it likewise seems to us that we sometimes act in ways disconnected to prior systems of cause. And even if it does seem that way to us, Speak wonders whether we have reason to trust such seemings. He concludes the chapter by questioning whether Swinburne has given adequate grounds for thinking we could never be justified in accepting a theory on which all of one's intentions are caused by brain events prior to the formation of one's intentions. Perhaps Swinburne has shown that we could have no good *scientific* grounds for thinking such a thing, but, wonders Speak, has he shown we could have no good grounds *period*? Perhaps there are other ways one could be justified in accepting such views. Chapter 9 comprises Swinburne's response.

In Chapter 10, "Neuroscience and the Human Person," philosophers Kevin Corcoran and Kevin Sharpe argue for physicalism on grounds that it fits recent neurobiological data better than does substance dualism. First, there is data regarding the enormously subtle and complex ways consciousness depends on the functioning of various subsystems spread throughout the brain. Corcoran and Sharpe argue that this is just what one would expect given the hypothesis of physicalism, but not at all what one would expect given the hypothesis of substance dualism. Second, there is the fact that brain science has explained quite a variety of features of our conscious life—for example, why selective memory loss occurs, how and why sleep cycles work as they do, why emotions work as they do—and that all of this is explainable without appeal to nonphysical souls, which look to be increasingly explanatorily irrelevant to the project of explaining the workings of consciousness. Corcoran and Sharpe further claim that physicalism fits much better than substance dualism what we know about the gradual evolutionary development of organisms and their capacities for consciousness.

Chapter 11, "Saving Our Souls from Materialism," is a reply to Corcoran and Sharpe by philosophers Eric LaRock and Robin Collins. They reject Corcoran and Sharpe's claim that, were substance dualism true, we should not expect to see the sort of systematic dependence of consciousness on brain functioning discovered by recent brain science. And they deny Corcoran and Sharpe's claim that postulation of souls is explanatorily superfluous, urging that postulation of souls saves one from having to postulate enormously complex laws governing which material systems are subjects of conscious experience and which aren't. Finally, they attempt to explain how it could be that immaterial souls without parts could develop new capacities over time. Corcoran and Sharpe's reply comes in Chapter 12, "Saving Materialism from a 'Souler' Eclipse."

Chapter 13, Eric LaRock's "Neuroscience and the Hard Problem of Consciousness," discusses what philosopher David Chalmers has dubbed the "hard problem of consciousness." An easy problem of consciousness, says Chalmers, is one susceptible to the usual explanatory methods of cognitive science in terms of computational or neural processes. The hard problem is the difficulty of explaining subjective conscious experience, the kind that goes with tasting an apple, feeling the pain of a pinch to the skin, having a visual experience. In each of these cases, there is *something it is like* to be in these states, to have these feelings, to undergo these experiences, but explaining this subjective aspect to our mental lives in terms of computational or neural mechanisms has turned out to be enormously difficult. LaRock's chapter focuses on one of the reasons for this difficulty, which has to do with the above-described unity on display in conscious experience. The variegated experience of sound, color, tactual feels, and kinesthetic sensations we enjoy at any given moment comes to us as highly unified: as part of a single, comprehensive experience, experienced by a single subject of experience. LaRock explores empirical grounds for doubting that this facet of conscious experience can be explained in terms of the usual reductive methodologies of neuroscience and proposes that the failure of such reductionism at explaining subjects and their conscious experience suggests the need for a new methodology of studying consciousness on which subjective features of the world are taken as fundamental, not reducible to anything more basic in the physical world.

Chapter 14, "Explaining Consciousness," is a reply to LaRock by Kevin Corcoran and Kevin Sharpe, who grant that it is difficult, perhaps even impossible, to reductively explain subjective conscious experience: to elaborate a mechanism, describable wholly in terms of computational and neural processes, and show how such a mechanism must give rise to subjective conscious experience. They argue, however, that "consciousness is susceptible to a kind of nonreductive explanation that's quite congenial to taking subjective data as fundamental and supports the broadly explanatory case for materialism" put forward in their essay in Chapter 10. Chapter 15, "From Non-Reductive Physicalism to Emergent Subject Dualism: A Rejoinder to Corcoran and Sharpe," LaRock's reply to Corcoran and Sharpe, critiques their proposed nonreductive explanation of consciousness and mounts an argument for an empirically informed version of dualism.

So far, the volume has covered the dialect between substance dualists and physicalists. In Chapter 16, "'Multidimensional Monism': A Constructive Theological Proposal for the Nature of Human Nature," systematic theologian Veli-Matti Kärkkäinen enters the fray, adumbrating his reasons for leaning away from traditional substance dualism, but also for rejecting the sort of nonreductive physicalism on display in O'Connor's, Runyan's, and Corcoran and Sharpe's chapters. Kärkkäinen proposes a third way in this chapter, arguing for a position he calls multidimensional monism, roughly, the view that reality comprises one basic sort of stuff (unlike the substance dualism of, say, Descartes on which reality is divided into two basic kinds of stuff, physical and mental), but that this stuff has many different aspects or dimensions: physical, mental, but others besides: inorganic, organic, spiritual, and more. Given his move away from traditional body-soul dualism, Kärkkäinen wonders whether traditional language of "soul" should be kept, arguing that indeed it should: suitably redefined, it should continue to have a place in our religious discourse. He concludes by considering the question of how to think about personal survival after death from the perspective of his anthropology, urging a view similar to one defended by John Polkinghorne, on which we survive into the eschaton by dint of the fact that God remembers the patterns that characterize us and re-embodies those patterns in the act of resurrection.

In Chapter 17, "'Multidimensional Monist': A Response to Kärkkäinen," philosopher Stewart Goetz takes issue with Kärkkäinen's suggestion that early Christian thought embraced substance dualism because of an unfortunate capitulation to Greek philosophy, suggesting rather that early Christian thinkers were dualists because, as certain contemporary cognitive scientists and psychologists have been arguing, humans naturally incline toward such belief: humans are born substance dualists. New Testament and early church writers weren't getting their substance dualism from Greek philosophy, but rather from common sense intuition. After animadversions on Kärkkäinen's positive case for multidimensional monism, he raises worries about Kärkkäinen's account of personal survival after death, suggesting that God's re-embodying a certain pattern is insufficient for the embodiment of that pattern's being *Stewart Goetz*, since in theory anyway, God could re-embody multiple copies of this pattern, but were God to do so, it wouldn't be that each of these is Stewart Goetz: it couldn't be that multiple people are identical with Stewart Goetz. Chapter 18 is Kärkkäinen's reply.

In Chapter 19, "Whose Interpretation? Which Anthropology? Biblical Hermeneutics, Scientific Naturalism, and the Body-Soul Debate," theologian John Cooper investigates the question: Whence the source of pervasive disagreement among contemporary interpreters of the Bible on the body-soul relation? Cooper contends that, historically, it wasn't this way: that there was general ecumenical agreement, throughout church history, on the basic outlines of biblical anthropology, that it was broadly dualistic, and that this was true of Orthodox, Roman Catholic, and most Protestant thinkers until relatively recently. Cooper argues that the explanation for the change turns on the fact of increasingly widespread adoption of certain scientific claims about human beings, arguing that biblical interpretation is a complex interaction between exegesis of the text, one's doctrinal commitments, and one's background commitments on other matters including scientific matters. Cooper proposes that the differences among biblical interpreters about the Bible's teaching on the body-soul relation is largely explainable by differing reactions to contemporary scientific and philosophical claims about evolutionary materialism and emergent physicalism.

Chapter 20, "Whose Interpretation? Which Anthropology? Indeed: A Response to John Cooper" is by theologian Brian Lugioyo. Lugioyo takes issue with Cooper's suggestion that the church, until recently, has uniformly embraced anthropological dualism, arguing that there has long been considerable diversity on the question. After critical interaction with Cooper's dualistic exegesis of various passages, Lugioyo concludes by suggesting that the recent turn to more monistic reads of the biblical texts owes not just to changing scientific views, but to a changing practical context in church life, characterized by increased sensitivity to abuses like slavery and sexism, which have led the church to more nuanced, non-dualistic reads of the text, reads less prone to lead to such abuses. Cooper responds in Chapter 21.

Such, in brief, are the essays in the volume. We think they nicely express the liveliness of current debate about body and soul among Christian thinkers and that they also advance that debate in important ways. For those who find themselves inclined to traditional belief in the soul but have wondered what to make of such belief in light of current brain science, we hope you'll find helpful resources here. So too for those who find themselves inclined to one or another of the Christian physicalisms under discussion here. And for those who aren't sure what to think, we think you too will be helped by the discussion. Finally, a word of heartfelt thanks to the John Templeton Foundation, whose generous funding made possible the research fellowship and conference that gave rise to the essays of this volume. The opinions expressed in the essays are those of their authors and do not necessarily reflect the views of the John Templeton Foundation or Biola's Center for Christian Thought.

Thomas M. Crisp
Steven L. Porter
Gregg A. Ten Elshof

PART 1

Recent Debate in Philosophy about the Mind-Body Problem

CHAPTER 1

Do My Quarks Enjoy Beethoven?

William Hasker

Do my quarks enjoy Beethoven? Perhaps that seems to you a strange question. If you were able to make any sense of it at all, you most likely thought of it as a rather extreme metonymy—a way of asking whether *I* enjoy Beethoven, somewhat as if someone had asked whether my taste-buds enjoy a medium-rare filet mignon. If that were the intended meaning, the answer would be an emphatic Yes—to both questions. In fact, however, I intended the question quite literally, as a question about the quarks in my body—those tiny particles that, combined in certain ways, make up the protons and neutrons that, together with electrons, compose the atoms that constitute that body. And my question is, do *those quarks* enjoy Beethoven, or don't they?

Given this, however, you may be returned to your initial state of bafflement, unable to understand the question in any sensible way. Nevertheless, I shall attempt to show you that the question is indeed deserving of our attention, at least if we have the aim to gain an understanding of the human mind. My project in this essay is to develop that puzzling question with reference to the philosophical view known as materialism. More precisely, the view to be considered is the doctrine of *material composition*—the claim that human beings, and other sentient organisms, consist of the physical stuff of the world and of nothing else. Now the doctrine of material composition is less demanding than some other views that go under the label of materialism. It does not require us to accept that there are no mental properties or mental states, or that mental properties are reducible to physical properties, or that mental states and properties have sufficient causes that are entirely physical in nature. All of these commitments are required by some of the currently popular forms of materialism, but material composition as such does not require them, though it is consistent with all of them. So material composition is a comparatively undemanding materialist view, and yet I will show that, when interrogated in terms of our question, it yields some extremely interesting results.

This paper has three parts. In the first part, I develop a version of compositional materialism, termed the theory of *emergent material persons* (EMP). This theory is largely based on the views of John Searle; towards the end I bring in some ideas from Timothy O'Connor. In the second part, I investigate further the EMP theory. First, I develop some implications of the theory concerning causation of and by mental states. Then, I raise the question: according to this theory, what is the subject of experience? It is here that the question about my quarks and Beethoven comes to the fore. A brief final section sums up the results and points to some direction for future research.

The Theory of Emergent Material Persons

We begin, then, by examining some ideas of John Searle. Searle is notable in that he is a committed naturalist who has nevertheless set out an unusually full and insightful account of the nature of consciousness.[1] Our task will be to see how he manages to accommodate this account of consciousness within his naturalistic commitments, including compositional materialism. For his account of consciousness, we may usefully begin with his article, "The self as a problem in philosophy and neurobiology." He begins with a definition: "consciousness consists of those states of feelings, sentience, or awareness that typically begin when we wake from a dreamless sleep and continue throughout the day until those feelings stop, until we go to sleep again, go into a coma, or otherwise become 'unconscious'" (Self, 141). This of course is not a scientific analysis; it merely "locates the target of our investigation," but as such it is hard to fault. He goes on to point out three essential features of consciousness:

1. See John Searle, *Rationality in Action* (Cambridge: MIT Press, 2001), ch. 9; "Free Will as a Problem in Neurobiology," in John Searle, *Freedom and Neurobiology: Reflections on Free Will, Language, and Political Power* (New York: Columbia University Press, 2007), 37-78, referenced in the text as "Free Will"; and "The self as a problem in philosophy and neurobiology," in John Searle, *Philosophy in a New Century* (Cambridge: Cambridge University Press, 2008), 137-51, referenced in the text as "Self." For a discussion of Searle's view of consciousness, see Neil C. Manson, "Consciousness," in Barry Smith, ed., *John Searle* (Cambridge: Cambridge University Press, 2003), 128-53. A more extensive consideration of various aspects of Searle's view may be found in Giuseppe Vicari, *Beyond Conceptual Dualism: Ontology of Consciousness, Mental Causation, and Holism in John R. Searle's Philosophy of Mind* (Amsterdam: Rodopi, 2008).

1. "Conscious states . . . are *qualitative* in the sense that there is always a certain qualitative feel to what it is like to be in one conscious state rather than another" (Self, 141).
2. "[C]onscious states are *subjective* in the sense that they only exist as experienced by a human or animal subject. Conscious states require a subject for their very existence" (Self, 141-42). The same point can be made by saying that these states have a "first-person ontology."
3. Conscious states are *unified:* "Conscious states always come to us as part of a unified conscious field." "[W]hen I am listening to Beethoven's Ninth Symphony while drinking beer, I do not just have the experience of listening and the experience of drinking, rather I have the experience of drinking and listening as part of one total conscious experience" (Self, 142).

These three features, moreover, are closely connected to each other: "You cannot have a qualitative experience such as tasting beer without that experience occurring as part of some subjective state of awareness, and you cannot have a subjective state of awareness except as part of a total field of awareness. . . . So we might say, initially at least, the problem of consciousness is precisely the problem of qualitative, unified subjectivity" (Self, 142).

A further important point made by Searle is that, as we consider these features of consciousness, we are forced to regard the subject of experiences as a "non-Humean self." "In order to make sense of our experiences," he tells us, "we have to suppose,

> There is some x such that
> x is conscious;
> x persists through time;
> x has perceptions and memories;
> x operates with reasons in the gap [i.e., between motives and the decision to act];
> x, in the gap, is capable of deciding and acting;
> x is responsible for at least some of its behavior" (Self, 148).

Searle insists, however, that this x is merely a "formal feature" of the conscious field, not a separate entity distinct from that field: we have to guard against "sounding like the worst kind of German philosophers (Was ist das Ich?)" (Self, 148).

Clearly, more could be said about each of these features of consciousness, but our present question is, how does Searle go about fitting them into his naturalistic worldview? As a first move, Searle repudiates the dichotomy between mental and physical states and properties, and with it the "property dualist" label that some readers have tended to attach to his views.[2] Conscious states are *biological* states; they are states of a biological (and therefore physical) organism. Mental properties are "higher-order" properties, grounded in the basic biological properties of the organism, in much the same way that solidity is a higher-order property of a physical object. When the molecules of an object are bound together in a certain way, so that they resist deformation and penetration by other objects, the object is said to be in the "solid state." Similarly, when a biological organism is functioning in a certain way—a way that as yet is not well understood, though it is being intensively studied by neuroscientists—the organism is in a certain conscious state. This can be described as a case of emergence, but it is an uncontroversial and relatively unexciting sort of emergence, one that is perfectly familiar in contexts unrelated to the mind and consciousness.

This parallel between mental properties and higher-order physical properties such as solidity does important work for Searle in his project of incorporating consciousness within his naturalistic worldview. But there is a significant difference between the two cases. Solidity and other higher-order physical properties are both ontologically and causally reducible to the microphysical base properties. When the molecules of a certain quantity of matter stand in such-and-such relations, it is in principle deducible that the matter in question will exhibit the behavior characteristic of solidity. Solidity, we can truthfully say, is "nothing but" those molecules standing in those relations to one another. And in general, the causal properties of the solid object are wholly deducible from the causal properties of the molecules, etc. of which it is composed. With consciousness, the situation is somewhat different. Mental properties, as was explained above, have a "first-person ontology"; that is to say, they can exist only as perceived by a subject. This is not true of the physical properties of the organism, and because of this mental states and properties are *not* deducible from, nor are they ontologically reducible to, the physical base properties. However, Searle holds that they are *causally* reducible; all the

2. I do not pursue here the question whether Searle is or is not a "property dualist." (See "Why I Am Not a Property Dualist," in *Philosophy in a New Century*, 152-60.) Searle gives a definition of property dualism according to which he definitely does not qualify as a property dualist. On the other hand, others may have different definitions of property dualism which would include Searle's position under that rubric. Unlike Searle himself, I doubt whether anything substantive turns on this terminological issue.

mental properties, events, and so on are completely accounted for in terms of the causal powers of the biological base properties. And this, he believes, is sufficient to enable his project of "biologizing" the mental to go through. He states: "from everything we know about the brain, consciousness is causally reducible to brain processes; and for that reason I deny that the ontological irreducibility of consciousness implies that consciousness is something 'over and above,' something distinct from, its neurobiological base" (Self, 156).

An important advantage Searle claims to derive from his view is that problems concerning epiphenomenalism, causal closure, and the like simply do not arise for him. He states, "Of course, the universe is causally closed, and we can call it 'physical' if we like, but that cannot mean 'physical' as opposed to 'mental'; because, equally obviously, the mental is part of the causal structure of the universe in the same way that the solidity of pistons is part of the causal structure of the universe; even though the solidity is entirely accounted for by molecular behaviour, and consciousness is entirely accounted for by neuronal behaviour" (Self, 157). No one objects on this account that solidity is epiphenomenal, so why is there a worry about consciousness as epiphenomenal? "Consciousness does not exist in a separate realm and it does not have any causal powers in addition to those of its neuronal base any more than solidity has any extra causal powers in addition to its molecular base" (Self, 158).

It may occur to us that Searle is moving a bit swiftly. If consciousness is not ontologically reducible to brain processes, it seems that only two alternatives are available: consciousness is something *other than* ("over and above") brain processes, or consciousness does not exist at all—and the latter option has clearly been ruled out. If consciousness involves properties other than the familiar physical and biological properties, the question does arise whether those additional properties convey any causal powers other than those that are entailed by the non-mental properties of the organism.[3] On the face of it, Searle's answer to this would seem to be "No"—he does, after all, affirm causal closure—and if so, the problem of epiphenomenalism seems to have returned.

In fact, Searle is himself forced to confront this problem, or a very similar problem, because of an additional feature of our conscious experience that has not been emphasized up until now. That is the experience of the "gap"—the "open space" in which decisions are made, without (apparently) being determined by anything that has gone before. Searle has long been aware that our experience as agents seems to provide support for a libertarian understanding

3. "Whether a feature is epiphenomenal depends on whether the *feature itself* functions causally" (Free Will, 67).

of free will. "For example, it seems that when I voted for a particular candidate and did so for a certain reason, well, all the same, I could have voted for the other candidate all other conditions remaining the same" (Free Will, 39). Furthermore, Searle believes that this "seeming" is deeply embedded in our experience as agents, so much so that we cannot really free ourselves from it even if we come to accept determinism as the truth. In his early work, *Minds, Brains, and Science*,[4] he was content to suppose that this impression of freedom is, in effect, a trick played on us by evolution, a persistent illusion which we cannot in practice overcome even when in theory we recognize its illusory character. But this is at best an uncomfortable position, and more recently he has come to entertain seriously the possibility that the intuition of freedom might be veridical.

A helpful discussion of this possibility is found in Searle's paper, "Free will as a problem in neurobiology." Consider the following situation: a person makes a decision that seems to be "free" in the sense described above. The person is aware of various motives for and against the decision actually made, but the motives do not seem to be causally sufficient to bring about the decision. Rather, there is a gap between the antecedent situation and the decision, and this gap is filled by the person herself, actually making the decision. By hypothesis, the conscious experience of making the decision is a higher-order property of the person's brain, which both causes and realizes the conscious states involved. Now, here is the question: Is the brain-process which causes and realizes the conscious decision-making itself deterministic in character, as most scientists and many philosophers would assume? Or is there also a gap on the neurobiological level, corresponding with the gap consciously experienced by the agent?

One possibility, the one Searle thinks most neurobiologists would assume to be the actual case, is that the brain-process is indeed deterministic. Searle, who apparently once accepted this view himself, now finds it to be problematic:

> But this is intellectually very unsatisfying, because it gives us a form of epiphenomenalism. It says that our experience of freedom plays no causal or explanatory role in our behavior. It is a complete illusion, because our behavior is entirely fixed by the neurobiology that determines the muscle contractions. On this view evolution played a massive trick on us. Evolution gives us the illusion of freedom, but it is nothing more than that—an illusion (Free Will, 62).

4. John Searle, *Minds, Brains, and Science* (Cambridge: Harvard University Press, 1984); see 87-88.

Note how the problem of epiphenomenalism, which supposedly had been banished by the view of consciousness as a higher-order property, now makes its reappearance. From now on I shall refer to this option as the *illusory-freedom* hypothesis.

But if this view is unsatisfying, what is the alternative? The key assumption in the alternative *real-freedom* hypothesis, and the one that creates the difficulties in formulating it coherently, is that the experience of freedom is *not* epiphenomenal, that *consciousness as such,* and our *conscious decision-making,* really make a difference in the functioning of the physical organism. In order to grasp this, we have to think of consciousness as a "system feature,"[5] one that is "literally present throughout those portions of the brain where consciousness is created and realized" (Free Will, 63). Further, we have to suppose that "the logical features of volitional consciousness of the entire system"—that is, I take it, the syntactic structure, semantic contents, affective components, and so on of the conscious state—"have effects on the elements of the system" (Free Will, 63). This hypothesis, then, involves three claims:

> First, the state of the brain at t_1 is not causally sufficient to determine the state of the brain at t_2 (Free Will, 64).

This is necessary to provide the gap in the chain of physical causation which is needed to match the experienced gap in the mental decision-process, thus allowing room for consciousness to have an effect on the physical sequence.

> Second, the movement from the state at t_1 to the state at t_2 can only be explained by features of the whole system, specifically by the operation of the conscious self (Free Will, 64-65).

In order to make this plausible, Searle returns once again to his example of solidity; clearly, he thinks, the behavior of the molecules in a solid object is affected by the object's solidity, a system feature which is analogous to consciousness.

> And third, all the features of the conscious self at any given instant are entirely determined by the state of the microelements, the neurons, etc. at that instant (Free Will, 65).

5. Searle asserts here that the language of "higher-level" properties, which he himself has used extensively, may be misleading because "It suggests that consciousness is, so to speak, like the varnish on the surface of the table" (Free Will, 63).

The third requirement is essential if we are to continue to hold, as Searle has insisted (and as is required for material composition), that the person is composed of those microelements and nothing else: any state of the person, then, must *be* a state of those microelements.

So far, this seems reasonably clear. We may note, however, that in order to avoid the threat of epiphenomenalism (a threat which previously was said to have been obviated by the doctrine of consciousness as a higher-order property) Searle appears to have adopted a form of "top-down causation," in the form of causation by consciousness, a "system feature" of the physical organism. Elsewhere Searle has claimed that his view involves only standard bottom-up causation, but it now appears that this claim cannot be sustained.[6] And he must also accept a stronger version of emergence than he has previously been willing to countenance. If the behavior of the micro-elements is affected by a system feature such as consciousness, we have in effect the emergence of new laws, or something analogous to new laws, for the behavior of those micro-elements. This is a far cry from the "emergence" of solidity and the like, which is based entirely on the operation of the micro-elements according to the standard laws of physics and chemistry. Note in this connection that the appeal to solidity as analogous to consciousness, a "system feature" which affects the functioning of the microelements, is misleading. Solidity does not "affect" the molecules, in the sense of causing them to act differently than they would have acted otherwise. Rather, solidity *just is* the behavior of the molecules as they bind together, obeying the fundamental laws of physics. The difference between ontological reducibility and non-reducibility, a difference whose importance Searle wants to minimize, becomes evident at this point.

All of this, however, still needs to be reconciled by what we take ourselves to know (or reasonably believe) about the functioning of complex physical systems like the brain. As already noted, the real-freedom hypothesis requires that "the state of the brain at t_1 is not causally sufficient to determine the state of the brain at t_2." Now, the only causal indeterminism we know about in the natural world is quantum indeterminism. This hypothesis requires, then, that "Consciousness manifests quantum indeterminism" (Free Will, 74-75). At present, however, neurological research on consciousness makes no appeal to quantum indeterminism. In order for the requirement to be satisfied, there must be some mechanism in the brain that, so to speak, "amplifies" quantum

6. "The form of causation is 'bottom up,' whereby the behaviour of lower-level elements, presumably neurons and synapses, causes higher-level or system features of consciousness and intentionality" ("Why I am not a property dualist," 152).

indeterminism, which manifests itself mostly at the level of elementary particles, so as to produce a different result on a larger scale, the scale at which conscious decision-making occurs. (This would be analogous to the way in which a Geiger counter "amplifies" a micro-event, the emission of a particle, so as to produce an audible click.) No such mechanism is known at present, though there have been speculative guesses as to what it might be. And even if this requirement can be satisfied, there is an additional difficulty:

> But even assuming we had a quantum mechanical explanation of consciousness, how do we get from indeterminism to rationality? If quantum indeterminacy amounts to randomness then quantum indeterminacy by itself seems useless in explaining the problem of free will because free actions are not random (Free Will, 75).

At this point we seem to have reached an impasse. Free will requires a causal gap in the functioning of the brain, a gap in which conscious decision-making can occur. The only candidate for such a gap is quantum indeterminacy. But quantum indeterminacy is random, and free choice cannot be random. The possibilities for the real-freedom hypothesis seem to have been exhausted, without success.

In response to this Searle resorts to a final defensive maneuver. He observes that "it is a fallacy of composition to suppose that the properties of the individual elements must be properties of the whole." In view of this, "the fact that individual micro-phenomena are random does not imply randomness at the system level. The indeterminacy at the micro level may (if [the real-freedom hypothesis] is true) explain the indeterminacy of the system, but *the randomness at the micro level does not by itself imply randomness at the system level*" (Free Will, 76; italics in original). Now, Searle is correct in that randomness at the level of elementary particles does not by itself entail randomness at the level of rational decision-making. But surely, more than this is needed for a credible defense of the real-freedom hypothesis. For such a defense, we need at least a sketch of the way in which randomness at the basic level leads to a result at the system level which, while still retaining indeterminism, satisfies the requirements for rational decision making.

Now, we do have examples in which randomness at a lower level leads to results at a higher level that are rational and non-random. The mutations which are essential to the evolutionary process are assumed to be random, but the operation of natural selection guarantees that the genetic changes that are preserved in the population will be on the whole beneficial. A skilled artist can flip her paint-laden brush at the canvas in a way that, from the random pattern of paint-spots thus produced, creates an impression that enhances the desired aesthetic effect. The random processes of coin-tossing, dice-rolling, card-shuffling and the like can produce highly predictable results; this is precisely what guarantees the ability of casinos to operate profitably.

Unfortunately, however, *none of these examples provides any help for the real-freedom hypothesis.* The reason for this is that, in each of the examples, the rational outcome of the random process emerges only as the result of a large number of individual instances. Any particular mutation, any particular paint-spot, any particular coin-flip, dice-roll, or card-shuffle remains entirely random. The rational outcomes that result depend on the cumulative effect of many such instances, as governed by the laws of probability and, in some instances, by guiding influences such as natural selection or the artist's aesthetic intentions. In rational decision-making, on the other hand, *rationality must be evident in the individual instance.* In Searle's own example of his decision to vote for Bush for President, it is *that particular decision* that must meet the requirements of rationality, and that must occur as a result of Searle's conscious decision. It is of no help to assert that out of, say, 35 instances in which Searle might make a similar choice, in 29 of them he would have voted for Bush—even assuming that such a scenario (involving multiple repetitions of what is in fact a unique individual event) makes sense at all.

Actually what is needed is fairly clear. In order for the real-freedom hypothesis to be viable, we need to assume that *the brain-processes are directly influenced by the agent's conscious decision-making.* If the indeterminism in the brain-process is quantum indeterminacy, it must be the case that *the quantum indeterminacy is resolved in one way rather than another because of the agent's thought-process.* But if this is the case, the resolution of the quantum indeterminacy cannot itself provide the explanation for the direction taken by thought-process. Nor is the resolution random, as physical theory says it must be. The thought-process must be given an *independent causal role* in determining the course of events. (Indeed, this seems to be implied by Searle's own statement that "the logical features of volitional consciousness of the entire system have effects on the elements of the system.") This, however, involves an ambitious version of emergence that he has never been willing to affirm.[7] The cost for Searle of such a hypothesis may well be forbiddingly high.

7. For Searle's views on emergence, see *The Rediscovery of the Mind* (Cambridge: MIT Press, 1992), 111-12. So far as I can see, he has never accepted any version of emergence beyond the ordinary causal emergence exemplified by such properties as solidity, liquidity, and transparency.

In the end, Searle declines to make a choice. He finds the illusory-freedom hypothesis disappointing and uninspiring, but it has the merit of being reasonably clear and also consistent with what we take ourselves to know scientifically about the functioning of the human organism. The real-freedom hypothesis, on the other hand, is intrinsically appealing, but it requires expensive metaphysical and, to some extent, scientific assumptions—assumptions which are not known to be true and which, in some instances, have not yet been fully clarified. Searle, one might say, is in the position of a man choosing between two similar "diamond" rings. One ring is well crafted from materials of certified quality, and carries a price-tag which is not exorbitant. However, the central stone of the ring is a fake diamond. The other ring, which superficially resembles the first, differs from it in having a genuine diamond—but this ring is very costly, and may in the end prove to be completely unaffordable. As things now stand, neither purchase has been made.

At this point, we turn for comparison to some ideas of Timothy O'Connor.[8] Unlike Searle, O'Connor is not a naturalist but rather a Christian theist, though he insists that his views are consistent with our developing scientific conception of the world. In spite of this difference, he has developed an understanding of consciousness that is strikingly similar to Searle's account, when that account is understood as incorporating the real-freedom hypothesis.[9] (Unless otherwise stated, subsequent reference to Searle's view should be understood as including the real-freedom hypothesis.) A comparison of the two should, I believe, yield some useful insights.

There is nothing in Searle's initial characterization of consciousness to which O'Connor would object. He would agree that consciousness is qualitative, subjective, and unified, and that the subject must be understood as

8. See Timothy O'Connor, "Emergent Properties," *American Philosophical Quarterly* 31 (April 1994), 91-104; "Agent Causation," in Timothy O'Connor, ed., *Agents, Causes, and Events: Essays on Indeterminism and Free Will* (New York: Oxford University Press, 1995), 173-200; *Persons and Causes: The Metaphysics of Free Will* (Oxford: Oxford University Press, 2000); "Causality, Mind, and Free Will," in Kevin Corcoran, ed., *Soul, Body, and Survival* (Ithaca: Cornell University Press, 2001), 44-58; and Timothy O'Connor and Jonathan D. Jacobs, "Emergent Individuals," *The Philosophical Quarterly* 53, no. 213 (October 2003), 540-55. I will not consider here O'Connor's ontology of immanent universals, which is introduced in the last-mentioned article. This ontology is not especially pertinent to the comparison with Searle, though it is consistent with O'Connor's other views as discussed here.

9. So far as I can tell, the similarities between Searle and O'Connor are the result of convergent research and not of direct influence. Searle is certainly not dependent on O'Connor, and I have not found in O'Connor's writings references to Searle or other indications of his influence.

a non-Humean self. He would agree that mental states and properties are not ontologically reducible to physical states and properties. And he would agree with Searle's characterization of our experience of the "gap," and the consequent intuition of freedom. Both Searle and O'Connor affirm material composition: human beings (and other sentient organisms) consist of ordinary material stuff and nothing else. The interesting differences between them arise with regard to the metaphysical implications of the experience of freedom. Searle, as we have seen, is ambivalent in his response to this experience; he clearly would like to accept it as veridical, but he holds back from making a definite judgment to that effect. O'Connor, on the other hand, unambiguously accepts the intuition of freedom as veridical; indeed he develops it with a careful and detailed analysis of libertarian free will, and of the theory of agent causation that goes with it.[10] O'Connor does not accept the physicalist doctrine of causal closure, as this is generally understood; Searle, once again, is ambiguous on this point.[11] O'Connor accepts a strong version of emergence, and backs it with an analysis of emergence which is, one has to say, considerably more nuanced and sophisticated than anything of the sort found in Searle's writings.[12] The central idea is this: ordinary physical stuff has within itself the potential and the tendency to produce mental states and properties of the sort we are familiar with in conscious experience. However, these tendencies remain latent until the matter achieves the sort of complex functional organization that is found in some living creatures. (Once again, it must be acknowledged that the precise nature of this organization still challenges our best scientific understanding.) Once that happens, consciousness emerges, and with it a new suite of properties and new kinds of behavior (including the behaviors involved in libertarian free will), that could not be predicted on the basis of the physico-chemical laws that describe the behavior of matter outside of these special situations. This amounts to a form of "top-down causation": consciousness, which is a higher-order, emergent property, has effects on the micro-level, and causes the microelements to behave dif-

10. See "Agent Causation," *Persons and Causes,* and "Causality, Mind, and Free Will."

11. Searle accepts that "the universe is causally closed," but it is not clear what is meant by this. A standard definition of causal closure is given by Jaegwon Kim: "Any physical event that has a cause at time t has a physical cause at t" ("The Myth of Nonreductive Materialism," in *Supervenience and Mind: Selected Philosophical Essays* [Cambridge: Cambridge University Press, 1991], 280). Here "physical cause" is understood to mean causation in terms of the standard laws of physics and chemistry. It is not clear to me whether Searle accepts this, or only the weaker claim that the ultimate source of causal power must be the physical stuff of the world.

12. See O'Connor's "Emergent Properties" and *Persons and Causes.*

ferently than would be predicted on the basis of the physico-chemical laws alone. (O'Connor is not committed to the view that this difference must be limited to the way in which quantum indeterminacy is resolved, though his views otherwise are consistent with this assumption.) This is a much stronger, and admittedly more controversial, sort of emergence than the emergence of solidity and similar properties about which Searle has so much to say. I believe, however, that Searle's claim that the less ambitious variety of emergence is sufficient cannot be sustained—not, at least, if the real-freedom version of his theory is accepted. An additional point made by O'Connor (but one that Searle might be willing to accept) is that some of the emergent properties are "non-structural"; that is, such that the property's instantiation "does not even partly consist of the instantiation of a plurality of more basic properties by the entity or its parts."[13]

Summing up all of this, I believe we can characterize the relationship between Searle's and O'Connor's views something like this: O'Connor has the sort of theory of consciousness that Searle could have (and arguably ought to have) if his naturalistic propensities did not inhibit him from embracing the metaphysical assumptions that are needed to make good sense of the real-freedom hypothesis. Furthermore, I venture the suggestion that the combined view—Searle's real-freedom theory together with the additional metaphysical underpinnings provided by O'Connor—offers the best available theory of consciousness consistent with their common assumption of the material composition of sentient beings. (I will not argue for this here, though I think the preceding discussion of their views provides some support for it.) For ease of reference, I shall label this the theory of *emergent material persons,* or the EMP theory. The second main section of this paper will consist of a further examination of this theory.

An Examination of the Theory of Emergent Material Persons

The EMP theory avoids many of the problems that beset Searle's original proposals, but it faces challenges of its own. I begin by summarizing, and extending somewhat, our conclusions about the way causality works in this theory. When a person makes a free decision, where should we locate the causal power—in O'Connor's terms, the causal "oomph"—that makes this happen? Suppose, in accordance with Searle's speculation, that the neuronal correlate

13. "Emergent Individuals," 541.

of the decision's being made in one way rather than another is that a particular quantum indeterminacy is resolved in one way rather than another. Shall we say that the quantum event is what determines, or causes, the decision to be made in that way? To say that is to say that the decision is random, as between the available alternatives, and both Searle and O'Connor would agree that a free decision cannot be in that sense random.[14] Rather, the decision must be a conscious, rational matter; it must be the rational-but-causally-undetermined outcome of the conscious state that precedes it. Consciousness, however, is a system feature of the organism; it consists of a certain complex way in which the organism (primarily, one assumes, the brain) is organized and functions. So the quantum event must itself be controlled by the non-Humean self. This is a non-physical form of control, one that is not mediated by the known forces of physics. This in turn means that causal closure, as normally understood, cannot be maintained.[15] Mind-body supervenience, furthermore, must also be abandoned: supervenience implies that the direction of determination is always physical-to-mental, rather than mental-to-physical.[16]

Once causal closure has been abandoned, however, it is difficult to see the point of insisting that the neural correlate of the free decision must be the resolution of a quantum indeterminacy. Searle has argued, to be sure, that this is the only kind of indeterminism we know about in the natural world. This observation has force, however, only if it is the case that, were there other sorts of indeterminism in the functioning of a brain that supports a conscious mind, we would know about it. It is precisely here that we should expect indeterminism to manifest itself, if the real-freedom hypothesis is correct. But we are very far from having the sort of knowledge of brain function that would enable us either to detect or to rule out the presence of such indeterminism.

14. Robert Kane is a philosopher who does think quantum randomness, properly construed, provides a good foundation for libertarian free will. (See his "Rethinking Free Will: New Perspectives on an Ancient Problem," in R. Kane, ed., *The Oxford Handbook of Free Will*, second edition [Oxford: Oxford University Press, 2011], 381-404.) Like Searle and O'Connor, I don't believe this is satisfactory, but one can't argue everything in a single essay. For the beginning of a critique, see my *The Emergent Self* (Ithaca: Cornell University Press, 1999), 94-99.

15. As noted previously, it may be that Searle endorses causal closure only in the sense that all of the causal power ultimately comes from the material stuff. In this sense, causal closure is simply a consequence of compositional materialism.

16. Yet another interesting result is that *we now have no empirical evidence whatsoever for determinism*. Searle has asserted (and rightly so, I believe) that psychological determinism has very little going for it; our psychological evidence rather supports libertarianism. What is left as a potentially viable candidate is physical determinism, but if consciousness exerts an independent causal function, physical determinism also has to be abandoned.

Our justified admiration for what has been learned concerning the workings of the brain must not be allowed to blind us to the enormous amount that remains unknown. Searle of all people should agree with this; he has argued forcefully that the brain cannot be a digital computer,[17] whereas all of the more ambitious projects in artificial intelligence assume that it is a digital computer, or something very similar.[18] Furthermore, he acknowledges that progress in the hunt for the neural correlate of consciousness has been painfully slow (Self, 144). So there is a huge amount still to be learned, and many surprises lie in wait for us. (Until recently the notion of a "grandmother neuron"—a single neuron which responds specifically to the presence or image of a particular, known individual—was something of a joke. It now turns out that we do indeed have grandmother neurons—or, in the case of one individual who was tested, a "Jennifer Aniston neuron"![19]) Nor are appeals to simplicity of much force here. Descartes might have argued—perhaps in effect he did argue—that the only form of physical causality of which we are clearly aware is action by contact (pushes and pulls), and that it is simpler to assume that all physical causality is of this sort than to propose other, more mysterious kinds of causal influence. Descartes simply did not know how much he did not know, and as a result his physics and physiology, unlike his philosophy, are now museum pieces, studied only by scholars of the period.

We may conclude, then, that (1) The real-freedom hypothesis requires the existence of a non-physical influence or causality that directs brain activity in one direction rather than another. (2) Such non-physical causality requires in turn a robust doctrine of emergence, as well as top-down causation. (3) Given this, the materialist doctrines of causal closure and mind-body supervenience cannot be maintained. (4) In view of (1)-(3), there is no good reason to assume that the neural correlate of a free decision must be the resolution of a quantum indeterminacy. These results by no means constitute a refutation of the EMP theory; they do, however, show something about the costs of such a theory, and about the difficulty (impossibility?) of accommodating it within the confines of a naturalistic worldview.

We turn now to an argument which challenges the core assumption of the EMP theory, the assumption that human beings (and other sentient organisms) consist of ordinary physical matter, and nothing else. This argument

17. See his APA Presidential Address, "Is the brain a digital computer?" in *Philosophy in a New Century,* 86-106.

18. See, for example, the "Blue Brain" project at http://bluebrain.epfl.ch/page-52063.html.

19. See Rodrigo Quian Quiroga, Izhak Fried, and Christof Koch, "Brain Cells for Grandmother," *Scientific American,* February 2013, 30-35.

begins by asking the question, "What is the self?"—the "non-Humean self" of which Searle has written. In asking this, to be sure, we may risk "sounding like the worst kind of German philosophers." A grave peril indeed! Still, we may wonder what exactly is so bad about asking what the self is (or "Was ist das Ich?," if the absurdity is supposed to be more evident in German). The unified conscious field can exist only as experienced by a self, so to say that the self is a "formal feature" of the field has a certain ring of circularity. More importantly, it is said of the self that it persists through time—including, we must assume, times when one is asleep or unconscious, times therefore at which there is no field of conscious experience. To be sure, the impression that the self persists through such times could be an illusion, just as the experience of the gap could be an illusion. But in either case it hardly seems appropriate to assume at the outset, without further discussion, that the deliverances of our experience are illusory.

The argument we are now considering asserts that the self, the subject of experience, cannot be a complex physical object such as the human body or brain. Instead, it must be a *simple substance*, one that has no parts that are themselves substances, and which cannot be divided into parts. For Descartes, this seemed evident:

> I first take notice here that there is a great difference between the mind and the body, in that the body, from its nature, is always divisible and the mind is completely indivisible. For in reality, when I consider the mind—that is, when I consider myself in so far as I am only a thinking being—I cannot distinguish any parts, but I recognize and conceive very clearly that I am a thing which is absolutely unitary and entire.[20]

Not everyone, to be sure, finds this as immediately obvious as Descartes did. Other philosophers have offered more by way of argument. Leibniz, for instance, wrote:

> In imagining that there is a machine whose construction would enable it to think, to sense, and to have perception, one could conceive it enlarged while retaining the same proportions, so that one could enter into it, just like into a windmill. Supposing this, one should, when visiting within it, find only parts pushing one another, and never anything by which to

20. René Descartes, *Meditations on First Philosophy,* trans. Laurence J. Lafleur (Indianapolis: The Liberal Arts Press, 1960), 81.

> explain a perception. Thus it is in the simple substance, and not in the composite or in the machine, that one must look for perception.[21]

It is a mistake to object to this because of the limitations of Leibniz's physics. If we find his "parts pushing one another" implausible as the vehicle of thoughts, how would replacing those parts with silicon chips, or with neurons, make things any better? The problem does not lie in the pushes and pulls but rather in the complexity of the machine, the fact that it is made up of many distinct parts, coupled with the fact that *a complex state of consciousness cannot exist distributed among the parts of a complex object.* The payoff of the argument comes in its final sentence: "it is in the simple substance, and not in the composite or in the machine, that one must look for perception." The same point is made more elaborately by Kant:

> Every *composite* substance is an aggregate of several substances, and the action of a composite, or whatever inheres in it as thus composite, is an aggregate of several actions or accidents, distributed among the plurality of the substances. Now an effect which arises from the concurrence of many acting substances is indeed possible, namely, when this effect is external only (as, for instance, the motion of a body is the combined motion of all its parts). But with thoughts, as internal accidents belonging to a thinking being, it is different. {Suppose a compound thing were to think. Then every part of that compound would have a part of that thought. The thought that the compound would then have would be composed of the thoughts of the parts of that compound.} But this cannot consistently be maintained. For representations (for instance, the single words of a verse), distributed among different beings, never make up a whole thought (a verse), and it is therefore impossible that a thought should inhere in what is essentially composite. It is therefore possible only in a *single* substance, which, not being an aggregate of many, is absolutely simple.[22]

21. Gottfried Wilhelm Leibniz, *Monadology*, in Nicholas Rescher, *G. W. Leibniz's* Monadology: *An Edition for Students* (Pittsburgh: University of Pittsburgh Press, 1991), par. 19.

22. Immanuel Kant, *Critique of Pure Reason*, trans. N. K. Smith (New York: St. Martin's, 1965), 335 (A 352). The sentences in brackets have been emended according to a suggestion of Roderick Chisholm ("On the Simplicity of the Soul," *Philosophical Perspectives* 5 [1991], 175). The Kemp Smith translation reads as follows: "For suppose it be the composite that thinks: then every part of it would be a part of the thought, and only all of them taken together would be the whole thought." It is difficult to make sense of this.

Kant's labeling of this argument as a "paralogism" is somewhat misleading; he does, in fact, view the argument as a conclusive refutation of the sort of materialism we are considering here. In the second edition of the *Critique of Pure Reason* he wrote, "From this [argument] follows the impossibility of any explanation in *materialist* terms of the constitution of the self as a merely thinking subject."[23] Henry Allison summarizes Kant's attitude towards the argument as follows:

> Thus, Kant's position seems to be that the unity of consciousness, which the rational psychologist (presumably Leibniz) uses erroneously to establish the positive metaphysical doctrine of the simplicity and hence incorruptibility of the soul, can be used legitimately to establish the weaker thesis of the impossibility of a materialist explanation of the conceptual activities of the mind.[24]

This unity-of-consciousness argument seems to have gone out of fashion in more recent philosophy, but perhaps it is on the verge of a comeback. An extremely interesting version is presented by Daniel Barnett in his paper, "You are Simple."[25] Barnett describes his argument as an "intuition pump"; he admits that it has escape routes, but expresses the hope that "By the end of the argument, the materialists just might find themselves having the intuition that they are wrong."[26] Barnett takes it as a datum that "for any pair of conscious beings, it is impossible for the pair *itself* to be conscious. Consider, for instance, the pair comprising you and me. You might pinch your arm and feel a pain. I might simultaneously pinch my arm and feel a qualitatively identical pain. But the pair we form would not feel a thing."[27] What, he asks, is the explanation for this datum? He considers the following possibilities: (1) Pairs of people lack a sufficient *number* of parts to be conscious; (2) they lack immediate parts capable of standing in the right sorts of *relations* to each other and their environment; (3) they lack immediate parts of the right *nature;* (4) pairs of people are not *structures;* (5) some combination of (1)-(4); and, finally, (6) pairs of people are not *simple.* He argues that none of (1)-(5) provides a plausible explanation of the datum, and therefore that (6) best explains that

23. *Critique of Pure Reason*, 376 (B 420).

24. Henry E. Allison, "Kant's Refutation of Materialism," *Monist* 79 (April 1989): 195.

25. In *The Waning of Materialism*, ed. Robert C. Koons and George Bealer (Oxford: Oxford University Press, 2010), 161-74.

26. "You are Simple," 161.

27. "You are Simple," 161.

datum. Readers who desire (or are willing to risk) having their intuitions pumped are advised to consult Barnett's article for the full story. I might add that I have myself presented and defended the unity-of-consciousness argument in several places.[28]

Perhaps due to the unfamiliarity of the argument in recent philosophy, it is difficult to find answers to it in defense of materialism. One notion that sometimes surfaces is that the subject of experience is just *the person as a whole*—that is, the body as a whole. This, I think, is surprising, because it ought to be obvious on a very little reflection that this simply does not constitute any kind of answer to the unity-of-consciousness argument. Referring to the body as a "whole" does not in any way get around the fact that the body is composed of a multitude of parts—organs, cells, chemical compounds, and ultimately of elementary particles. Whatever the body does must ultimately come about through the actions and interactions of those micro-elements; without some account of those actions and interactions, the claim that the body as a whole does such-and-such is at best a promissory note.

A more interesting response to the argument is found in the writings of Franz Brentano.[29] Brentano initially considers the argument, which can be found in Descartes, that the self must be simple and immaterial because no multiplicity or other physical characteristics can be detected in our conscious experience. Brentano rejects this on the highly plausible ground that we have no assurance that our conscious experience gives us complete information about the nature of the experiencing self. (To be sure, Descartes can also be read as claiming a direct intuition of the simplicity of the self: "I recognize and conceive very clearly that I am a thing which is absolutely unitary and entire." But not everyone shares this intuition, so more than this is needed for a compelling argument.)

Brentano, however, is clearly aware of the central point stressed by the unity-of-consciousness argument:

> What we directly perceive of mental activities appears to be very complicated but to belong, despite all the complication, to one real unity. . . . If, when we see and hear, the seeing were the property of one thing and the

28. See "Emergentism," *Religious Studies* 18 (1982), 473-88; *The Emergent Self* (Ithaca: Cornell University Press, 1999); and "Persons and the Unity of Consciousness," in Koons and Bealer, eds., *The Waning of Materialism*, 175-90.

29. See Franz Brentano, *On the Existence of God: Lectures given at the Universities of Würzburg and Vienna (1868-1891)*, ed. and trans. Susan F. Kranz (Dordrecht: Martinus Nijhoff, 1987), 290-99. My thanks to Dean Zimmerman for calling this material to my attention.

> hearing the property of another, then how could there be a comparison between colors and sounds? (It would be just as impossible as it is for two people, one of whom sees the color and the other of whom hears the sound, etc.) This is the fact of the unity of consciousness.[30]

This of course is also the point made by Searle, in emphasizing the unity of the field of awareness. Brentano contends, however, that this fact does not immediately establish the immateriality of the self:

> It is true, of course, that a mental function having no parts cannot be distributed piece by piece onto the parts of a body. And, again, it is true that a mental function cannot attach to a single point of the body as long as all the other points do not carry out the same function or one just infinitesimally different from it. However, it is not so obviously absurd as Aristotle believed for this mental function to recur in a continuum by steady repetition point for point, as indeed other properties do, e.g., red, when a whole surface is red.[31]

The idea is that a mental function, that is to say a conscious experience, might exist uniformly throughout an extended body, rather than parts of the experience occurring in parts of the body. One might say, then, that with regard to that experience the body is *functionally simple*—it has no parts to which different functions can be assigned—even though it is complex in the sense that, like all bodies, it does consist of distinct parts. We might picture this by saying that the conscious experience is like peanut butter which is spread uniformly over a piece of toast, in this case the brain.

This then is the objection which, according to Brentano, keeps the unity-of-consciousness argument from reaching its goal immediately. Nevertheless the argument does, according to him, succeed in reaching its goal. By the late nineteenth century research had begun to reveal the localization of various functions within the brain:

> [I]f we regarded the cerebrum as the subject of thought and, as would then be necessary, if we attributed the same cognitive function to it part by part and point by point, we would completely contradict what the materialists among physiologists believe. That is, they believe they have demon-

30. *Existence of God*, 293.
31. *Existence of God*, 295.

> strated specific cognitive functions to be functions of different parts of the cerebrum; thus, for example, the phenomena of memory, indeed very specialized ones by means of the remarkable phenomena of amnesia. . . . And everything which goes to show that the different parts of the brain perform different functions for our thinking therefore results in a fresh proof that their function does not consist in their being themselves the subject of thought, but rather in their being a condition of thought in a different subject.[32]

Brentano triumphantly concludes, "And so it is now really, rigorously proved, as Descartes and others had prematurely assumed, that what thinks in us is not something corporeal, that it must rather be held to be something spiritual."[33]

Brentano may have been too quick in declaring victory over his own objection. Note that the mind's conscious experience involves two distinct phases. There is what Brentano calls the brain's "being a condition of thought in a different subject"; for us it is natural to call this the *data-processing phase.* And then there is the "thought" itself; we may term this the *phase of conscious experience.* We normally do not concern ourselves much with the distinction between these phases, but they are conceptually distinguishable, and even to some extent separable. This clearly happens, for example, in blindsight, where there is no conscious experience of sight, yet the data processing obviously does occur, as shown by the ability of a subject to state accurately certain facts about the objects within his "field of vision"—objects, however, of which he has no conscious experience whatever.

Now, a substance dualist like Brentano will be happy to assign these phases to different subjects—the data-processing phase to the brain, and the conscious experience to the immaterial mind. An EMP theorist, on the other hand, must of necessity assign both phases to the same entity, namely the brain. But here is the point: *There is no evident necessity why the brain must function in the same way in both phases.* In processing the data, the brain clearly functions by having various operations performed by parts of the brain—neurons and so on—precisely as neuroscience is progressively finding to be the case. The unity-of-consciousness argument, on the other hand, shows that in order to be the subject of consciousness the brain must function holistically, in the manner described by Brentano. The possibility that he overlooked is that the same brain might function in these two different ways, in accomplishing both

32. *Existence of God,* 297.
33. *Existence of God,* 297.

the data-processing phase and the phase of conscious experience. Something like this, it seems, is what the EMP theorist is obliged to say.

We may say, then, that the brain according to this hypothesis has a *double aspect;* there is the *particulate aspect,* in virtue of which the various neurons and other tissues process data in the complex ways that are now being studied, and there is the *holistic aspect,* in which the brain (or a relevant portion thereof) operates in a way that is *functionally simple* in undergoing the conscious experiences. Yet these two aspects are, on this view, aspects of the *very same entity,* namely the brain.

Now let us ask another question: what is the *spatial location* of this holistic aspect of the brain? (Recall Searle's dictum: consciousness is "literally present throughout those portions of the brain where consciousness is created and realized.") My interest here is not in the external boundary of this region of the brain; that is something that may well be left undecided, pending further research. Rather, my question is, within that boundary, where exactly is consciousness present? No doubt the natural answer is, "everywhere." But this answer has a problem. We learn from physics that the ultimate physical constituents of the brain, the elementary particles, are not packed in, so to speak, cheek to jowl, like riders in a crowded subway train. Rather, these particles are separated by comparatively vast amounts of empty space.[34] Now, if we suppose that the holistic aspect occupies all of the space within the boundaries of the relevant brain-region, we encounter the fact that *in most of this space no material particles exist.* And yet, the brain consists precisely of those particles and nothing else. But if conscious experience literally exists in the interstices between the particles, it must nevertheless inhere in *something,* must it not? (To say that it need not inhere in anything is in effect to make consciousness a substance in itself, which is hardly a move a materialist will want to make.) So if consciousness exists in all of the space in the relevant brain-region, including the interstices between the particles, it must inhere in something other than the physical brain—and if so, what more is needed to make this hypothesis explicitly dualistic?

It would seem, then, that the EMP theorist needs to say that consciousness exists *in the brain's particles and nowhere else;* in particular, not in the comparatively vast empty spaces between the particles. And yet these particles

34. Electrons and quarks are each approximately 1 attometer (10^{-18} meters) in size; protons and neutrons one femtometer (10^{-15} meters); a hydrogen atom is 25 picometers (25×10^{-12} meters). The diameter of the hydrogen atom, and therefore the orbit of its one electron, is around 25 million times the size of that electron! This is roughly equivalent to a single golf ball tracing an orbit 600 miles in diameter. It's lonely in there!

are linked together in such a way that the very same conscious state occurs in all of them simultaneously *without there being any physical communication of information between the particles.*[35] (This could be seen as analogous to the "entanglement" of particles in quantum mechanics, where whatever happens to one of a pair of entangled particles instantaneously affects the other, even across a considerable distance.) To say the very least, this situation strikes us as remarkable, but it is not, so far as I can see, logically incoherent.

Now, consider just one of the particles in my body, a quark named Jeremy. Jeremy is a Down quark which is combined with two Up quarks to make up one of the protons in the nucleus of a particular carbon atom in my brain. Like Searle in his own example, I am listening, with great enjoyment, to the triumphant final movement of Beethoven's Ninth Symphony. Pursuing our previous line of thought, we may ask, *What is going on in the tiny region of space occupied by Jeremy?* There is no question that part of the answer must be that this region of space contains the conscious state, *listening with enjoyment to the Ninth Symphony of Beethoven.* (The unity-of-consciousness argument has shown that it can't contain just *part* of that conscious state—and if it contains none of the state (and the same is true of the other regions that are relevant), then the state just doesn't exist anywhere in that spatial region, which is to say it is not a state of any material object.) We go on to ask, *Who or what is the subject of this conscious state?* Our initial answer, no doubt, will be that the subject of the state is I myself, the person doing the listening. By hypothesis, however, this person consists of a certain physical body and nothing else. And of that body, nothing exists in the region in question except for the quark Jeremy. I, the person, am present in that region of space, and my presence there *consists entirely of the presence there of Jeremy.* Look at it this way: there is a property, *enjoying Beethoven,* which literally is exemplified in that region of space. There is nothing physical in that region of space except for the quark, Jeremy. And there is nothing non-physical in that region of space that might exemplify the property, *enjoying Beethoven.* The conclusion seems ineluctable: if the experience of enjoying Beethoven occurs in the space occupied by the quark Jeremy, the subject of that enjoyment must be Jeremy itself.[36] It looks very much, then, as if the EMP theorist is obliged to say that yes, my quarks do, quite literally

35. There will, of course, be the normal forces and interactions that occur between the microelements of any material thing whatever. It is not credible, however, that the information of the conscious field is transmitted by those forces and interactions.

36. Recall Brentano's observation that if we "regarded the cerebrum as the subject of thought" we must then "attribute the same cognitive function to it part by part" or, we might now say, "particle by particle"!

and not as a matter of any figure of speech, enjoy Beethoven! EMP theorists are cordially invited either to acknowledge and embrace this consequence of their view, or explain why it does not follow.

Summary and Prospects

In the first section of this essay we developed a theory of consciousness, the theory of emergent material persons. We began with the assumption that human beings, and other sentient organisms, are entirely composed of ordinary matter. Next came some insights concerning the nature of consciousness taken from John Searle. Consciousness involves qualitative experience; for any conscious experience, there is something it is like to have that experience. Consciousness has a first-person ontology: conscious states can exist only as experienced by a subject, a non-Humean self. Consciousness is essentially unified: any particular conscious state can exist only as part of a unified field of awareness. Finally, Searle calls our attention to the experience of the gap: as we make decisions, the antecedent circumstances do not seem sufficient to bring about the resulting decision. Rather it is we ourselves who fill the gap by actually making the decision. This raises the question whether there is a causal gap in the brain corresponding to the experience of the gap, or whether our experience of indeterminism is an illusion and the underlying brain process is deterministic. Searle is attracted to the idea that the indeterminism is real in the brain, allowing our apparently free decision-making to genuinely affect the world rather than being relegated to epiphenomenal status. However, he has difficulty arriving at a plausible metaphysical account that will allow this to be the case.

At this point we introduced some metaphysical ideas from Timothy O'Connor which enable us to regard the gap, and free will, as physically real. These include a strong doctrine of emergence coupled with top-down causation, as well as the rejection of the materialist doctrines of causal closure and supervenience, which entail the one-sided determination of conscious states and events by the brain. This results in a theory of consciousness which affirms and vindicates the insights concerning the nature of consciousness that we found in Searle, but which he has difficulty in taking at full face value.

In the second main section we confronted the EMP theory with the unity-of-consciousness argument which seeks to show that the subject of conscious awareness cannot be a material thing. Through a series of plausible moves we arrived at the conclusion that a compositional materialist such as the EMP theorist is forced to ascribe to the tiniest particles in a person's brain that person's entire conscious state, such as the state of enjoying a Beethoven symphony. Without doubt this conclusion will strike many as bizarre and incredible, and will motivate a search for an escape route from the argument that led to it. I agree that the conclusion is bizarre, but the escape route may be difficult to discover. A principle which is implicit in the argument as given is the principle of *localized property instantiation:*

> (LPI) The intrinsic (non-relational) properties of a material thing are instantiated in the space occupied by that thing.

Upon reflection, LPI looks very much like a tautology. Whatever else may be true of material things, they are paradigmatically spatial entities; we have no way of making sense of the idea that there is a material thing that is not located anywhere in space. (That is not the same as saying that *only* material things can be located in space.) A material thing must have some intrinsic properties (whether known to us or not), and where would these properties be instantiated, if not in the space occupied by the thing? It makes no sense to suppose that the thing is in New York, but its F-ness is in Los Angeles (always supposing that F-ness is an intrinsic, non-relational property). Whatever exists must instantiate properties, and vice versa, and nothing material can instantiate non-relational properties in a place where it does not exist. (At this juncture there is no need to decide what we should say about putative non-material entities such as spirits or God.) So at least it seems; and I propose that LPI can properly be taken as an axiom as we reflect on our present topic.

Now, let us return to our friend, the quark Jeremy. The ever-changing conscious state designated as *enjoying Beethoven's Ninth Symphony* is, we assume, instantiated in the tiny bit of space occupied by Jeremy. (If not there, where else could it be instantiated?[37]) It follows at once, given LPI, that Jeremy is at least

37. A possible answer to this question has been suggested in correspondence by Thomas Crisp. He writes,

> I should think it possible that C [an event of awareness] occurs in the sum S of the regions occupied by the particles that compose B [the physical object that has the awareness], but not in any of the subregions of S. It occurs in S, but not by dint of partly or wholly occurring in proper subregions of S.

He adds, "Being a dualist, I don't think things in fact work this way, but this seems to me a coherent picture." He goes on,

> The agent's having C is a process comprising a succession of events. Events constitutive

a candidate for being the individual in which that state is instantiated. There are of course all the other parts of my body, in particular of my brain—organs, cells, and ultimately sub-atomic particles. But according to LPI, each of these instantiates its own intrinsic properties in the space which it occupies, and not in the different region of space occupied by Jeremy. Is there another candidate? It might occur to us at this point that I, myself, am such a candidate. But I, by hypothesis, am a wholly material being, consisting of these organs, cells, and

---

> of C are structured things: something's-having-a-property. . . . The "thing constituent" of each such event is the organism O; the "property constituent" is a mental property. Each such mental property is instantiated by the mereological sum of the particles that compose O, but is not instantiated by any part or parts of O.

He agrees that

> There are no [other] events occurring in the region S, or in any other of the regions occupied by the particles, such that the occurrence of those events constitutes the agent's having C.

This is true, he surmises,

> by dint of the fact that the mental properties involved are fundamental. In the nature of the case, the having of these properties can't be conceived of as constituted by more basic property-havings, property-havings by parts of the organism, or the like.

He adds,

> No doubt it will be nomologically necessary that C occurs only in the presence of various other events, but these events won't be such as to *constitute* the having of mental properties.

In terms of our example, the process of enjoying Beethoven occurs in the space occupied by my body, but not in any subregion of that space, nor are there other events occurring in my body that constitute my enjoying Beethoven. Switching to our illustration, it's as though, when we examine the piece of toast bit by bit (perhaps with a magnifying glass), no peanut butter is to be seen, yet the toast as a whole is entirely covered with peanut butter!

I must confess that I am unable to make anything of this; I cannot see that this is in any way possible. But perhaps we don't have to leave the matter at this point of sheer incomprehension. Let O be the organism that is enjoying Beethoven; the enjoyment is taking place in the organism as a whole, but not in any proper part of that organism. Now, let O_1 be one-half of that organism, divided down the middle or in any other way one chooses. Neither the enjoyment of Beethoven, nor any other events constitutive of that enjoyment, is going on in O_1. Let O_2 be O_1 plus one-half of the remainder of O, let O_3 be O_2 plus one-half of the remainder, and so on. Finally, we get to O_n, which comprises all of O except for the quark Jeremy. No enjoyment of Beethoven is occurring in O_n—and of course, in this scenario neither does Jeremy enjoy Beethoven. But now we combine Jeremy with O_n, and suddenly, in this (*very* slightly) enlarged region, we have the enjoyment of Beethoven occurring in all its musical glory. If (and only if) *this* seems possible to you, you should feel free to accept Crisp's scenario as a real possibility.

particles, and nothing else. My presence—my literal, physical presence—at any particular point in space consists entirely of the presence there of one of my parts. My presence in the space occupied by Jeremy *just is* Jeremy's presence in that space, and there is no material being in that space other than Jeremy that could be the subject of the experience, *enjoying Beethoven.*

But is it really so absurd to suppose that Jeremy enjoys Beethoven? Perhaps this possibility merits another look, in view of the apparent lack of viable alternatives. Let us then consider some further remarks of Brentano on this very topic:

> The mental activities such as we carry out in an instant present themselves as a very complicated whole even in the variety of simultaneous sensations and affections, and still more so in the conceptual thought and judgement and emotion which are tied to them. And this whole is by no means something, like the shape assumed by a body, which persists by itself until it happens to be transformed into another shape; rather in order to continue to exist it must be actualized anew at each moment. Now how could the brain accomplish this without quite a varied functioning of the individual parts, each of which makes its peculiar contribution? The richness and order which is present in our psychological thought would have to be conceived of as the effect, not of the complicated structure of the brain, but of a quite immeasurable complication which would be given at each individual point.[38]

Now, we are supposing, unlike Brentano in this passage, that the whole of the conscious experience exists at each point not *instead of,* but rather *along with,* the data-processing function carried on by the different parts of the brain in all their marvelous complexity. It will nevertheless still be true that there is this "quite immeasurable complication" of subjective, conscious experience at each and every point in the brain, in spite of the fact that *the various points do not receive the information from the different processing units of the brain through any known causal process, nor is there any physical process occurring at those points that would correspond to the complexity of the conscious experience.* At this point I merely ask the reader to consider: does this not strain one's credulity to the breaking point, and beyond?

My own conviction, for what it is worth, is that it is the assumption of material composition that needs to be abandoned. But if so, what should take

38. *The Existence of God,* 297.

its place? This question launches us on a journey that promises to be difficult, and will no doubt abound with surprises. A natural direction, for those who have seen the need to abandon materialism in its pure form, is towards panpsychism.[39] If the "hard problem" of explaining consciousness is just *too* hard, then why not obviate the problem by positing that consciousness—at least, some form of awareness, however simple and impoverished—is there right from the beginning? Panpsychism, however, advances the cause of understanding less than we might wish. Panpsychism may give us "mind-dust," to borrow an expression from James Van Cleve.[40] But we can't be satisfied with mind-dust—that is, with tiny fragments of mentality inherent in the tiny fragments of material stuff. What we need is a *single* mind, and a single field of conscious awareness, for each sentient being;[41] that is one of the lessons of the story concerning Jeremy, and of the unity-of-consciousness argument. Panpsychism leaves this need unmet, and we would still need an explanation of the process by which those bits of mind-dust are fused into a single conscious mind. But given that this need would remain, not much is gained by postulating the mind-dust to begin with. What we need, in Searle's own words, is to know "how the brain produces the peculiar organization of experiences that expresses the existence of the self" (Self, 136).[42] We have seen, however, that (contrary to Searle's own intention) it is unlikely that an account of this can be given within the boundaries set by the doctrines of biological naturalism and material composition. In raising these issues, however, we are approaching the frontier of some very dangerous territory—the territory that on maps is marked with the skull-and-crossbones symbol as well as with the ominous words, **Substance Dualism**. But the guidebook for that portion of the journey, if indeed we are to go there, must be found elsewhere; this essay has already exhausted the patience of both editors and readers.

39. Thomas Nagel, having argued (tentatively) for the view in his paper "Panpsychism" (in *Mortal Questions* [New York: Cambridge, 1979], 181-95), returns to it in his recent book, *Mind and Cosmos* (Oxford: Oxford University Press, 2012); see 57-63.

40. James Van Cleve, "Mind-Dust or Magic? Panpsychism versus Emergence," *Philosophical Perspectives* 4 (1990).

41. Though possibly one that could be divided due to exceptional circumstances such as commissurotomy; for discussion see my "Persons and the Unity of Consciousness."

42. That is, we need this if we eschew creationist versions of dualism. I believe those versions are worthy of serious consideration, but also involve formidable difficulties. See *The Emergent Self*, ch. 6; also, "The Dialectic of Soul and Body," in Andrea Lavazza and Howard Robinson, eds., *Contemporary Dualism: A Defense* (London: Routledge, 2013), 204-19.

CHAPTER 2

Materially-Composed Persons and the Unity of Consciousness: A Reply to Hasker

Timothy O'Connor

William Hasker and I agree that conscious experience and agency are in no way "reducible to" bio-physical phenomena. He argues persuasively that John Searle's longstanding position on this matter is at best an unstable one. By maintaining that consciousness is *causally* reducible to neurophysiological processes, Searle's spirited contention that it is *ontologically* irreducible is revealed to be less than it first appears. Although Searle resists explicating his view in terms commonly used by other philosophers, it seems to be very much in the neighborhood of the fashionable-in-the-90s "non-reductive physicalism" which held that mental states are type-distinct but token-identical to physical phenomena. (The distinctiveness of Searle's view rests not on the strength of its "nonreductionism" but on his claim that mentality in all its varieties is intimately tied to consciousness.)

Setting aside Searlian exegesis, Hasker and I think the truth of the matter as concerns the phenomena of consciousness lies in the direction of a strong form of ontological emergence. On such a view, when physical elements are organized in the right sorts of ways (including, but for all we know not limited to, certain kinds of properly-functioning neurophysiological structures), they give rise to—cause—wholly distinct mental phenomena. These mental phenomena are token-distinct, physically unstructured states that in turn do fundamental causal work, affecting the very neural processes that sustain them.

This broad-strokes characterization leaves open many questions regarding, e.g., the details of mental-physical causal interaction, the intentionality of unconscious states, and how to think about human agency and free will. It also is silent on the question of chief interest to Hasker: what is the nature of the *subject* of conscious experience? Are creaturely subjects necessarily distinct entities from the organized material systems that are involved in generating and sustaining conscious experiences, or might some or all of them be wholly materially composed? Hasker argues that careful reflection on the puzzling and seemingly *sui generis* unity of conscious experience should lead us to conclude that humans and other sentient beings are not materially composed—the unity of conscious experience points to an ontological simplicity of the experiencing subject.

I believe that Hasker's argument for this conclusion is mistaken, but in a way that is instructive. As we will see, responding to it properly forces one to be explicit about assumptions concerning basic ontology, specifically, the nature of properties, states, and individuals. It also raises interesting issues concerning the trans-temporal identity conditions of composed objects that manifest strongly emergent properties.

Following a long line of thinkers, Hasker argues that the conscious experience of a sentient being, while encompassing several modalities (visual, auditory, etc) that manifest an array of elements structured in various ways, are unified in that they are co-experienced by the thinking subject, *and not by way of distribution among the subject's parts* (if such there be) (29). That is, the immediate subject of the elements of my current visual experience (as of, among other things, a computer, table, mug, and much less focally the painting on the wall in front of me, all spatially arrayed in a particular way) is me, and not, e.g., the different processing units in my visual cortex proximally responsible for those elements being part of my overall experience. Similarly, the subject of the *total* visual aspect of my current experience is me (and not my visual cortex), as is the subject of my auditory experience (and not my auditory cortex), and my conscious thoughts (and not my frontal lobe). If these claims are correct (and I believe that they are), what follows concerning the kind of thing I might be?

Hasker argues that a way to answer this question is to consider the claim that I am materially composed and then to ask what, on this supposition, "is the spatial location of this [conscious experience] of the brain?" (34)—in what does it "inhere", where does it "exist" (34)? And he argues that once we do ask this question, we will be led to say that it inheres in each and every material particle of the brain that in some way underwrites the experience, and so exists in (and only in) every location those particles occupy. Given the unity of consciousness, it cannot do so by way of distribution (with distinct "parts" of the experience located in each of the various particle locations). So it must do so by being wholly located in all of them. If (to switch Hasker's example) I am currently enjoying Radiohead's *Electioneering*, then so is each and every one of innumerable particles of my brain. Clearly, something has gone wrong, and it's not just my taste in music. That something, says Hasker, is the assumption that I am materially composed. Composition is inhospitable to the unity of consciousness.

As Hasker notes, his argument rests on a general thesis of "localized property instantiation" (LPI):

> (LPI) The intrinsic (non-relational) properties of a material thing are instantiated in the space occupied by that thing.

This thesis is hardly the tautology that Hasker suggests. For a Platonist, no properties of any kind exist or inhere in a spatial location, even though some properties are instantiated by objects that have locations. One might say that the object's having or instantiating an intrinsic property occurs in the region the object occupies, but (for the Platonist) this is not to say anything more than that the object is so located. (The *sui generis* relation of instantiation is not so located.) But Hasker presumably is assuming a view on which certain universals (or perhaps tropes) are immanent to their bearers. Given this alternative view, LPI appears to be plausible. As it happens, I am myself partial to this immanentist thesis. In any case, let us assume it for the sake of assessing Hasker's argument.

In a long footnote, Hasker considers a reply to his argument that suggests that, for an emergentist who accepts material composition, conscious mental properties occur in an extended region of the experiencer's brain, but not in any of its subregions. My enjoyment of Radiohead's up-tempo, bleak-message song is ontologically emergent: as a fundamental property, it is instantiated by me as a whole, while being instantiated by my basic parts neither in part *nor* in whole. I enjoy the tune, but none of my fundamental parts do. If there is anything deeply puzzling here, it is aesthetic, not ontological.

Hasker's rejoinder to this reply runs as follows:

> Let O be the organism that is enjoying [Radiohead]; the enjoyment is taking place in the organism as a whole, but not in any proper part of that organism. Now, let O_1 be one-half of that organism, divided down the middle or in any other way one chooses. Neither the enjoyment of [Radiohead], nor any other events constitutive of that enjoyment, is going on in O_1. Let O_2 be O_1 plus one-half of the remainder of O, let O_3 be O_2 plus one-half of the remainder, and so on. Finally, we get to O_n, which comprises all of O except for the quark Jeremy. No enjoyment of [Radio-

> head] is occurring in O_n—and of course, in this scenario neither does Jeremy enjoy [Radiohead]. But now we combine Jeremy with O_n, and suddenly, in this (*very* slightly) enlarged region, we have the enjoyment of [Radiohead] occurring in all its musical glory. If (and only if) *this* seems possible to you, you should feel free to accept [the proposed] scenario as a real possibility. (38, n.37)

What shall one who endorses the "Theory of Emergent Material Persons" (EMP) say in response to this sorites-style argument? We should start by noting that nothing peculiar to consciousness (and its unity) drives the argument. It aims to bring out an absurdity in the very idea of an ontologically emergent property had by a materially composed system. If, e.g., it turned out that certain systems-level control features of living organisms were ontologically emergent in the way that some seem to suggest,[1] then we should be led to posit an entelechy that is the bearer of such primitive holistic properties. Fundamental, structurally-simple intrinsic properties cannot be instantiated by complex systems, on pain of supposing that every constituent of the system also instantiates the property.

Having noted the argument's generality, I suggest that any tendency one may have to find the argument a forceful one is a result of its illicitly inviting us to understand EMP as committed to the claim that anything short of the entire configuration of my brain is *insufficient* for my having the experience I do (or anything similar to it). This is quite evidently absurd, on empirical grounds, but it is not something that EMP need accept. It is highly plausible for empirical reasons that no fundamental particle that is bound up in the comparatively large-scale, nested processes that causally sustain my present conscious experience is causally necessary for it: its role is not only negligible, it is (likely) redundant. Were God to annihilate one such particle, my experience would remain unchanged. Annihilate enough of them, though, and there will be changes in the intrinsic character of my experience; annihilate still more, and all experience would cease, at least for me. Reversing the series in accordance with Hasker's example, if God were to miraculously augment an incomplete brain system, particle by particle (and keep it from, e.g., bleeding out until it reaches full organismic integrity), at some point conscious experience would arrive on the scene. As we near the end of the sequence, the conscious experiences would be highly similar and then precisely similar to those had at the final step. Or so we may assume. This is an empirical issue, and

1. Denis Noble, *The Music of Life: Biology Beyond Genes* (Oxford University Press, 2008).

there may be points at which cognitive functional integrity depends on fairly small additions—there is no reason to suppose that the change in experience would be uniformly "smooth."

Now, the target of Hasker's reflection is synchronic, not diachronic. I note the latter scenario because distinguishing the two is important to judging whether it is absurd, as Hasker thinks, to maintain that conscious experience occurs in a largish region of the brain but not in any of its sub-regions. I am a unified, albeit composed individual. I have conscious experiences through the collective activity of organized regions of my brain generating and sustaining them. (Note well, the relation between their activity and my experience is causation, not identity, realization, or any other purely formal relation.) There is only one subject of experience associated with the region of space occupied by my body, not many overlapping ones. *Were* a few of the particles of my brain not to have existed, everything else remaining fixed, then the unified individual I am would have been (slightly) differently composed, and so the spatial region in which my thought occurred would have (slightly) differed. But as things stand, it is the larger region. (Of course, one may doubt, on empirical grounds, that there is a reference-frame invariant fact of what is happening at an instant; or that the sustaining activity, which is biological in nature, can be thought of as "built up" out of instantaneous events; or that there is, even over an interval, a precise location had by any individual particle.) The best we can say is that it is that region encompassing all and only those particles making any causal contribution to sustaining the experience in question.

To be sure, thorny questions remain, although they are not Hasker's: For example: is the conscious subject *merely* a system of parts, albeit one distinguished from many other stable composites by virtue of having some emergent properties? My own view is that, at least when it comes to human persons, there is an interconnected array of emergent capacities, and this strongly suggests that we are true, i.e., basic individuals, no less than fundamental particles are or would be. Explicating this further requires us to go into the murky waters of the ontology of individuals more generally. On the sort of constituent ontology I favor, this implies that there is a distinctive particularizing element, or substratum, to the human person that is wholly distinct from the substrata of the person's basic parts. In a slogan, composed, emergent individuals without emergent substance dualism.[2]

2. For attempts to develop such a view, see a pair of papers I co-authored with Jonathan D. Jacobs: "Emergent Individuals", *Philosophical Quarterly* 53 (2003), 540–55, and "Emergent Individuals and the Resurrection", *European Journal for Philosophy of Religion* 2 (2010), 69–88.

A second, related question is, what are the boundaries of the composed individual that I am? On the account just gestured at, my individuality is a result of emergent capacities and their manifestations. So far as we know, all of these are associated with conscious thought and experience (or perhaps mentality more generally), and only parts of my brain and nervous system are involved in sustaining my mental life. So which other elements are, in strict truth, parts of me, and why? And is there a determinate answer to this question? The best answer, I believe, is that I am indeed a biological organism. Elements that do not directly contribute to sustaining emergent capacities and their manifestations are parts of me in virtue of their functional integration into the overall system necessary to sustain those purely psychological aspects of myself. Given what we know about the interface of the scales of particle physics and basic biology, it seems inevitable that there will be degrees of functional integration on the outer peripheries of our bodies, and perhaps of individual organs as well. This is indeed theoretically puzzling, but it seems fitting to close a paper in basic ontology by opening a large can of worms.

CHAPTER 3

A Rejoinder to O'Connor

William Hasker

I want to thank Timothy O'Connor for his thoughtful reply to my essay. It is gratifying to have his confirmation that there is a good deal of agreement between us. We agree about the problems inherent in Searle's philosophy of mind, and we agree on the need for strong ontological emergence as a remedy for those problems. And however much I may deplore his apparent preference for Radiohead over Beethoven, this does not constitute a *philosophical* difference between us!

Such a difference does arise, however, in the doctrine that human beings are wholly composed of material particles, a doctrine that O'Connor upholds and that I have attacked. In defending this view, O'Connor presents his answer to the unity-of-consciousness argument, an argument I have deployed in my essay and in a number of other publications. This, then, is what we need to discuss.

O'Connor initially makes heavy weather over my principle of "localized property instantiation," but eventually he accepts it.[1] And by accepting it, he accepts the requirement of specifying the spatial region in which his enjoyment of Radiohead's music occurs. Not surprisingly, he rejects the notion that his quarks individually enjoy Radiohead, or that mine enjoy Beethoven. He agrees with me that his experience cannot exist in the form of bits distributed

1. I do not believe the LPI principle is problematic for Platonists in the way stated by O'Connor. It is true that, on their view, neither properties nor the instantiation relation are spatially located. But the instantiation of a property is an event that occurs in space—and if the property is an intrinsic property of a material object, the instantiation had better occur where the object is located.

among the various sub-units of his cerebral mechanism. But he endorses the proposal that the experience "is instantiated by me as a whole, while being instantiated by my basic parts neither in part *nor* in whole." This seems to be equivalent to Thomas Crisp's suggestion, quoted in my essay, that it is

> possible that C [an event of awareness] occurs in the sum S of the regions occupied by the particles that compose B [the physical object that has the awareness], but not in any of the subregions of S. It occurs in S, but not by dint of partly or wholly occurring in proper subregions of S.

I responded to this by generating (what I took to be) a *reductio* scenario, in which the "subregion" comprises the whole of the organism, except for the minuscule region of space occupied by a single quark. In this entire subregion there is no experience at all going on, but in the *very* slightly larger region obtained by including the space occupied by the quark in question, the full experience of musical enjoyment is taking place. But this, I think, is incredible.

O'Connor's response to this is hard to understand. He writes,

> I suggest that any tendency one may have to find the argument a forceful one is a result of its illicitly inviting us to understand EMP as committed to the claim that anything short of the entire configuration of my brain is *insufficient* for my having the experience I do (or anything similar to it).

It is hard to make sense of this. Why should my argument lead anyone to misunderstand EMP in this way? O'Connor's proposed "misunderstanding" concerns the *causation* of mental experiences, but my argument says nothing about causation; it is exclusively concerned with the *location* in which the experiences take place. Questions about causation and questions about location are distinct: for instance, it's clear that the causation of mental experiences involves the distributed activity of a large number of different brain-structures, but O'Connor and I are agreed that the experiences themselves cannot be distributed in this way.[2] The possibility of the scenario arises directly from the claim, endorsed by O'Connor, that the experience is located in the organism as a whole but not in any subregion thereof. This does not suggest anything

2. This allows us to raise a question about O'Connor's assumption that "the spatial region in which my thought occurred . . . is that region encompassing all and only those particles making any causal contribution to sustaining the experience in question." This might be correct, but it's not at all obvious that it is; in principle, the region in which the thought occurs might be either larger or smaller than the region from which the causal contributions emanate.

like the claim of causal dependence suggested by O'Connor—a claim that is, as he says, extremely implausible. But furthermore, even if someone were to be misled in the way he proposes, it is hard to see how this is relevant to the argument I gave. If someone believed that "anything short of the entire configuration of my brain is [causally] *insufficient* for my having the experience I do," this would entail that, in the absence of the quark Jeremy, the experience could not occur. But my argument does not suppose that Jeremy is absent. On the contrary, Jeremy is right there doing its thing (whatever that may be), and the experience is flowing along: the argument, however, considers only where it is that the experience is located. So how is O'Connor's supposition even relevant? But having proposed this implausible misreading of the EMP theory, O'Connor proceeds to refute it, and seems to suppose that in doing so he has erased any difficulty that might be posed by my scenario. On the contrary: since the misreading has nothing to do with my argument, refuting the misreading does nothing to lessen the argument's force.[3]

What seems to be the case here is that O'Connor *does not* find anything especially implausible in the supposition that no experience whatsoever is going on in the region occupied by the organism minus the tiny space enclosing a single quark, but that once that space is included we have the entire, rich experience of listening to the music, plus of course whatever else one might be experiencing at the same time. Faced with this, my inclination is just to step back and invite readers to judge for themselves. I strongly suspect that any further argument designed to show that this situation is implausible or incredible would not be more convincing than the sheer oddity of the situation itself.

There is, however, one additional point made by O'Connor that deserves a reply. He states that "nothing peculiar to consciousness (and its unity) drives the argument. It aims to bring out an absurdity in the very idea of an ontologically emergent property had by a materially composed system." This is incorrect. If "certain systems-level control features of living organisms were ontologically emergent," this would *not* mean that "we should be led to posit an entelechy that is the bearer of such primitive holistic properties." The behavior of the organism, while guided by the systems-level control features, would consist entirely of the behavior of the organs, cells, molecules, and ultimately the fundamental particles of which the organism is composed; there is no need here for an entelechy. Kant made the essential point here long ago: "Now an

3. For what it's worth, in O'Connor's reverse scenario, in which God builds up a brain particle by particle, the predictions made by my emergent substance dualist view correspond exactly to O'Connor's. His scenario does nothing to distinguish between our respective views.

effect which arises from the concurrence of many acting substances is indeed possible, namely, when this effect is external only (as, for instance, the motion of a body is the combined motion of all its parts). But with thoughts, as the internal accidents of a thinking being, it is different."[4]

It may be helpful to try and figure just why it is that O'Connor finds the scenario I've proposed unmysterious. The key to this, I submit, lies in his claim that "I am a unified, albeit composed individual." Once the "unified individual" has been brought onto the stage, the action proceeds smoothly and without paradox. But the question that needs to be raised is, *where did that unified individual come from?* All we initially have to work with is a structure composed of microphysical particles hooked up together in complicated ways. Just how have we managed to generate, from those organized particles, a unified subject? Let me point out that O'Connor does not take up my challenge, as to whether the experience takes place in the entirety of the space occupied (as we would normally say) by the organism, or only in the tiny, scattered portions of that space occupied by the elementary particles. If there is something strictly and literally occupying the whole of the space, then (as our mutual friend Dean Zimmerman once remarked) this is beginning to look a lot like dualism—albeit a non-standard brand of dualism, one in which minds exist in space. But if there is, strictly and literally, nothing there but the particles in their interconnections, this raises all the more forcefully the question, how do we get from those lonely particles to a unified self? That is the puzzle posed for the EMP theory by the unity-of-consciousness argument, and so far as I can see O'Connor has done nothing to resolve it.[5]

4. Immanuel Kant, *Critique of Pure Reason,* trans. N. Kemp Smith (New York: St. Martin's 1965), 335 (A 352).

5. Though this has not been a theme of the present exchange, some readers will be interested in the question about the relationship between the EMP theory and the doctrine of bodily resurrection. This is developed in O'Connor's paper with Jonathan Jacobs, "Emergent Individuals and the Resurrection"; for a critique, see my "Materialism and the Resurrection: Are the Prospects Improving?," *European Journal for the Philosophy of Religion* 3:1 (Spring 2011), 83–103.

CHAPTER 4

Why Top-Down Causation Does Not Provide Adequate Support for Mental Causation

J. P. Moreland

Many think that top-down causation is essential for preserving the causal efficacy of the mental. Thus, Nancey Murphy claims that top-down causation is crucial for avoiding causal reduction and, accordingly, leaving room for mental causation and responsible agency (Murphy 2006, 71–110). Now it seems to me that the causal efficacy of the self and its various mental states is correct. Indeed, I believe that this is a properly basic belief grounded in (defeasible) knowledge by acquaintance with the self's and its mental states' causal activities. But I am not so sanguine about top-down causation, at least when it is located against a certain metaphysical framework to be mentioned below. When properly interpreted, I do not believe there are any clear examples of it, and I think there is a persuasive case against top-down causation. In order to clarify and defend these claims, I shall, first, lay out three preliminary considerations relevant to what follows; second, show why I do not believe alleged examples of top-down causation are convincing in a way that is pertinent to mental causation; third, present a case for why there is no top-down mental causation; fourth, suggest an important option for moving forward in preserving what we all know to be the case—that mental causation is real.

Three Preliminary Areas of Clarification

1. *Causal powers*

In this article I shall assume a causal-powers view of causation according to which the essence of causation is causal production, the bringing-about of an effect, by an exercise of active power or the triggering of a passive liability.[1] In a causal-powers view, causation cannot be reduced to non-causal notions (e.g., constant conjunction.) There are three reasons why I shall assume this analysis of causation. First, the fundamental, commonsense notion of agency is one in which the self or its mental states bring about various effects and, because of this, the agent stands as a responsible actor. In my view, fundamental, commonsense notions should be preserved if at all possible.[2] Second, a causal-powers/dispositions position provides a metaphysical ground for other causal views (e.g., Humean regularities, counterfactual analyses, and the obtaining of a second-order causal relation between first-order properties of causes and effects), and this seems preferable to leaving these other causal accounts as unanalyzable, brute facts. Third, the view provides a treatment of how the laws of nature connect to their relata that is superior to categoricalism. According to categoricalism, all properties are categorical, and the dispositional character of a property is contingently imposed on that property by the laws of nature. Not only does categoricalism fail to ground why particulars stand in the laws they do, but it also entails that the same entity, say an electron, could enter into radically different laws in different possible worlds. By contrast, dispositionalism holds that some properties are essentially dispositional, and among those are the dispositional properties that ground counterfactual and regularity-treatments of laws.[3]

2. *Parts and wholes*

Part/whole relations are important metaphysical topics, and there are two kinds of parts relevant to our discussion—separable and inseparable.[4]

1. Eric LaRock has pointed out to me that there is another sense of causal powers that is directly relevant to the issue of mental causation, namely, formal causation. The soul has the causal power to organize the structures and functions of the brain through sustained conscious effort. It seems to me that formal causation would include the soul's causal production in organizing the structures and function in view.

2. For a defense of the role of commonsense in intellectual debate, along with its impact on shifting the burden of proof against advocates of revisionist metaphysics, see Kelly 2008.

3. For a defense of dispositional essentialism vs. categoricalism, see Bird 2005. For a defense of a mitigated version of dispositional essentialism, see Moreland 2012. For more on a causal-powers view, see Timothy O'Connor and John Ross Churchill 2010, 262–65.

4. Owen Flanagan seems unfamiliar with this distinction. In rebutting the idea that the soul is simple and indivisible, he points out that "souls" contain various non-identical faculties—e.g., reason, imagination, will—that undermine this claim. See Flanagan 2002, 174–75. However, given

p is a *separable part* of some whole W $=_{def.}$ p is a particular, p is a part of W, and p can exist if it is not a part of W.

p is an *inseparable part* of some whole W $=_{def.}$ p is a particular, p is a part of W, and p cannot exist if it is not a part of W.

In contemporary philosophy, inseparable parts were most fruitfully analyzed in the writings of Brentano, Husserl, and their followers. The paradigm case of an inseparable part in this tradition is a (monadic) property-instance or relation-instance. In our discussion, inseparable parts will play no role. The focus will be on separable parts because they are the entities that constitute the higher-level individuals and structural properties (see below) in the standard mereological hierarchy.

3. *Supervenience*

There are three different kinds of properties that are involved in three different types of supervenience. The first is a functional property: F is a functional property $=_{def.}$ F is a functional concept that is constituted by role R. Moreover, F supervenes on some entity e if and only if e plays (realizes) role R. In my view, Jaegwon Kim has argued persuasively that there are no functional properties that characterize things in the mind-independent world. (Kim 1996, 120–22; 1998, 103–06) Rather, functional "properties" are functional concepts, ways of describing or taking something for certain purposes. For example, a certain piece of paper exemplifies being rectangular, but it realizes the functional concept "being a dollar bill." One virtue of Kim's approach is that it simplifies our ontology when compared to a more abundant view of properties. On such a view, a dollar bill actually has the property of being a dollar bill that, in turn, could be identified with the property of being such as to play role R. And in the right circumstances, people would also take a certain piece of paper to play role R by having the concept of playing role R. Kim's approach simplifies our ontology by reducing the property of being a dollar bill to the concept of playing role R and that is one reason I prefer to go with Kim here.

Given his view, Kim has offered the Causal Inheritance Principle that en-

---

an ontology of inseparable parts, these faculties are such and the soul retains its simplicity and indivisibility regarding separable parts.

tails the epiphenomenal nature of functional "properties" when compared to their realizers: "If a second-order property F is realized on a given occasion by a first-order property H . . . , then the causal powers of this particular instance of F are identical with (or a subset of) the causal powers of H (or of this instance of H)" (Kim 1998, 54). The causal powers of a functional "property" just are those of its realizer, and a causal description is actually epiphenomenal—it does not carve the world at the joints nor does it correctly ascribe unique, new causal powers to an entity that it didn't already have independently of that causal description. Thus, since we are interested in attempts to preserve distinctively mental causation, functional "properties" will not be in focus in what follows.[5]

To understand the other two kinds of properties, it will be helpful to clarify the difference between emergent and structural properties and supervenience. An emergent property is a completely unique, new kind of property different from those that characterize its subvenient base. Accordingly, emergent supervenience is the view that the supervenient property is a mereologically simple, intrinsically characterizeable, novel property different from and not composed of the parts, properties, relations, and events at the subvenient level. We may clarify the sense in which emergent properties are novel as follows:

Property P is a novel emergent property of some particular x at level l_n just in case P is an emergent property, x exemplifies P, and there are no determinates P′ of the same determinable D as P such that some particular at levels lower than n exemplifies P or P′.

By contrast, a structural property is one that is constituted by the parts, properties, relations, and events at the subvenient level. A structural property is identical to a configurational pattern among the subvenient entities. It is not a new kind of property; it is a new pattern, a new configuration of subvenient entities. And many philosophers would characterize emergent and structural supervenience as causal and constitutive, respectively. Since I am contrasting emergent and structural supervenient properties, I will use the notion of an emergent property as a simple, novel, *sui generis* property.

5. David Wilson points out that Nancey Murphy and Warren S. Brown conflate a top-down, even lawlike description, and explanation for a top-down cause (Wilson 2008, 382). This could be due to confusing causation with lawlike regularities or counterfactual dependencies. It could also be due to conflating a functionalist, epistemic notion of the levels in the mereological hierarchy with an ontological depiction of them. According to the former, there are no new causal powers at each level; there are new lawlike descriptions that are pragmatically useful in an anti-realist way in predicting and explaining phenomena. Philip Clayton seems erroneously to equate new causal activities at a level with the presence of an explanatorily and predictively useful law at that level. See Clayton 2004, 52.

In addition, a few words need to be said about the nature and modal force of supervenience relevant to our topic. Since the literature focuses on property supervenience, I will set aside global supervenience and focus on property supervenience. And, given my comments about causal powers above, I shall be employing "supervenience" to express strong property supervenience with a modal force of either metaphysical or nomological necessity. Thus, Jaegwon Kim's characterization accurately captures my conception of strong property supervenience (stated in terms of the supervenience of mental on physical properties): "Mental properties strongly supervene on physical/biological properties. That is, if any system s instantiates a mental property P at t, there necessarily exists a physical property P such that s instantiates P at t, and necessarily, anything instantiating P at any time instantiates M at that time" (Kim 2005, 33).

Top-Down Causation

There is a ubiquitously presented argument for top-down causation among those who accept both a standard presentation of the mereological hierarchy and various supervenient properties at levels above the micro-physical: Throughout the natural world, there are numerous examples of emergent properties that exhibit top-down causation, and this fact establishes a context and plausibility structure for justifying the belief in and understanding of mental causation. (Cf. Steward 2012, 233–43.) In reply, I shall argue that the analogy between the mental case and the others is a poor one and, thus, even if we accept the reality of the other examples, that provides no evidence for mental top-down causation. To understand and evaluate this dialectic, we need to get clear on two things: the mereological hierarchy and the actual nature of top-down causation.

1. *The mereological hierarchy*

Let us construe the mereological hierarchy ontologically and stipulate that there is, in fact, a basic level which is the micro-physical tier of atomic simples (cf. Peterson 2006; Huttemann 2004, 5–15). Three things are important about the hierarchy. First, there is an ontological dependency relation between levels n+1 and n with the former supervening on and being grounded in the latter, terminating with the bedrock, micro-physical level. Everything is dependent on/determined by the micro-physical, and micro-physical processes are causally closed to efficient causal intervention from higher levels.

Second, in the category of individual, ontological reduction is accepted in the sense that there are no non-physical particulars—souls, entelechies, and so forth—in that category.[6] The relation between entities at level n and those at n+1 is the separable-parts/whole relation. Moreover, all particulars above the level of micro-physics are mereological aggregates, systems of parts standing in various instantiations of structural relations. Here is a definition of a mereological aggregate: It is a particular whole that is constituted by (at least) separable parts and external relation-instances between and among those separable parts (there is a debate as to whether or not one should add an additional constituent, viz., a surface or boundary to the analysis). Nancey Murphy's views may be taken as representative in this regard, and she seems to agree that living things are mereological aggregates. She acknowledges that all one needs ". . . is the proper functioning of a suitably complex entity and it would be alive. Life is an emergent property that is dependent on complex organization, not on an additional entity or non-material stuff. . . . Thus, a sphere of proteins and other large molecules is living if . . . it has a membrane separating it from its environment . . ."[7] (Murphy 2006, 57).

The third important feature of the hierarchy is the existence and nature of emergent properties. The first two features of the hierarchy would be accepted by my dialectical opponents and me. However, from my reading of this literature, the main advocates of the view I am criticizing (see below) fail to distinguish structural and emergent supervenience and, accordingly, merge both kinds of supervenience under the category of emergent properties. But as we shall see below, this is a serious mistake. In the category of property, virtually all the properties above the level of micro-physics are structural and not emergent properties.

To illustrate my charge, in his widely referenced work *The Emergence of Everything*, Harold Morowitz cites twenty-eight examples of "emergence" (e.g., the emergence of stars from collections of primordial matter, the emergence of chemical elements from a combination of more elementary particles, the emergence of new cell structures in the evolution of eukaryotes from prokaryotes), and all of them except the emergence of thought/spirit are cases

6. A noteworthy exception to this is Thomas Nagel, who has recently argued that matter should be construed in a panpsychist way and endowed with teleological potentialities to actualize conscious, rational, valuable agents (Nagel 2012).

7. In context, Murphy also adds that the whole must be able to take in nutrients, engage in self-repair, and reproduce. But these features of life are not relevant to my present concerns.

of structural supervenience (Morowitz 2002, 1–38). Citing Terrence Deacon approvingly, Philip Clayton claims that in the process of evolution, we regularly see complex, new kinds of combinatorial novelty (Clayton 2004, 84). Clayton lists numerous examples of emergence, and as far as I can tell, every one of them is structural, not emergent, with the main exception being that of consciousness, which he treats as a genuinely emergent property as I characterized an emergent property above (Clayton 2004, 65–106). Nancey Murphy uses these locutions to describe "emergent" properties: they exhibit a new sort of organization, a larger pattern or system of causal powers at the new level, a unique set of relational properties composed of the system's constituents (Murphy 2007). And when Murphy and Warren Brown categorize different types of "emergent" properties, all of them are structural in nature (Murphy and Brown 2010, 78–85).

At this point, I want to mention briefly two problems. First, given that higher-level properties are structural, it is hard to resist the notion that they are decomposable into the micro-physical level except for exhibiting new relation-instances (and the same is true of the mereological aggregates in the category of individual). Accordingly, Andrew Bailey calls structural supervenient properties "group-level" properties, and says: "It makes some intuitive sense to continue thinking of group-level properties as being at a higher level than the properties of their components, but, in fact, they are really just very complex concatenations of so-called bottom-level properties" (Bailey 1998, 581).

Moreover, the pattern of top-down causation is established with reference to numerous examples of structurally supervenient properties, but as we shall see below, if consciousness is emergent, then the analogy between the former and the latter is not a good one in this sense: Even if, in some way or another, structural properties exhibit top-down causation, it does not immediately follow that emergent properties do. Given that the mental is emergent, more work needs to be done to establish mental causation besides citing examples of structural supervenience.[8]

2. *The real nature of top-down causation*

Two aspects of top-down causation are important for my purposes: the direction and the precise function of such causality. Let's begin by focusing on the

8. For a critique of Nancey Murphy's idiosyncratic view of supervenience and its employment to support "top-down" causation, see Bielfeldt 1999; Wacome 2004, 332–34.

direction of top-down causation. In this regard, Clayton says that top-down causation is "the process whereby some whole has an active non-additive causal influence on its parts" (Clayton 2004, 49). Clayton's (ontological) characterization may fairly be taken as canonical such that top-down causation is widely depicted as moving from wholes to parts.

The main problem with calling whole-to-parts causation "top-down" is that it is not top-down; it's outside-in. The mereological "hierarchy" doesn't go up; it goes out. From micro-physical particles to atoms, molecules, cells, organisms, ecosystems, etc., the movement is towards wider and wider configurational patterns at the same level of reality, towards larger units of interaction. Thus, all the examples of structural supervenience are not examples of genuine top-down causation, but of outside-in causation. For example, in illustrating "top-down" causation, Helen Steward advances the frequently used molecule-in-a-wheel case (Steward 2012, 233–43). When force is applied to a molecule outside a wheel, it will travel along a certain path, but if it is part of a rolling wheel, its path will be determined in a "top-down" way by the wheel of which it is a part. Now, it should be clear that a wheel structurally supervenes on a collection of subvenient parts and this example is outside-in, not genuine top-down causation.

It is crucial to keep in mind that examples of structural supervenience are cases of outside-in and not top-down causation, because if there really are causally efficacious emergent properties, their causal activities would, indeed, be examples of top-down causation. Why? Because the instantiation of an emergent property is a state of affairs whose coming-to-be and continued existence and nature are either efficiently caused by (Searle 1992, 124–26) or, at a minimum, ontologically dependent on and determined by the lower subvenient level. Such emergent properties "rest on top" of the subvenient entities that sustain them in existence. And if they are to exhibit causal power, it must be from the emergent to the subvenient level by intervening into the chain of events at that level. It is important to note that the disanalogy between outside-in vs. top-down causation means that piling up more and more examples of the former does not in the least show that the latter is possible.

The distinction between outside-in causation between a mereological whole and it parts (or between a structurally supervenient property and the subvenient properties, parts, and relations that constitute it) on the one hand, and top-down causation between a simple emergent property and its subvenient base on the other hand, is an important one. Those who think the mereological hierarchy goes up such that individuals (or supervenient properties) at higher levels rest on top of and exert top-down causation with respect to individuals (or subvenient properties) at lower levels fail to make this distinction. Moreover, they fail to distinguish two different, disanalogous ways that higher-level entities are ontologically dependent on lower levels. Mereological wholes (and structurally supervenient properties) are relational structures that are dependent on certain parts because they are composed of those parts. By contrast, an emergent supervenient property is a mereologically simple quality that is dependent on its subvenient base because that base brings the quality about and sustains it in existence without composing it.

So much for the direction of causality. Regarding the precise function of "top-down" causality, there is a view according to which wholes exert efficient causality on their parts by intervening into the chain of subvenient events and changing the direction of that chain. In this sense, top-down efficient causation involves causal activities that "push and pull the lower level components of the system" (Clayton 2004, 24). As far as I can tell, this view is universally rejected by the advocates of top-down causation I am seeking to criticize.[9] Nancey Murphy argues that such a notion of "top-down" causation may require the postulation of spooky new entities, it threatens the integrity of the special sciences, and it smacks of interventionism according to which wholes intervene in the course of micro-physical processes and, as it were, interrupt them (Murphy 2007, 27–29). Helen Steward opines that this notion of causation is "spooky, magical, dualistic, and otherwise metaphysically problematic . . ." (Steward 2012, 228).

In light of these remarks by Murphy and Steward, an alternative view of "top-down" causation is offered: "Top-down" causation for structural supervenient properties should be cashed out, not in terms of efficient causality, but in terms of causal constraints. Various distributions of a whole's parts are consistent with micro-physical laws, but that one distribution was selected as opposed to another must be explained by referring to "higher-level" entities. Thus, "top-down" causation functions as "a larger system of causal factors hav-

9. The issue of "law-violation" enters into discussions of alleged top-down causation in two ways. First, there is the issue of top-down intervention into causal chains that I have just mentioned. Second, there is the issue of parts exhibiting different causal activities or following different laws of nature when in wholes than when in isolation from those wholes. William Robinson defines this sort of "downward" causation as follows: Xs (e.g., brains) downwardly cause ys (e.g., neurons) to have property F (e.g., a new reactive tendency) if ys have F when parts of x but don't have F when not parts of x (Robinson 2005, 119). In my view it is the former notion of "law-violation" that is relevant to genuine emergent top-down causation. And the latter notion is usually combined with a causal constraints view of "top-down" causation to be discussed shortly. For more on this latter notion of "law-violation" see Steward 2012, 229–32.

ing a *selective* effect on lower-level entities and processes" (Murphy, 2007, 29; cf. Steward 2012, 232–45). Further, higher-level entities (e.g., wholes, processes, relational configurations) provide context-sensitive constraints, e.g., boundary conditions, feedback loops, non-linear factors, on the parts at "lower" levels, and higher-level entities are what sustain the sequence of synchronous arrangements of subvenient parts (e.g., reference to a whirlpool and its "top-down" causal influence must be made if we are to explain the relatively stable sequencing through time of subvenient parts arranged whirlpooly).[10]

By contrast with the view just presented, if we grant a causal-powers view and a rejection of causal overdetermination, a genuinely emergent property with causal efficacy will exert top-down causation in such a way that physical causal closure is violated and the exercise of causal power by the emergent property changes the flow of events at the subvenient level.[11]

It is time to summarize what we have learned in this section. The mereological system of reality depicts all levels as dependent on micro-physics in that the laws governing that level are not gappy with outside intervention, the hierarchy goes out not up and, accordingly, complex individuals are mereological aggregates with structurally supervenient properties that exhibit outside-in causal constraints and selection on their parts. While acknowledging a disanalogy between emergent mental and other emergent properties, Philip Clayton nevertheless asserts that "understanding the relationship between mind and

10. Philip Clayton goes beyond the causal-constraints view and advocates a position in which top-down causation involves treating wholes as causal agents in their own right (Clayton 2004, 65). In this sense, the causal activity of such higher-level wholes involves distinct laws and causal influences of the wholes at the higher level (52). I will not discus Clayton's unique position further because I am interested in exposing problems with a depiction of mental causation on a causal-powers view such that it involves genuine top-down intervention in the chain of subvenient base events. Clayton's position is different from this. As far as I can tell, all of Clayton's examples of top-down causation (besides that of conscious states) are outside-in and not top-down. Moreover, he rejects the causal interventionist view of efficient causality that I take to be characteristic of top-down causation exercised by genuine emergent properties (24), and he seems to embrace a counterfactual analysis of causation and not a causal-powers view (57).

11. William Hasker offers a helpful discussion of top-down causation with a causal-powers view and the impact such causation makes on the flow of events at the subvenient level. His discussion is carried out in terms of libertarian actions, but I don't think that such actions are necessary for his general observations to be applicable. See Hasker 1999, 197–201. Richard Swinburne would be another advocate of a view of this sort. See Swinburne 2011, 63–69. Interestingly, neither Hasker nor Swinburne advocate the top-down causal efficacy of mere emergent properties. Each believes in mental substances whose powers enable them to intervene into chains of physical events in the lower levels of the brain.

brain—between consciousness and its neural correlates—requires understanding the multi-leveled structure of the natural world. On this view, the appearance of mental causes is, in one sense, just another case of emergence—just another case in which a complicated natural system gives rise to unexpected causal patterns and properties" (Clayton 2004, 107–08). As I have already suggested, nothing could be further from the truth. Other examples of supervenience are structural; conscious properties are (alleged to be) emergent. Other examples involve outside-in causation; conscious properties involve top-down causation. Other examples exhibit selective and constraining causal influence; conscious properties exhibit efficient, interventionist causality.

Mental Causation as Top-Down Causation

In the previous section, we examined the following argument: Throughout the natural world, there are numerous examples of emergent properties that exhibit top-down causation, and this fact establishes a context and plausibility structure for justifying the belief in and understanding of mental causation. I believe this argument is a total failure, and I have provided a defeater for it.

Is there a positive case against the top-down causal efficacy of emergent mental properties? I believe there is, and before we examine it, let us look at the dialectical context. For the sake of argument, let us grant that mental and value (aesthetic, moral, epistemic) properties are emergent, and let us also grant that secondary qualities are emergent categorical properties that objectively characterize mind-independent entities. So far as I can tell, given the mereological hierarchy, these are the only examples of genuine emergent properties. Now it seems that secondary qualities and value properties are epiphenomenal; their exemplification by an object either does not bestow any causal powers on that object or else those powers are never actualized.

It may be that a bull reacts to seeing red and that a person acts a certain way upon recognizing an object's value properties. In these cases, we have a pretty detailed story to tell at the micro-physical level regarding, e.g., how light is absorbed/reflected by the object, and how the reflected light interacts with the sense organs on to the brain. Given this story and the mereological hierarchy, it is plausible to say that it is this micro-physical story and not the secondary quality redness that is causally responsible for the sensation of red in the bull. Whether or not the sensation of red causes the bull to react is a case of the general issue before us.

For now, I note that if the other two cases of emergent properties are epiphenomenal (secondary qualities, value properties), this fact would seem to place a substantial burden of proof on those arguing for the causal efficacy of mental properties construed as emergent. So far as I can tell, mental properties provide the only case of emergent properties that can plausibly be taken to exert genuine top-down causation. In this regard, it is important to note that in the best current defense of genuine top-down causation regarding emergent properties, O'Connor and Churchill acknowledge that the only clear candidates for such causation are emergent mental properties (O'Connor and Churchill 2010, 278–79).

The positive argument against top-down causation I have in mind is one that appropriates certain insights from a general case against such causation by Jaegwon Kim (Kim 2005, 32–69; cf. Buckareff 2012). Kim's supervenience argument (a.k.a. the exclusion argument) purportedly shows that, given the irreducibility of the mental, there can be no mental causation in a world that is fundamentally physical as depicted in the mereological hierarchy, and according to Kim, this raises serious problems regarding cognition and agency, two features of our lives that are hard to give up. The supervenience argument, says Kim, may be construed to show that mental causation is inconsistent with the conjunction of four theses: (1) closure; (2) exclusion (no overdetermination); (3) supervenience; (4) mental irreducibility. Kim invites us to consider two physical events, p and p*, along with two mental events, m and m* such that (1) m and m* supervene on p and p* respectively (where supervenience includes the notion of dependence and determination, even if this is not taken to be efficient causality) and (2) p causes p*.

The argument proceeds in two stages. Stage 1: Focus on m to m* causation. Since m* obtains in virtue of p*, if m is going to cause m* it must do so by causing p*. Stage 2: Kim offers two different ways to complete the argument, the first of which is most relevant for our purposes. Assuming causal closure and exclusion (no causal overdetermination), p will be the cause of p* and there is no room for m to be involved in bringing about p*. We have m and m* supervening on p and p*, respectively, and p causing p*, nothing more and nothing less.

This argument has been widely discussed, but what have garnered less attention are certain background issues Kim advances prior to formulating the supervenience argument. According to Kim, the fundamental idea behind the argument is what he calls (Jonathan) Edwards's dictum: Vertical determination excludes horizontal causation (Kim 2005, 36). In support of the dictum, Kim invites us to consider a lump of bronze whose macro-properties such as color, density, or shape are dependent on and determined by its synchronous micro-structure. Now, suppose the lump is yellow at time t. Why is this the case? Two answers are possible: (1) Its micro-structure at t causes the color to emerge. (2) It was yellow at t-Δt. Unfortunately, says Kim, there is a tension between the two such that there is neither need nor room for the second explanation. I would add that this seems especially correct, given a causal-powers view of causation. The lump at t will be yellow, given its micro-structure, no matter what was the case at t-Δt.

Kim advances a second illustration taken from Edwards. The successive images of an object in a glass do not remain the same nor do earlier images cause latter ones. Rather, each successive image is caused by and the series of images is constantly renewed with respect to a sequence of new light rays that bring about each image. Again, there is neither need nor room for each image to cause its successor or to exert top-down causation.

In the arguments to follow, I will be employing Edwards's dictum and the two cases used to illustrate it in my arguments against top-down emergent-property causation, and we will be considering situations in which a mental property emergently supervenes on a subvenient physical base. Some might think that these supervenient situations are not analogous with the second case (the glass-image case) above. Why? Of the two cases, the latter one (the glass-image example) is a case of efficient causality and the former one (the bronze-color case) is a case of synchronous supervenience. And, the objection continues, efficient causality is just different from emergent supervenience so the glass-image case is not relevantly analogous with cases of emergent supervenience. Now some take synchronous supervenience to be an example of efficient causality, but even if we don't agree with this opinion, the glass-image case is still relevantly analogous with the emergent supervenient situations because both sorts of cases (efficient causality and the relation between cause and effect; emergent supervenience and the relation between emergent and subvenient properties) involve an ontological dependence/determination of one entity on another (diachronically, synchronically) and I believe it will become evident below that this is the important analogous feature between the two cases for my purposes.

Note that Edwards's dictum and the two supporting illustrations are not defeated by the truth of a causal-powers view of causation and properties. For example, even if the instantiation of secondary qualities brings along their individuating causal powers, those powers are preempted and never actualized. Moreover, given a rejection of overdetermination, it is important to see that in both of these cases, top-down causation is eliminated without a fundamental commitment to the closure of the physical, a commitment I do not embrace.

It is emergence as depicted in the mereological hierarchy that does the trick, along with the fact that we have a pretty good micro-physical story depicting sequences of change at that level as a causal chain. Instantiations of properties at the emergent level are completely dependent on and determined by instantiations of properties at the micro-level; changes at the emergent level are due to changes at the micro-level. Given emergent dependence, the emergent level becomes a series of epiphenomenal states synchronously dependent on the micro-level. Diachronic causation at the emergent level is preempted. And given that there is a causal chain at the micro-level, there is neither need nor room for top-down causation. In light of Kim's background considerations just mentioned, it would seem that the culprit regarding top-down causation is emergence. Granting the mereological hierarchy's twin commitments to the micro-physical level being basic and to genuinely emergent properties, these properties, or, rather, their instantiations, seem to be a series of epiphenomenal states. This surely appears to be the case with secondary qualities and value properties, and it would be odd, to say the least, to make an exception in the case of mental properties. Even if the instantiation of these three sorts of properties brings along their causal powers, there doesn't seem to be a need or room for their exercise.

In the remarks just offered and in the arguments to follow, I am presupposing that there is no such thing as causal overdetermination (COD), especially in cases in which one cause (a baseball) is ontologically dependent on the other cause (a collection of micro-physical parts composing, or allegedly composing, the ball). But COD has been defended by Theodore Sider in the context of discussing Trenton Merricks's eliminativism regarding non-living macro-objects (Sider 2003, 719–26). Now it seems to me that many, perhaps most, philosophers reject COD. Accordingly, I am tempted to rest content with limiting the effectiveness of my arguments to those who agree with me in this regard. But I believe there is more to be said here, and I want to raise two difficulties with the notion of COD.

To understand the first difficulty, consider the following statements from Helen Steward: "Supposing that substance causation does indeed make sense, there is a question whether substance causation by a big and complex substance like an animal could ever fail to be constituted by causation going on at the level of the much smaller and simpler substances that are the animal's *parts* . . . that is to say, whether we can really understand what might be called *top-down* causation, where causality by the complex does not merely reduce to the sum total of a lot of causality by the simple" (Steward 2012, 206). Elsewhere she states: "The challenge, as I see it, is to understand how on earth it can be that the animal has any real, independent efficacy *of its own*: an efficacy that does not merely reduce to the efficacy of its various parts" (Steward 2012, 227).

Steward's worry can be expressed in the following principle of complex whole causation (CWC):

> CWC: The functioning of some complex object O composed of separable parts $e_1, e_2, \ldots, e_n$ to produce some effect E consists in the coordinated functioning of $e_1, e_2, \ldots, e_n$ (or some relevant subset) each of which produces a sub-effect of E and E just is the sum of such sub-effects.

Given this principle, it seems that the causal work in, say, breaking a window is accomplished by its atomic constituents, and there is no work for the ball as a whole to do, and no room for that work. Indeed, when we say that the ball broke the glass, we would more accurately say that the ball broke the glass in virtue of its atomic constituents, and this second assertion seems straightforwardly to give way to a paraphrase along the lines of CWC in which the atomic constituents themselves are identified as the true cause without remainder. And if we add to CWC an epistemic principle of simplicity, then given that we have a clear story about the causal role of the baseball's constituents in breaking the glass, we have no epistemic justification for multiplying causes and postulating the baseball as a whole as an additional cause.

Sider responds by saying that on several views of causation, the baseball and its atomic constituents qualify as causes: counterfactual, covering law, probability-raising, primitive-causal-relation analyses. Now while this may be true, I am assuming a causal-powers analysis of causation, and Sider does not explicitly mention it. And a causal-powers view seems to support a rejection of COD because if, say, the atomic constituents of a ball actually bring about an effect, there just does not seem to be need or room for the ball as a whole to do anything. This claim can, perhaps, be clarified by considering a view of causation that Sider mentions in order to set aside. On this view, causation is a kind of fluid divided among the various potential causes of an effect. If one such cause produces the effect, the fluid is used up and no other potential cause can act. Atoms that break a glass use up the available fluid, leaving none for the baseball itself to use. Now while the fluid example is too crude a picture of causation to be accepted, it does bear an important analogy with a causal-powers position. Just as the fluid in Sider's example brings about or produces its effect, so causes on a causal-powers view bring about or produce their effect. In the fluid case, the problem is not that there would be no fluid left over for another purported cause to use. Rather, the problem is that if one stream of fluid is adequate to produce an effect, say water from a hose knocking a quarter off of a fence, there would not be room or need for a second stream of fluid to do anything, especially if that second stream was somehow ontologically dependent on the first one.

In addition, Sider does take up the epistemic problem of simplicity, but he does so in the context of someone wielding the principle to deny the existence of macro-objects like balls. His response is that the epistemic principle is not an argument against the existence of macro-objects—after all, we may have other reasons besides causality to believe in their existence—rather, it is an argument against one argument for them, viz., that they must exist because they exhibit causal activity in their own right. But I am not using CWC to argue against the existence of macro-objects. I am arguing that such wholes do not have causal powers in addition to those of their atomic parts such that COD is exhibited. And Sider seems to agree that the epistemic argument does, in fact, count to some degree against COD.

My second argument against COD is this: Granting (as I do) the existence of macro-objects such as a baseball, the metaphysical constituents added to their atomic simples to give such macro-objects being are not the sorts of entities that ground additional causal powers for such objects besides those that follow from their atomic simples. The sorts of macro-objects of interest are mereological aggregates. Here is a definition of a mereological aggregate: It is a particular whole that is constituted by (at least) separable parts and external relation-instances between and among those separable parts (there is a debate as to whether or not one should add an additional constituent, viz., a surface or boundary to the analysis). Now a baseball breaks a glass due to the additive causal powers of its atomic simples. The relational structure (and its surface) is not the sort of entity that adds to the ball's causal powers. It could be argued that this point counts against alleged cases of COD that involve entities like baseballs because they just are a collection of parts standing in a structure. But when it comes to the instantiation of genuine emergent properties, such as mental properties, these mental states are not structural wholes composed of atomic simples, and these states, or more precisely, their properties, bring along with them their own causal powers when instantiated, and such powers could, at least in principle, be exercised, maybe even in ways that satisfy COD. It is to this issue that we now turn.

O'Connor and Churchill advance the following Kim-style argument against non-reductive physicalism that is important for our discussion (what follows is a summary of their argument; 2010):

(1) Causal nonreductionism (causation is a real, irreducible relation)
(2) Production account of causation (causation consists in the exercise of causal powers)
(3) Causal theory of properties (properties are individuated with respect to causal powers)
(1)-(3) unpack a causal powers ontology according to which causality is irreducibly real, it consists in the production of an effect, and causal powers are part of the identity conditions for properties.
(4) Supervenience thesis (mental properties strongly supervene on physical properties)
(5) Realization thesis (mental properties are realized by physical properties)
(6) Completeness/causal closure of physics (every physical event that has a cause has a complete physical cause)
(4)-(6) unpack nonreductive physicalism in which mental properties are either functionally or structurally supervenient. (1)-(6) are inconsistent with (7):
(7) A mental property, M, is distinct from its physical realizer property (or properties), P, and each event that consists of M's being instantiated exercises a distinctive form of causality that in one way or another impinges on the realm of physical events. (assumption for reductio)
(8) The instance of M either (a) directly produces a subsequent mental event, M*, or (b) it directly produces a wholly physical event, P*.
(5) (the realization thesis) and (2) (causal production) seem to rule out (8a) because they jointly imply that M has to cause P* on which M* is ontologically dependent; M cannot directly cause M*. So,
(9) Not (8a)
(6) (completeness/causal closure) implies:
(10) If (8b), then the physical event P* is overdetermined by M and some other physical event.
Now, P* could be counterfactually dependent on M&P, but since we are assuming a causal production view of causation, there is no need or room for M in light of P. So we get:
(11) There is not systematic mental-physical overdetermination, as the consequent of (10) implies.
(11) and the consequent of (10) implies not (8b) by *modus tollens*. Therefore,
(12) M does not make a distinctive contribution to occurrences in the physical world, whether wholly physical or supervening mental occurrences.

O'Connor and Churchill conclude by claiming that since (3) (the causal theory of properties) rules out epiphenomenalism, we should either identify M with P or just deny that M is a genuine property.

Now I believe this argument is successful against nonreductive physicalism. But my purpose in presenting the argument is not to evaluate it on that score. Rather, I want to adjust the argument and try to show that the adjusted version is successful against the causal efficacy of emergent property dualism. Let's begin with a few observations. First, as far as I can tell, the argument does not make or, at least, require explicit use of the supervenience thesis (4). In (12), the phrase "supervening mental occurrences" could just as well have been "realizable mental occurrences." And the argument's move from (8) to (9) employs realization, not supervenience. In my view, realization is sufficient to go from (8) to (9), but it is not necessary. Our investigation of Edwards's dictum above suggested that supervenience, especially emergent supervenience, alone, without the need to appeal to closure, will justify the move from (8) to (9). The problem with the causal efficacy of an instantiation of an emergent property is that it is a state of affairs totally dependent on and determined by its subvenient state.

But what about O'Connor and Churchill's claim that (3) (the causal theory of properties) rules out epiphenomenalism? Now if this were the case, it would count against (3). Why? Because we have strong intuitions that there is a relevant possible world in which epiphenomenalism is true, say, a world in which a mental property's causal powers are not, and perhaps cannot be, exercised, even though they are present. In such a world, those powers are real but preempted. Remember, it is not enough to avoid epiphenomenalism that an instantiated emergent property has causal powers. Those powers must be capable of being actualized, and if for some reason or another—such as Edwards's dictum and the two supporting illustrations cited above—that cannot happen, we have both (3) and epiphenomenalism. Thus, I think their premise (7) should be replaced with (7′) (I have italicized my changes to (7)):

(7′) A mental property, M, is distinct from its physical *subvenient* property (or properties), P, and each event that consists of M's being instantiated *has the per se capacity to exercise* a distinctive form of causality that one way or another impinges on the realm of physical events.

According to (7′), a causal theory of properties means that the instantiation of a mental property M carries with it the capacity for M's unique causal powers to be exercised, a capacity that can be blocked or preempted by other factors. In light of these observations, I believe a causal-powers Kim-style argument can be developed against the causal efficacy of emergent mental properties along the lines of the O'Connor/Churchill argument. This argument accepts premises (1)-(4) (with a slight adjustment to (4)), sets aside (5) and (6) and uses (7′) instead of (7). It also involves stating a new premise NP for the purposes of reductio. Here is the argument:

(1)-(3) as before (a causal powers ontology)

(4′) The conjunction of the supervenience thesis and the mereological hierarchy's depiction of the micro-physical level as basic and its sequence of events as a causal sequence.

(7′) A mental property, M, is distinct from its physical *subvenient* property (or properties), P, and each event that consists of M's being instantiated *has the per se capacity to exercise* a distinctive form of causality that one way or another impinges on the realm of physical events.

(NP) An instance of M makes a distinctive contribution to occurrences in the physical world, whether wholly physical or supervening mental occurrences.

(8) An instance of M either (a) directly produces a subsequent mental event, M*, or (b) it directly produces a wholly physical event, P*.

(4′) (the supervenience and mereological-hierarchy thesis) and (2) (causal production) seem to rule out (8a).[12] So,

12. Another way to see why supervenience rules out M to M* causation is to consider the fact that on a causal-powers view, a cause produces an effect in virtue of the actualization of the cause's dispositional powers. Now, such an actualization will require the disposition to pass from potency to actuality through some time frame of t1 to t2. From t1 to t2, the dispositional power passes through various degrees of actualization until it reaches full actuality at t2. Suppose at t1, M has the dispositional potential Dp to bring about M*, and at t2, M has Da, the full actualization of Dp. What is happening at the subvenient physical level during the interval from t1 to t2? It seems like two scenarios are possible. *Scenario one*: The subvenient state remains the same. But if this is true, supervenience is violated because the subvenient state at t1 underlying M&Dp is the same as that underlying M&Da at t2. In this case, there is a mental difference without a subvenient physical difference and this physical base is not sufficient to fix the supervenient state. *Scenario two*: At each degreed state between t1 and t2 in which Dp is increasingly becoming more and more actualized until Da is reached, there is a different subvenient state. However, in this scenario, the transition between Dp and Da is not the actualization of a genuine causal power. Rather, it is just a series of gradually different epiphenomenal states fully dependent on/determined by the graded differences at the subvenient level. Thus, supervenience rules out M to M* causation because in scenario one, supervenience would be violated. And in scenario two, the transition between M&Dp to M&Da is like a series of shadows. All the ontological work is being done at the subvenient level.

(9) Not (8a).
(10) If (8b), then the physical event P* is overdetermined by M and some other physical event.

Assuming a causal production view of causation and (4′), there is no need or room for M's causal activity in light of P. So we get:

(11) There is not systematic mental-physical overdetermination, as the consequence of (10) implies.

So we conclude that not (8b) and, more generally,

(12) An instance of M does not make a distinctive contribution to occurrences in the physical world, whether wholly physical or supervening mental occurrences.

(12) is inconsistent with (NP) and, thus, (12) completes our reductio. Epiphenomenalism follows for all possible worlds in which mental properties satisfy (4′). This is consistent with (1)-(3). In these possible worlds, mental properties, as it were, bring their defining mental powers along with them. It's just that emergent supervenience and the mereological hierarchy preempt their actualization.[13]

13. Cynthia and Graham Macdonald attempt to provide an account of a specific form of downward causation for emergent properties (specifically, the instances of such properties) in the special sciences, including mental properties, that preserves the causal closure of the physical. See Macdonald and Macdonald 2010. Working within a framework of immanent universals and a Lombardian account of event existence and identity, they claim the following: (1) The extensionality of causality (x and y stand in the causal relation to each other irrespective of the descriptions under which they fall). (2) Just as the exemplifying of a determinable (being a color) and one of its determinates (being red) constitutes a single event that is one exemplifying of two properties, so there is a single event consisting in the exemplifying of a supervenient (e.g., mental) property and a subvenient (e.g., physical) property (the Co-Instantiation Thesis—two or more properties of an event can be co-instantiated in a single instance). (3) By extensionality, if the physical event (the instantiating of the subvenient physical property) is causally relevant/efficacious, so is the mental one (since they are the same event). (4) If a property has instances that are causally efficacious, then the property has causal powers, so mental properties have causal powers. (5) In this way, the causal relevance of mental properties is preserved without violating physical causal closure. Here is my brief response to the Macdonalds: First, the instantiation of being a color at a time is not identical to the event of the instantiation of being red at that time. Rather the former is an essential constituent of the latter. Second, the determinable/determinate relation

A Way Forward

My arguments against the causal efficacy of emergent, especially mental, properties have not appealed to physical causal closure.[14] In my view, closure is not basic; it follows from emergence and the standard mereological hierarchy. The same may be true of the rejection of overdetermination—it may not be basic—but, since I accept that rejection, I won't weigh in on this matter here. As I mentioned in this article's introduction, belief in the self's and its mental states' causal efficacy is properly basic. Almost all of us know that this efficacy is true. So where do we go from here?

From what we have seen, the problem resides in treating mental properties as emergent ones against the backdrop of the standard mereological hierarchy. I believe this standpoint should be rejected with regard to providing an ontological analysis of causally efficacious mental subjects. Instead, we should depict mental properties as kind-defining properties that constitute the essence of the objects that instantiate them. Those objects will be genuine substances, which may have inseparable parts, but which are not mereological aggregates composed of separable parts. In short, we should be substance dualists of some form or another regarding causally efficacious mental subjects. In this way, mental properties or their instantiations are not emergent. They and their powers are basic characteristics of the substances that have them. Edwards's dictum and the supporting illustrations do not apply to ba-

is a bad analogy for the emergent supervenient property/subvenient property relation. The former is a constituent/whole relation and the latter is a dependency relation between two different properties and their instantiations. Even if the instantiation of a case of the former is regarded as one event, an instantiation of the latter is two distinct events standing in a dependency relation. Some (e.g., John Searle) take the relationship between an emergent-property event and a subvenient-property event to be causal. Even if this is wrong, it is not unintelligible. If the emergent-property event was identical to the subvenient-property event, then the causal interpretation would, in fact, be unintelligible since a causal event is not identical to an effect event. And given a causal-powers ontology, emergence, the hierarchy and closure, the physical event and not the mental event is causally efficacious. Finally, if one insists on taking the instantiation of the two properties to be a single event, it still seems that this event is efficient-causally efficacious qua being physical and not qua being mental, even if the mental property tracks (e.g., due to multiple-realizability) a different causal profile than the former. In light of a causal powers approach, it is the causal efficacy, not the causal relevance, of the mental that is required to preserve mental causation and responsible agency. For a brief discussion of the difference between causal efficacy and relevance, see Ravenscroft 2005, 144–55.

14. For a detailed treatment of the difficulties in stating a version of physical closure that is empirically testable, see E. J. Lowe 2008, 41–57.

sic mental substances. Rather, they target emergent properties. At the basic level of the hierarchy, we have not only micro-physical entities that compose relevant objects (rocks, bodies, etc.), we also have mental subjects. Obviously, I cannot undertake an evaluation of all the pros and cons of such an ontology (cf. William Hasker 2012) relative to non-reductive physicalism or emergent property dualism. But if we limit our focus to the causal efficacy of the mental, then I believe substance dualism—or some view that is so close to it that its differences from substance dualism are largely verbal—is the best, perhaps, the only way out, given the other two views, or so I have argued.[15]

REFERENCES

Bailey, Andrew. (1998) The Five Kinds of Levels of Description. In Stuart R. Hameroff, Alfred W. Kaszniak, Alwyn C. Scott, eds., *Towards a Science of Consciousness II: The Second Tucson Discussions and Debates*, 577–83. Cambridge, Massachusetts: MIT Press.

Biefeldt, Dennis. (1999) Nancey Murphy's Nonreductive Physicalism. *Zygon* 34, 619–28.

Bird, Alexander. (2005) Laws and Essences. *Ratio* XVIII, 437–61.

Buckareff, Andrei. (2012) An Action Theoretic Problem for Intralevel Mental Causation. *Philosophical Issues* 22, 89–105.

Clayton, Philip. (2004) *Mind & Emergence*. Oxford: Oxford University Press.

Flanagan, Owen. (2002) *The Problem of the Soul*. New York: Basic Books.

Hasker, William. (1999) *The Emergent Self*. Ithaca, New York: Cornell University Press.

———. (2012) Is Materialism Equivalent to Dualism? In Benedikt Paul Gocke, ed., *After Physicalism*, 180–99. Notre Dame, Indiana: University of Notre Dame Press.

Huttemann, Andreas. (2004) *What's Wrong with Microphysicalism?* London: Routledge.

Kelly, Thomas. (2008) Common Sense as Evidence: Against Revisionary Ontology and Skepticism. *Midwest Studies in Philosophy* XXXII, 53–78.

Kim, Jaegwon. (1996) *Philosophy of Mind*, 1st. ed. Boulder, Colorado: Westview Press.

———. (1998) *Mind in a Physical World*. Cambridge, Massachusetts: MIT Press.

———. (2005) *Physicalism, or Something Near Enough*. Princeton, New Jersey: Princeton University Press.

———. (2006) *Philosophy of Mind*, 2d. ed. Cambridge, Massachusetts: Westview Press.

Lowe, E. J. (2008) *Personal Agency: The Metaphysics of Mind and Action*. Oxford: Oxford University Press.

Macdonald, Cynthia, and Graham Macdonald. (2010) Emergence and Downward

15. I want to thank my co-fellows at the Biola Center for Christian Thought for their helpful feedback on an earlier draft of the paper. Special thanks go to Emily Esch, Jason Runyan, Eric LaRock, Gregg TenElshof, Tom Crisp, and Steven Porter.

Causation. In Cynthia Macdonald and Graham Macdonald, eds., *Emergence in Mind*, 139–68. Oxford: Oxford University Press.

Moreland, J. P. (2012) God and the Argument from Consciousness: A Response to Lim. *European Journal for Philosophy of Religion* 3, 243–51.

Morowitz, Harold. (2002) *The Emergence of Everything*. Oxford: Oxford University Press.

Murphy, Nancey. (2006) *Bodies and Souls, or Spirited Bodies?* Cambridge: Cambridge University Press.

———. (2007) Reductionism: How Did We Fall Into It and Can We Emerge From It? In Nancey Murphy and William R. Stoeger, eds., *Evolution and Emergence: Systems, Organisms, Persons*, 19–39. Oxford: Oxford University Press.

———. (2009) Introduction and Overview. In Nancey Murphy, George F. R. Ellis, and Timothy O'Connor, eds., *Downward Causation and the Neurobiology of Free Will*, 1–28. Berlin: Springer.

———, and Warren S. Brown. (2010) *Did My Neurons Make Me Do It?* Oxford: Oxford University Press.

Nagel, Thomas. (2012) *Mind and Cosmos*. New York: Oxford University Press.

O'Connor, Timothy, and John Ross Churchill. (2010) Nonreductive Physicalism or Emergent Dualism? The Argument from Mental Causation. In Robert C. Koons and George Bealer, eds., *The Waning of Materialism*, 261–79. Oxford: Oxford University Press.

Peterson, Gregory R. (2006) Species of Emergence. *Zygon* 41, 689–712.

Ravenscroft, Ian. (2005) *Philosophy of Mind: A Beginner's Guide*. Oxford: Oxford University Press.

Robinson, William. (2005) Zooming in on Downward Causation. *Biology and Philosophy* 20, 117–36.

Searle, John. (1992) *The Rediscovery of the Mind*. Cambridge, Massachusetts: MIT Press.

Sider, Theodore. (2003) What's So Bad about Overdetermination? *Philosophy and Phenomenological Research* 27, 719–26.

Steward, Helen. (2012) *A Metaphysics for Freedom*. Oxford: Oxford University Press.

Swinburne, Richard. (2011) Dualism and the determination of action. In Richard Swinburne, ed., *Free Will and Modern Science*, 63–83. Oxford: Oxford University Press.

Wacome, Donald H. (2004) Reductionism's Demise: Cold Comfort. *Zygon* 39, 321–37.

Wilson, David L. (2008). Neurobiology of Human Action: Is Downward Causation Necessary? *The Quarterly Review of Biology* 83, 381–84.

CHAPTER 5

Emergence and Causal Powers: A Reply to Moreland

Jason D. Runyan

J. P. Moreland believes in mental causation. However, in his chapter, he expresses doubt about whether there is any evidence of top-down causation. He also provides an argument for why there is no top-down mental causation. This is posed as a problem for emergentists, who resist the elimination, or reduction, of mental causes but don't endorse traditional substance dualism; or, that is, the idea that we are, or are partially composed of, a substance or entity with mental characteristics but without physical characteristics. The upshot, according to Moreland, is that if we want to uphold mental causation we should be traditional substance dualists.

In what follows I summarize, and respond to, the two main prongs of Moreland's argument against top-down mental causation: (1) that there are no other examples of the type of top-down causation of which top-down mental causation could at least *prima facie* be a subtype; and (2) that top-down causation can't actually support mental causation given emergentist commitments, thus emergentism leads to epiphenomenalism.

A distinction can be drawn between "strong" emergence, or the emergence of a distinct efficient cause, and "weak" emergence, or the emergence of that which isn't a distinct efficient cause. As I hope to make clear, I think Moreland discusses good reasons to doubt that mental causes can *weakly* emerge, as some (maybe most) emergentists postulate. I will, however, argue that he doesn't provide a successful argument against the idea that mental causes do, or can, *strongly* emerge. For one thing, I argue that alterations must be made to his argument for (2) if it's to apply to strong emergentism; and the most straightforward way of doing so makes it equally apply to the view that immaterial substances, or entities, with mental characteristics are causes of physical occurrences—a view Moreland wishes to uphold. I, however, will also sketch out why I think there are no good grounds for this alteration.

The overall consequence of what I argue here is that Moreland has presented us with no reason to doubt that mental causes are emergent. He has, however, given good reasons for thinking that weak emergentism leads to epiphenomenalism.

In his chapter, after making some clarifications, Moreland takes aim at those who want to uphold top-down mental causation while upholding what he calls "the mereological hierarchy." According to this hierarchy:

> there is an ontological dependency relation between levels n+1 and n with the former supervening on and being grounded in the latter, terminating with the bedrock, micro-physical level. Everything is dependent on/determined by the micro-physical, and *micro-physical processes are causally closed to efficient causal intervention from higher levels.* (55-56)[1]

There are two claims contained here that I want to focus on: (a) anything that exists at a "higher" level of emergent phenomena depends upon what exists on a "lower," basal level such that, if the basal level didn't exist as it does, neither would the emergent level. So if there is a change in the emergent level there will be a change in the basal level.[2] Additionally, (b) the "bedrock, micro-physical level," or some basal level of phenomena, is causally closed such that all that happens on that level, and has an efficient cause, can be given a complete, efficient, and accurate causal explanation in terms of the phenomena that occur at that level or lower.[3]

We should, at the outset, note that the truth of (a) doesn't entail the truth of (b). To illustrate, my ability to raise my hand may, under normal circum-

1. My emphasis.

2. We shouldn't make the mistake of thinking that this dependency relationship entails that all that occurs mentally is determined by what occurs physically. We should remember that dependency relationships are—and supervenience is—at its core about property co-variation and a dependency relationship (cf. Kim 1998, 14). And the fact that two phenomena co-occur, and that the occurrence of one depends upon the other also occurring, doesn't, on its own, establish which occurrence determines the other.

3. Here, I should point out that a growing number of philosophers of biology argue that the idea that the world is made up of "levels" of phenomena (in the way depicted in "the mereological hierarchy") is artificial, and that upholding emergentism doesn't require upholding such a view; cf. J. Dupré 1993; I. Brigandt 2010; C. Waters 2013. Though I will often adopt the "levels" language used in the works to which I am replying, the central arguments I develop here don't hinge on whether such ways of speaking prove artificial. I thank J. Churchill for suggesting I mention this point.

stances, depend upon the occurrence of certain neural activity states in the motor cortex and elsewhere (the latter being necessary for the former), without this entailing that there is a complete, efficient, and accurate causal explanation in terms of neurophysiological causes for the raising of my hand when I raise it. Also, this dependency relationship, along with the lack of a complete, efficient, and accurate causal explanation in terms of neurophysiological causes, doesn't entail that a substance lacking physical characteristics is doing some of the work. There are more possibilities.

Even if the existence of emergent phenomena depends upon what exists at basal levels, it may be that distinct efficient causes come about when the right things are organized just right at basal levels. (It seems that Aristotle held something along these lines—at least, some historical philosophers think so [cf. Johansen 2012].) In this case, at least some basal entities would have, among their properties, the property of having the potential of being a part of an entity that has a distinct causal power not possessed by any of its constitutive parts. And by causal powers—consistent with Moreland—I am thinking of powers to, when given the opportunity, produce some change. The exercise of such a power is the producing of some change that wouldn't otherwise occur. So to exercise a causal power is to be an efficient cause of something.

However—as Moreland notes—to think there are emergent mental causal powers along the lines outlined above is to part ways with many emergentist theorists, such as Nancey Murphy, who want to uphold top-down mental causation, and yet maintain that thinking some efficient causes are not those of interest in the natural sciences (e.g., physics, chemistry) requires thinking there are "spooky new entities" that interrupt normal, underlying processes (cf. Murphy 2007, 27–29; 2011, 8). What, however, is assumed in such characterizations is—as Moreland points out—that a level of phenomena underlying mental phenomena is normally causally closed in the way described in what I designated as claim (b) of "the mereological hierarchy." In this case, given claim (a) of the hierarchy (see above), the exercise of a distinct efficient mental causal power would result in an unusual, or exceptional, interruption of normal brain processes. Equally, all other efficient causes would be found within a constricted range of lower levels, and so to introduce any more efficient causes, at some higher level of phenomena, would be to make a special exception, thereby introducing something mysterious.

Instead of introducing something "spooky," Murphy endorses what is sometimes called "whole-part constraint" (cf. Murphy 2011, 12). Moreland correctly characterizes this as a type of "outside-in," rather than top-down, causation since all causes exist at a basal level (or within a certain set of basal levels) of phenomena, studied in the natural sciences—a level of phenomena that, according to emergentists, underlies mental phenomena. It's just that, according to such theories, our nervous systems (and all other configurations of complex *physical* systems) are dynamic, and probabilistic, "systems" that place "constraints" on the operation of the causes studied in the natural sciences (cf. Murphy 2007, 29; Murphy 2011, 13). So any work being done can be completely and accurately explained in physical terms (cf. Murphy 2011, 12–13).

At this point, we should remember that what has led Murphy, and others, down the "whole-part constraint" path (and to characterize the idea of a distinct efficient mental cause as an idea about something spooky that would have to interrupt normal underlying processes) is the assumption that, along with claim (a), claim (b) of "the mereological hierarchy" is true. So some level of phenomena underlying mental phenomena is causally closed. But do we have good reason to think this? This is a point to which we will have to return.

Regardless of their basis, as Moreland observes, the problem with "whole-part constraint" theories is they don't actually allow for the emergence of mental causes. They may, perhaps, allow for the emergence of genuine mental phenomena, but none of these emergent phenomena are causes in the way needed for top-down mental causation. All causation of the kind needed for top-down mental causation (i.e. efficient causation) is reduced to some basal level of phenomena (58-60). Further, as Moreland also observes, for *true* top-down mental causation, emergent mental phenomena must produce change at basal levels (60). And in this case, barring systematic overdetermination by mental and physical causes, the causal closure principle of the physical is violated (or at least certain versions of it are; see below). Something "whole-part constraint" folks, like Murphy, deny.

The central argument Moreland goes on to make from all of this is that granted there really is top-down mental causation it's a lone wolf. It's one of a kind. All other supposed cases of top-down causation that have been wheeled out are, when it comes down to it, simply cases of outside-in causation. However, only if claim (b) of "the mereological hierarchy" is true except for cases of top-down mental causation is Moreland right—top-down mental causation would be a lone wolf. This is because he is right only if, in all other cases, (c) all that physically occurs, and has an efficient cause, can be given a complete, efficient, and accurate causal explanation in terms of what occurs at some "bedrock" level; and (in keeping with points already made) (b) is true only if (c) is true. There are, however, good reasons to be skeptical about the warrant for thinking either is true.

Whether we put aside possible cases of top-down mental causation or not, the idea that all that physically occurs, and has an efficient cause, can be given a complete, efficient, and accurate explanation in the terms of physics (or even of some set of natural sciences) isn't an *a priori* truth. And, at present, it seems unwarranted from our empirical observations. Rather, its widespread acceptance seems the result of over-exuberance about what we can legitimately and confidently conclude from the fact that we can devise laws that can be used to explain what happens under certain, clearly defined circumstances. And the fact that we can design complex artifacts (e.g., computers) that are, under certain conditions, rather reliable and useful, and operate according to such laws, seems to fan the flame of this over-exuberance.

The truth of the matter, however, is that science, on the whole, is a messy set of disciplines. The ways that what is learned from these disciplines comes to be integrated (when it has been) is anything but formulaic. The more we meticulously study the phenomena of interest in our various scientific disciplines, the more specialized and divergent these disciplines become. The implication is that, as Nancy Cartwright has extensively argued, by all appearances our world is

> rich in different things, with different natures, behaving in different ways. The laws that describe this world are a patchwork, not a pyramid. They do not take after the simple, elegant and abstract structure of a system of axioms and theorems. Rather they look like—and steadfastly stick to looking like—science as we know it: apportioned into disciplines, apparently arbitrarily grown up; governing different sets of properties at different levels of abstraction; pockets of great precision; large parcels of qualitative maxims resisting precise formulation; erratic overlaps; here and there, once in a while, corners that line up, but mostly ragged edges; and always the cover of law just loosely attached to the jumbled world of material things. (Cartwright 1999, 1)

Given that Cartwright and likeminded philosophers of science are correct, we have biology as a distinct discipline out of more than mere convention, as we do psychology, sociology, ecology, etc. What happens at the level of phenomena of interest in these various disciplines is not merely the result of what happens at a more fundamental level. All the work being done isn't being done at some fundamental level(s).

In each scientific discipline we develop theories. And we only have a basis for thinking that even the best, and most precise, of these apply where they are useful—e.g., where they are successfully used to model, make predictions, make successful and purposeful manipulations, and/or to construct artifacts (cf. Cartwright 1999, 9). Since the utility of a scientific theory is limited in scope, so is the range of circumstances wherein we have reason to think it applies. Basically, we have reason to think a theory applies within the range of circumstances consulted when formulating the theory. And that this range is limited should be clear from the fact that the conditions of our experiments, and contraptions, have to be arranged "*just so* to fit the well-conformed and well-established models of the theory" being used, or tested (Cartwright 1999, 2). Thus, we encapsulate our contraptions, and often conduct our experiments in sealed spaces, being sure to limit, or stop, factors not considered, or taken into account, when developing the theory being used or tested. And even then, external factors sometimes intervene such that our contraptions behave unexpectedly, or our experiments fail.

Further, the laws we develop in our scientific disciplines, physics included, by all appearances "hold only *ceteris paribus*" (all things being equal) (Cartwright 1999, 4). We only have warrant for thinking these laws are true given certain, prescribed circumstances. Our scientific, and technological, advances support the truth of these laws but not their universality. Like our theories, we have reason to believe these laws apply within the range of circumstances consulted when formulating them.

So there is a good argument to be made that we have our various scientific disciplines (including biology, psychology, and sociology), and will continue to have them, out of more than mere convention. It seems perfectly valid to think each discipline focuses on distinct phenomena with their own distinct efficient causes. It seems unwarranted to think all our various scientific disciplines except physics are focused on structures, or systems, that merely constrain causes in operation at some basal level.

It, of course, may be true that thinking all efficient causes are at some basal level may be consistent with what we currently know. However, my point isn't that a consistent position along these lines can't be articulated. My point is that thinking thus is unwarranted. The current state of the sciences is what we should expect if there are distinct efficient causes—some emergent—sprinkled throughout the domains of interest in our various sciences, psychology and sociology included. To borrow an illustration used by Michael Gazzaniga (2010), it seems likely that if an impartial, rational alien were to land on our planet they would be left wondering what basis we have for thinking that all efficient causes are in operation at some basal level of phenomena. They may even find such a postulation quite surprising given the common, everyday evidence that our universe is quite stratified, varied, and even surprising.

The point is—putting aside possible cases of top-down mental causation or not—whether all efficient causes exist at some "bedrock" level of phenomena seems to be left underdetermined; and may always be so, if not ruled out at some point. We may always be able to develop a depiction of our universe, consistent with what we know, wherein all efficient causes exist at some basal level. And the same may be true for a depiction wherein various types of distinct emergent efficient causes exist. It, equally, remains a possibility that the idea that all efficient causes exist at some "bedrock" level of phenomena (e.g., the level studied by physicists) will turn out to be merely a detour in our intellectual advancement resulting from over-exuberance about what conclusions are warranted by our incredible scientific, and technological, advancements over the past several 100 years. We may find it problematic the more we unpack the implications upholding such a view has in various disciplines, including psychology (cf. Runyan 2013, ch. 8).

Generally speaking, I, like Moreland, think we should hold on to "commonsense notions" unless there are good reasons to do otherwise. But I think this approach should be taken more widely, and not reserved for discussions about the mental. And, given this *modus operandi*, it seems unwarranted to think our universe isn't teeming with various types of strongly emergent entities, or substances, that, under certain circumstances, are efficient causes. All our various scientific disciplines aren't *prima facia* aimed at uncovering structures, or systems, that merely "constrain" the causes studied by physicists. And, as of yet, there seems no good reason to think there aren't all kinds of emergent substances, and entities, that exercise their own distinct causal powers—the exercise of which is not merely the conjoined exercise of causal powers by their constitutive parts.

But, as a brief aside, what about the principle of causal closure of the physical? Earlier we noted that upholding this principle along with the idea that there are distinct efficient mental causes leads to problems. And shouldn't we be hesitant to give up this principle?

E. J. Lowe noted that there are a variety of causal closure principles, some stronger than others (Lowe 2010, 41–57). The ones typically used against the idea that there are distinct efficient mental causes go something like this:

> For any physical event *e*, if *e* has a cause at time *t*, then *e* has a wholly physical sufficient cause at *t*. (Lowe 2010, 63)

It's true that principles of this strength (though not weaker versions; Lowe 2010, 41–57) are inconsistent with the idea that there are efficient mental causes that produce physical change. But what is the warrant for such principles? They aren't *a priori* truths. Further, the empirical basis for quantum physics provides evidence that they are false. We have evidence that certain occurrences have physical causes at some earlier time *t* even though there is no sufficient physical cause at *t*, as we can have all knowledge of the physical causal factors at *t* and yet only probabilistically predict the occurrence (cf. Lowe 2010, 65–68). One reply might be that we have no reason to think that what applies to the quantum level applies elsewhere. But, equally, we don't have a good reason to think it doesn't.

There are all kinds of things that we can only probabilistically predict even though they have a cause—e.g., the weather, the pattern with which flames lick wood, the path a water molecule takes as it moves downstream, certain behaviors, and even brain activity patterns. It has become commonplace to assume that, in every case, this is because we don't have all the facts. And such assumptions may have seemed to have a basis when Newtonian physics reigned supreme. But, given quantum physics, this basis seems to have been swept away, and such assumptions seem to be left suspended in thin air.

With particular reference to brain activity patterns (because it's closest to the topic at hand), given what we presently know, it seems that—within the conscious, behaving individual—we can only probabilistically predict how brain activities will unfold given all the neurophysiological variables (cf. Runyan 2013, 134–44). It also seems that there will be differences in the relevant brain activities between instances of an individual engaging in some conduct, mental or otherwise. Now, it could be that we may simply not have all the neurophysiological facts; or that this activity is, to a certain extent, left up to chance. However, it could equally be that there may be no sufficient neurophysiological cause for certain changes. Rather, *the individual*—whose brain we are examining after all—may produce certain physical brain changes that would not otherwise occur by exercising mental causal powers. In this case, it may be that an emergent agent is an efficient cause for certain changes that occur in, or to, their constitutive parts.

In sum, the main point I wish to make is that, whether or not we put aside possible cases of top-down mental causation, thinking that (c) all that physically occurs, and has an efficient cause, can be given a complete, efficient, and accurate causal explanation in terms of what occurs at some "bedrock" level is unwarranted. The same is, thus, the case for thinking claim (b) of "the mereological hierarchy" is true. Given this—in agreement with Moreland—we should be skeptical of "whole-part" constraint theories, and weak emergentism. However, for the same reason, we should be skeptical of the conclusion that there are no other examples of the type of top-down causation of which top-down mental causation could at least *prima facie* be a subtype. That is, we have reason to find the first prong of Moreland's two-pronged argument against top-down mental causation unconvincing as an argument against *all* forms of top-down mental causation. Moreland has, however, focused our attention on serious problems for a weak emergentist account of mental causation.

Let's now turn to the second prong of Moreland's argument.

To develop a positive account against top-down mental causation, Moreland adjusts an argument put forth by Timothy O'Connor and John Churchill (2010) in support of the idea that the mental is ontologically emergent from the physical. This general line of argument stems from Jaegwon Kim's famous exclusion argument (cf. Kim 2005, 32–69). The argument, as adjusted by Moreland, can be summarized as follows:

We should think that:

(i) Causal powers are "irreducibly real," fundamental, and their exercise produces change. (We should uphold a causal power view of causation along the lines of the one I summarized earlier.)

Given that emergentism is true:

(ii) The mental strongly supervenes on the physical such that "if any system s instantiates a mental property M at t, there necessarily exists a physical property P such that s instantiates P at t, and necessarily, anything instantiating P at any time instantiates M at that time" (Kim 2005, 33);[4] and "the mereological hierarchy" (see above) holds.

Given (ii):

(iii) The exercise of a mental causal power "does not make a distinct contribution to occurrences in the physical world, whether wholly physical or supervening mental occurrences."

Ultimately, (iii)—as a consequence of (ii)—should lead us to realize that, given (i) and (ii), there is never the opportunity for a mental causal power to be exercised as no physical change is ever produced as a result of exercising such a power. The mental is, in effect, epiphenomenal.

Here, I have attempted to streamline Moreland's argument while retain-

4. Here, it should be noted that T. O'Connor and H. Wong (2005) have argued that emergence doesn't require the "strong" supervenience conditions it's often thought to require. I am indebted to J. Churchill for bringing this point to my attention. I, however, will leave this point aside.

ing what I ascertain to be its key features. It should, nevertheless, be clear that his argument (whether successful or not) only applies to positions that uphold "the mereological hierarchy"—a pivotal piece of premise (ii) (Moreland's premise (4′)). But, as I have argued above, upholding this hierarchy is unwarranted, and emergentists needn't endorse it (though, as Moreland has pointed out, many do).

For example, this hierarchy wouldn't be endorsed by the kind of emergentist who maintains that the existence of emergent phenomena depends upon what exists at basal levels, while also upholding the idea that some substances, or entities, at basal levels of phenomena have, among their properties, the potential of being a part of an emergent substance that has a distinct causal power not possessed by any of its constitutive parts. They would be the kind of emergentist that endorses the idea that substances, which have and exercise distinct causal powers, emerge when states-of-affairs are just right at basal levels. As I mentioned earlier, positions of this kind, or close to it, are not new. Ostensibly they have been around since Aristotle. And according to such accounts, distinct types of substances or entities—e.g., human beings—possess mental causal powers, and when they exercise these powers they produce change, physical and mental, that wouldn't otherwise occur.

What differentiates the emergentist (and we might say "Aristotelian") position sketched above from traditional substance dualism (which some might refer to as "Cartesian") is that, according to the former, at least some substances that possess mental causal powers, and other mental attributes (e.g., human beings), also possess physical attributes. What also differentiates this position from traditional substance dualism is that, according to this position, there are numerous types of substances with causal powers, some basal, some emergent. Mental causal powers are a subtype of causal power.

The most straightforward way to modify Moreland's positive argument against emergentism so that it applies to accounts like the one outlined above would be to replace "the mereological hierarchy" piece of premise (ii), above, with a strong enough principle of causal closure of the physical. (That is, it would be to convert it back to something close to Kim's original exclusion argument.) However, we would, then, also have on our hands an argument against the idea that substances without physical attributes are causes of physical occurrences. But, as we saw earlier with Lowe's help, there are good reasons to be deeply skeptical of the warrant for such principles—principles Moreland also rejects. Nevertheless, it doesn't seem that Moreland has provided any good reason as to why we should accept traditional substance dualism over emergentist accounts that include the emergence of distinct efficient mental causes. He has, however, pointed out serious problems facing weak emergentist accounts of mental causation.[5] And this is a significant contribution.

REFERENCES

Brigandt, I. "Beyond Reduction and Pluralism: Toward an Epistemology of Explanatory Integration in Biology," *Erkenntnis* 73 (2010), 295–311.

Cartwright, N. *The Dappled World.* Cambridge University Press, 1999.

Dupré, J. *The Disorder of Things: Metaphysical Foundations of the Disunity of Science.* Harvard University Press, 1995.

Gazzaniga, M. "Neuroscience and the Correct Level of Explanation for Understanding Mind," *Trends in Cognitive Science* 14 (2010), 291–92.

Johansen, T. J. *The Powers of Aristotle's Soul.* Oxford University Press, 2012.

Kim, J. *Mind in a Physical World: An Essay on the Mind-Body Problem and Mental Causation.* MIT Press, 1998.

Kim, J. *Physicalism, or Something Near Enough.* Princeton University Press, 2005.

Lowe, E. J. *Personal Agency: The Metaphysics of Mind and Action.* Oxford University Press, 2010.

Murphy, N. "Reductionism: How Did We Fall Into It and Can We Emerge From It?" In *Evolution and Emergence: Systems, Organizations, Persons*, ed. N. Murphy and W. Stoeger, 19–39. Oxford University Press, 2007.

Murphy, N. "Did My Neurons Make Me Do It?", *Christians in Science and Technology Presentation*, Australia, August 2011. Retrieved from http://www.iscast.org/presentations/murphy_n_2011-08_annual_lecture.pdf (accessed 1/17/14).

O'Connor, T., and H. Wong. "The Metaphysics of Emergentism," *Noûs* 39 (2005), 658–78.

O'Connor, T., and J. R. Churchill. "Nonreductive Physicalism or Emergent Dualism? The Argument from Mental Causation." In *The Waning of Materialism*, ed. R. Koons and G. Bealer, 261–80. Oxford University Press, 2010.

Runyan, J. D., *Human Agency and Neural Causes: Philosophy of Action and the Neuroscience of Voluntary Agency.* Palgrave Macmillan, 2013.

Walter, C. "Shifting Attention from Theory to Practice in Philosophy of Biology." Preprint. Retrieved from http://philsci-archive.pitt.edu/id/eprint/10009 (accessed 1/15/14).

5. I am grateful to John Churchill and Sameer Yadav for helpful comments and suggestions.

CHAPTER 6

A Rejoinder to Runyan

J. P. Moreland

I thank my friend Jason Runyan for his critique of my chapter. Unfortunately—and it pains me to say this—his critique misrepresents several of my paper's main arguments. And in those places where he does accurately represent my position, his arguments are far from persuasive.

The Target of My Paper

I explicitly limit my critique to those who, like Kim (Kim 1998, 15–19) and Murphy (Murphy et. al. 2009, 1–28), accept the standard presentation of the mereological hierarchy as I depict it. Since my project is so limited, it is simply irrelevant that an ontologically pluralist scheme like Runyan's can be developed so as to include causally efficacious emergent entities. Runyan rejects the hierarchy, but so do I. However, this is beside the point. The vast majority working in this area accept the hierarchy as I present it, so if I can undermine this view, that would be a decent day's work. It would affect a lot of thinking about these matters. Now Runyan thinks that I do, in fact, present a strong case against these thinkers, e.g., Nancey Murphy. Since that was my aim, given that much of Runyan's case is devoted to the charge that I don't provide defeaters for ontological pluralism or other models, he is, sadly, chasing after windmills.

But, one may ask, why limit my critique as I do? There are two reasons for this—one practical and one philosophical. Practically, since my limited target is the one held by the vast majority of philosophers working in this field, given space limitations, it is enough for a short paper to attempt to defeat the majority view.

Second, the hierarchy is not presented in a philosophical vacuum. Indeed, it is an expression of philosophical naturalism (and even embraced by those theists who have naturalized important aspects of their ontology) that rightly employs serious and not shopping list metaphysics (Runyan and I are both shopping listers). Why is this the correct employment for naturalists? For one thing, it claims the virtues of epistemic and ontological simplicity. As Frank Jackson (Jackson 2000, 1–27) and Colin McGinn (McGinn 1999, 77–83) point out, after the Big Bang, the history of the cosmos is constituted by the formation of larger and more complicated aggregates with structural properties, and all of this can be explained by rearrangement according to natural laws. The resulting ontology: the mereological hierarchy. For another thing, this approach solves the location problem by either reducing or eliminating the problematic entity, and emergent properties are among the chief targets of such activity. By adopting this strategy, a naturalist can provide a simple etiological account of how all things came-to-be in light of a combinatorial story. The resulting ontology: the mereological hierarchy. Since my paper is part of a life-long research program to defeat naturalism (and those theists who absorb too much of what naturalists say), the mereological hierarchy is an excellent target. By contrast, Runyan's ontology is of little interest to me.

The Hierarchy and My Employment of Causal Closure

As I see it, Runyan's critique is plagued by at least three confusions regarding the hierarchy and my employment of causal closure. First, Runyan spends a fair amount of time criticizing the causal closure principle and its role in excluding top-down causation, and he explicitly states that I embrace the closure principle as an essential part of the mereological hierarchy. This is just false and I state repeatedly that neither I nor my arguments depend on the closure principle. My employment of Kim's two illustrations and my adjustment of O'Connor and Churchill's syllogism explicitly state that the argument against top-down causation need make no reference whatever to closure. The issues, as I argued, are (1) the diachronic depiction of the bottom level as a (deterministic or probabilistic; it doesn't matter) causal sequence and (2) the ontological dependence of level n+1 on n and, ultimately, on the micro-physical bottom. The two commitments imply that there is neither need nor room for top-down causation, and this conclusion is reached without any appeal to closure.

Perhaps Runyan missed this because of a second confusion: the nature of the dependence of level n+1 on n. Runyan is at pains to show that, given the dependence of a "higher" level of emergent phenomena on a "lower" basal level, it doesn't follow that the basal level is causally closed such that all that happens causally at that "higher" level can be given a complete, accurate causal explanation solely in terms of that lower level. His argument consists in an illustration: one's ability to raise one's hand, under normal circumstances, depends upon certain neural activities, but this does not entail that a complete, accurate causal explanation exists at the neurophysiological level. It could easily be the case that an immaterial substance is also doing some of the work (e.g., intending, exercising active power).

Unfortunately, this illustration entirely fails as an argument. Why? In the illustration, the dependency of raising the hand on neurophysiological factors is only partial; these necessary causal conditions require supplementation by additional causal conditions (the mental ones) to form the entire set of sufficient dependency conditions for the hand to be raised. But the dependency between levels of the hierarchy is sufficient in itself without need or room for supplementation from anywhere. What happens at n is sufficient to fix what happens at n+1; and something different may happen at n+1 only if something different happens at n. Here we have full, not partial dependence. I conclude, then, that Runyan's argument is wide of the mark.

Third, Runyan seems confused about the nature of emergence as depicted by those who accept the hierarchy, namely, they quantify over emergent properties—not emergent substances—from lower levels (and ultimately traced to the micro-physical level). Indeed, the whole debate in my paper was whether or not such emergent properties could, once instantiated, exert top-down causation. Runyan says that some emergentists may escape the hierarchy by embracing emergent substances/entities with their own causal powers. At least some basal entities would have, among their properties, the property of having the potential of being a part of an entity that has distinct causal powers. Such a part would clearly be a particular, as would the new whole constituted by it. Further, Runyan says that it's plausible to hold that Aristotle held something along these lines.

It is far from clear that this should be called emergentism. For centuries, emergentism has been associated with emergent properties. And even if some, e.g., William Hasker (Hasker 1999), believe new substances can emerge, one must be careful in calling this "emergentism" without giving a lot of qualification, something Runyan does not do. Moreover, there are two reasons for thinking that Runyan's view is closer to cases of substantial change and not emergence. First, he claims that his view is Aristotelean, but as Richard Connell has demonstrated (Connell 1988), for Aristotle and those who followed him, the appearance of a new property signals substantial change, not emergence. And as we will see below, Runyan's scientific pluralism undercuts the depiction of a universal basal level. On this account, emergence is unneeded, and substantial change is just as available as emergence.

My Adjusted Syllogism against Top-Down Causation

As far as I can tell, Runyan presents two main arguments against this part of my paper: (1) I explicitly state in my paper that my argument applies only to those who uphold the mereological hierarchy and not to those who reject the hierarchy and adopt a different version of emergence. But as I mentioned earlier, this is simply irrelevant to my paper since I explicitly limited my critique to hierarchy advocates. I did not try to provide defeaters for every version of emergence in sight.

(2) Runyan states that I could modify my argument against emergentist top-down causation and thereby make it effective, not only against hierarchy advocates, but also those who hold emergentist views like Runyan's. The modification would be to remove "the mereological hierarchy" from premise (ii) (premise 4′ in my paper) and replace it with a strong enough principle of causal closure. But such a move would defeat my own view since it would imply that immaterial substances cannot themselves be efficient causes of physical occurrences.

I offer three brief responses to this argument. First, I reject closure and the hierarchy, so as far as my personal views go, I am not in trouble here. Second, suppose I did accept a version of the hierarchy slightly different from the standard one. On this version, there is still no top-down causation because everything depends on the bottom level, and there is no need or room for such causation. But the bottom level need not be physical. Rather, it consists in entities that are not mereologically composed by more basic entities. Now a mental substance would be such an entity and, thus, besides atomic simples, the bottom level would include other simple substances, in this case, causally-efficacious mental ones because they are at the bottom.

Third, I would reject Runyan's emergentism in favor of a preferable view. To this last issue we turn.

An Alternative to Runyan's Philosophy of Science

Runyan's emergentism is an aspect of his general philosophy of science. Now he cannot be faulted for not developing this aspect of his thought because space is limited and he had a lot of other things to say. And while I could be wrong about this, from what he does say, I suggest that his views are virtually identical to those of Steven Horst (Horst 2007). Most of Runyan's statements are at the core of Horst's views which, Horst says, allows one to avoid the mereological hierarchy and its reductionist overtones. Here is some of what Runyan says: "science, on the whole, is a messy set of disciplines"; "[integration] of these disciplines is anything but formulaic"; "the more we meticulously study the phenomena of interest in our various scientific disciplines, the more specialized and divergent these disciplines become"; ". . . we only have a basis for thinking that even the best, and most precise, of these [developed disciplinary-relative theories] apply where they are *useful*—e.g., where they are *successfully used to model, make predictions, make successful and purposeful manipulations, and/or to construct artifacts*" (italics mine). Runyan goes on to say that the utility of a scientific theory is limited in scope as are the circumstances wherein we have reason to think it applies. Each discipline focuses on distinct phenomena with their own distinct efficient causes. Now Runyan does say that the laws we discover are true, all things being equal, with application only relative to our theories and the circumstances they depict.

Now all of this sounds like Horst, who claims that these positions support a cognitive pluralist view of science and the "world" according to which we approach things from a sort of Kantian or pragmatic constructivism. Our carving of the world isn't bedrock to the way the mind-independent world is. Rather, it reflects how our cognitive modeling faculties work, and our interests determine the form of our models (Horst 2007, 5, 121–203). If this is, indeed, Runyan's view, then it will be rejected by many philosophers, including me, who cannot follow him in this regard.

Moreover, on the assumption that this is, indeed, his view, Runyan still uses emergentist language, implying that in each fairly autonomous theory domain, there is a central emergent property constitutive of that domain. But, given his pluralism, along with a rejection of the hierarchy, there is no longer a need to call *sui generis* entities emergent properties. Instead, why not go with some sort of Aristotelianism according to which there is a plurality of unique substances, and the various new properties aren't emergent but, rather, attributes of new substances according to their natures.

Interestingly, Horst points out that besides the hierarchy and his cognitivist-pragmatic pluralism, there is a realist pluralism the most viable of which is a contemporary extension of Aristotelian metaphysics. Perhaps Runyan is some sort of metaphysical realist. If so, then, given his rejection of the hierarchy, I urge him to reject a superfluous emergentism, and go with the Aristotelian view, especially since he expresses some sympathy with that view.

This, then, is my attempt to respond to what I take to be the central concerns of Runyan's critique. As I said at the beginning of this response, he is a friend and colleague, and his critique forced me to do some serious thinking. And, for that, I am, indeed, grateful.

REFERENCES

Connell, Richard. (1988) *Substance and Modern Science.* Houston: Center for Thomistic Studies.

Hasker, William (1999) *The Emergent Self.* Ithaca, New York: Cornell University Press.

Horst, Steven. (2007) *Beyond Reduction.* Oxford: Oxford University Press.

Jackson, Frank. (2000) *From Metaphysics to Ethics.* New York: Oxford University Press.

Kim, Jaegwon. (1998) *Mind in a Physical World.* Cambridge, Massachusetts: MIT Press.

McGinn, Colin. (1999) *The Mysterious Flame.* New York: Basic Books.

Murphy, Nancey. (2009) Introduction and Overview. In Nancey Murphy, George F. R. Ellis, and Timothy O'Connor, eds., *Downward Causation and the Neurobiology of Free Will.* Berlin: Springer-Verlag.

PART 2

Recent Debate about the Bearing of Contemporary Brain Sciences on the Mind-Body Problem

CHAPTER 7

The Impossibility of Proving That Human Behavior Is Determined

Richard Swinburne

I argue in this paper that it is immensely improbable that there could ever be a well-justified deterministic theory of how humans are caused to perform all the intentional actions which they perform, because our very criteria for a well-justified scientific theory make it almost impossible for a theory of this kind to be well justified. It follows that since there cannot be counter-evidence to what seems to us to be the case (that it is often up to us, uncaused by prior causes, how we will behave), we should—by the Principle of Credulity—believe that things are as they seem to be: that is, that we often have freedom to perform intentional actions, not caused to do so by prior causes.

I begin with a crucial assumption, which I cannot justify adequately within the compass of a short paper, but which I have justified elsewhere:[1] mind-body event dualism. I understand by a mental event, one to the occurrence of which the person in whom it is an event has privileged access (by experiencing it); and by a physical event, one to whom no person has such privileged access. Among physical events are brain events. Some mental events entail the occurrence of physical events—"My seeing a desk" is a mental event, but it entails the existence of a desk—a physical event. I understand by a "pure mental event" one which does not entail the occurrence of any physical event—for example the event of me seeming to see a desk. Pure mental events

1. See Swinburne (2013), chapter 3.

This paper summarizes some of the arguments contained in Swinburne (2013). The main part of the paper is taken from an earlier paper of mine, Swinburne (2011), and reused here by kind permission of the British Academy.

include both conscious events and continuing mental states. Conscious events are events of which the person whose they are is conscious as they occur. They include sensations (patterns of color in our visual field, feelings of warmth, etc.), occurrent thoughts, and also our intentions in our actions (that is, what we are trying to achieve by what we are doing intentionally). Continuing mental states include beliefs and desires (in the sense of involuntary inclinations to do actions); they are states of ourselves to which we have privileged access, but continue to exist while we are not conscious of them. Clearly all of such states occur innumerably often. It follows from this account of the nature of physical and mental events, that mental events are not identical to physical events, and do not supervene (metaphysically) on them (that is, it is metaphysically possible that any mental event can occur or not occur, whatever physical events do or do not occur).

I understand by a theory being (epistemically) "well-justified" that it is made probable by the total available evidence. Philosophers of science give different accounts of the criteria for evidence making a theory probable, but there are surely at least two crucial criteria. The first is what I will call the "predictive criterion"—that the theory must have made probable much observed evidence and no evidence observed to be false; and the second criterion is what I will call the "simplicity criterion"—that the theory must be simple in the sense of having only a few laws relating only a few kinds of properties in relatively simple ways. It cannot consist of innumerable independent laws each having predicted only one or two phenomena.

A deterministic theory of human behavior seeks to explain the immediate causes of such behaviour in the brains and conscious lives of humans. There are two possible kinds of such theories. The first kind of theory is an epiphenomenalist theory which claims that brain events alone cause human behavior, and are themselves caused only by other brain events or more generally physical events; and so our mental events, and in particular our conscious intentions, never cause brain events, and so never affect which intentional actions we perform. The second kind of theory is a psychophysical theory which acknowledges that our intentions often cause the brain events which cause our intentional actions, but claims that our intentions are caused (normally via other mental events) ultimately by brain and other physical events. I argue in this paper that any epiphenomenalist theory will (inevitably) fail the predictive criterion, and any psychophysical theory will (with immense probability) fail the simplicity criterion.

Many neuroscientists claim that recent scientific work, developed from the pioneering work of Benjamin Libet, supports an epiphenomenalist theory.

Libet did experiments in which subjects were instructed to perform a simple bodily movement (e.g., move a hand) at a moment of their choice within some subsequent interval (e.g., twenty seconds). He found that half a second before subjects formed their intention there was always a brain event of a correlated kind. Many neuroscientists interpreted such results as showing generally (not just in this experimental situation) that any intention to perform some intentional bodily movement occurs subsequently to a brain event which causes a train of brain events, the last member of which causes the bodily movement, and that a person's intention makes no difference to whether the bodily movement occurs. Rather, they have claimed, when we perform movements which we believe to be intentional, the intention is itself caused by one of the train of brain events which lead to the bodily movement, leading the agent to have the false belief that his or her intention caused these movements. However, such experiments could only show this if they predicted correctly if and when (relative to brain events) intentions occur. In all the neuroscientific experiments this information was provided by subjects who watch a very fast clock and subsequently report at what time by the clock they formed the relevant intention. But why should the scientists believe what the subjects report? Scientists reasonably assume that the subjects are trying to convey (that is, have the intention of conveying) by the words which come out of their mouths, their beliefs about the time registered on the clock when they formed the relevant intention. That is, scientists assume that a subject's intention (together with his belief) causes the words to come out of the subject's mouth. But if epiphenomenalism were true, that could not be happening; it must be brain events which alone cause these words to be uttered, quite independently of whether or not subjects have the relevant intentions or beliefs. And what applies to Libet's own experiments applies to all subsequent more sophisticated experimental work designed to establish some epiphenomenalist theory, which relies on subjects' claims about when they formed some intention or other conscious event.[2] Subjects' claims can only be trusted on the assumption that the words coming out of their mouths are caused by their beliefs (that they had formed a certain intention at a certain time) and their intentions to convey those beliefs. But no theory can be rendered probable by evidence which can only be trusted on the assumption that the theory is false. (Of course a scientist could show by means of Libet-type experiments that our intentions do not cause actions of particular kinds which we had supposed to be intentional actions, but only

2. For a short description of Libet's experiment and relevant subsequent experimental work, and some of the detailed problems involved in assessing its results, see Haggard (2011).

on the assumption that our intentions do cause actions of other kinds, such as our actions of reporting our conscious events. What cannot be done is to show that no intentions cause brain events.)

We make a causal assumption in all reliance on testimony or memory. We trust someone's testimony to have done this or seen that, because we believe that (via his memory) his past experiences cause his present belief about what happened, and that his intention to tell the truth about his present belief together with that belief cause the words of his testimony to come out his mouth. And we rely on our own memories because we believe that they are caused by our past experiences. We have learnt that any memories about events more than a few minutes earlier are available to us only because our brain events cause us to have these memories, which we then trust because we believe that past experiences caused the brain events which cause the present memories. If epiphenomenalism were true, that trust would be unjustified. So even if a scientist were himself to become a subject and purport to remember when he formed an intention, for any intention about an event more than a few minutes earlier, he too would be relying on an assumption that conscious events cause brain events; and mere knowledge that his theory correctly predicted one or two intentions occurring only a few minutes ago is not going to provide enough evidence to make his theory very probable. So even a solitary scientist cannot have much justification for believing a theory of this epiphenomenalist kind. I conclude that no work of this kind which depends for its justification on predictions about if and when conscious events occur could make it probable that no conscious events cause brain events, because our knowledge that the predicted events occurred must depend on an assumption that some conscious events do cause brain events.

But could it not be shown that no conscious events cause brain events, simply by studying brain events and finding for each brain event a necessary and sufficient immediately precedent cause of its occurrence in a prior brain or other physical event—that is, by establishing thereby what is called "the causal closure of the physical"? If we could show that, we would have shown that conscious events make no difference to what happens. It is true that scientists could come to know that some brain event occurred without assuming that any conscious event caused any brain event; they could just observe the brain event. But in order to know that the theory made true predictions, we need to know that the theory predicted those brain events. It is a complicated matter to work out what a theory predicts. A scientist who does it must rely on his memory of the early stages of his calculations (and even if the calculations are written down, he relies on his memory that he believed what he wrote down). And anyway scientists need to confirm their calculations by asking other scientists to check them, and so they rely on what other scientists tell them (that their calculations were correct); and that involves assuming that the words come out of the other scientists' mouths because their intentions cause them to do so. And we, non-scientists, need to rely on the scientists' assurances that what was observed was what they believed to be predicted by their theory. So we would all need to rely on memory and testimony for the justification of any belief in a theory of the causal closure of the physical; and again we can only trust such memory and testimony on the assumption that conscious events (this time, the conscious beliefs of scientists and their intentions to report them) cause brain events. So again, no scientific theory to the effect that mental events never cause brain events, and so intentional actions, could ever be epistemically justified. In summary this is because it will always fail the prediction criterion—we can never know that it predicts successfully without assuming its falsity.

So, to be well justified, any deterministic theory of human intentional actions would need to be a psychophysical theory showing how brain events cause mental events, and how mental events (and in particular intentions) cause brain events. I now argue that it is immensely unlikely that there could be any well-justified theory of this kind, because it will almost certainly fail the other criterion, the simplicity criterion, for the probable truth of a scientific theory.

To construct such a theory we need data about the mental events of many humans. Before I come to the simplicity issue, I must comment that—even granted that mental events do affect our behavior, and that subjects do not seek to deceive investigators about their mental lives—there are two major obstacles in the way of getting the requisite data from subjects about their conscious events, the occurrence of which the theory would need to predict. The first obstacle concerns the "propositional" mental events—occurrent thoughts, desires, beliefs, and intentions. I call them "propositional events"[3] because they involve an attitude to a proposition (which forms the content of the attitude). A belief is a belief that such-and-such a proposition is true; a desire is a desire that such-and-such a proposition be true, and so on. The problem is that while the content of most of these events can be described in a public language, its words are often understood in slightly different senses by different speakers. One person's thought which he describes as the occurrent

3. They are sometimes called "intentional" events, but I avoid this label since it leads to confusion between intentions and the wider class of "intentional events."

thought that scientists are "narrow-minded," or the belief that there is a "table" in the next room, has a slightly different content from another person's thought or belief, described in the same way. What one person thinks of as "narrow-minded" another person doesn't; and some of us count any surfaces with legs as "tables," whereas others discriminate between desks, sideboards, and tables.[4] This obstacle can be overcome, by questioning subjects about exactly what they mean by certain words. But it has the consequence that, since beliefs etc. are the beliefs they are in virtue of the way their owners think of them, far fewer people have exactly the same particular beliefs, desires, etc. as anyone else than one might initially suppose—which makes the kind of experimental repetition which scientists require to establish their theories much harder to obtain. And it seems most unlikely that any two humans understand all their words in exactly the same way, and so have exactly the same concepts as each other.

There is, however, a much larger obstacle to understanding what people tell us about their sensations. This is that we can understand what they say only on the assumption that the sensations of anyone else are the same as we would ourselves have in the same circumstances—and that is often a highly dubious assumption. This obstacle applies to all experiences of color, sound, taste, and smell (the "secondary qualities"). We can recognize when someone makes the same discriminations as we do between the public properties of color etc., but we cannot check whether they make the discriminations on the basis of the same sensations as we do. While it might seem counter-intuitive to suppose that green things look to one group of people just like red things look to another group of people, while red things look to the first group just like green things look to the second group, other possibilities seem less counter-intuitive. Maybe green things look a little redder to some people than they do to others,[5] or colored things look fainter to some people than to others, when neither of these differences affect their abilities to make the same discriminations.

We could rule out such possibilities on grounds of simplicity (that it is simpler and so more probable to suppose that these things do not happen), if it were the case that which neurons have to fire in which sequence at which rate in order to produce a sensation which subjects call "green" (or whatever)

4. Though it hardly needs such support, this point is borne out by recent experiments showing that presenting some image to a group of subjects produced in all subjects similar patterns of activity in different regions, but slightly different patterns for each subject. See Shinkareva et al. (2008).

5. Even if two groups of subjects typically agree in the percentage of "redness" shown by greenish color samples, that won't show that the "pure green" or "pure red" samples look the same to both groups, and so that a "10% red" sample looks the same to both groups.

were exactly the same in all humans. But in view of the differences between the brains of different humans, that seems very improbable. It's much more likely that sometimes for two different people, different neurons produce a sensation which they both call "green." The different reactions which people often have to the same input from the senses supports the hypothesis that the sensations caused thereby are sometimes different in different people. Some people like the taste of curry, others don't. There are two possible hypotheses to explain this: curry tastes the same to everyone but some people like and some people don't like this taste, or curry tastes different to different people. It would seem highly arbitrary to suppose that the first explanation is correct—let alone to suppose that a similar explanation applies to all different reactions to tastes.

So, bearing in mind these limits to the kinds of mental data we can have to support any psychophysical theory, the even greater difficulty in the way of getting a well-justified psychophysical theory is that it will be almost impossible to satisfy the simplicity criterion. What makes a scientific theory such as a theory of mechanics able to explain a diverse set of mechanical phenomena is that the laws of mechanics all deal with the same sort of thing—material objects—and concern only a few of their properties—their mass, shape, size, and position, which differ from each other in measurable ways (one has twice as much mass as another, or is three times as long as another.) Because the values of these measurable properties are affected only by the values of a few other such properties, we can have a few general laws which relate two or more such measured properties in all objects by a mathematical formula. We do not merely have to say that, when an inelastic object of 100 gm mass and 10 m/sec velocity collides with an inelastic object of 200 gm mass and 5 m/sec velocity, such and such results, with unconnected formulae for the results of collisions of innumerable inelastic objects of different masses and velocities. We can have a general formula, a law saying that for every pair of inelastic material objects in collision the quantity of the sum of the mass of the first multiplied by its velocity plus the mass of the second multiplied by its velocity is always conserved. But that can hold only if mass and velocity can be measured on scales—for example, of grams and meters per second. And we can extend mechanics to a general physics including a few more measurable quantities (charge, spin, color charge, etc.) which interact with mechanical quantities, to construct a theory which makes testable predictions.

A mind-brain theory, however, would need to deal with things of very different kinds. Brain events differ from each other in the chemical elements involved in them (which in turn differ from each other in measurable ways) and in the velocity and direction of the transmission of electric charge. But mental events do not have any of these properties. The propositional events (beliefs, desires, etc.) are what they are, and have the influence they do in virtue of their propositional content, often expressible in language, but a language which—I noted earlier—has a content and rules differing slightly for each person. (And note that while the meaning of a public sentence is a matter of how the words of the language are used, the content of a propositional event such as a thought is intrinsic to it; it has the content it does, however the subject or others may use words on other occasions.) Propositional events have relations of deductive logic to each other; and some of those deductive relations determine the identity of the propositional event. My belief that all men are mortal wouldn't be that belief if I also believed that Socrates was an immortal man; and my thought that "2 = 1 + 1, and 3 = 2 + 1, and 4 = 3 + 1" wouldn't be the thought normally expressed by those equations if I denied that it followed from them that "2 + 2 = 4." And so generally, much of the content of the mental life cannot be described except in terms of the content of propositional events; and that cannot be done except by some language (slightly different for each person) with semantic and syntactic features somewhat analogous to those of a public language. The rules of a language which relate the concepts of that language to each other cannot be captured by a few "laws of language" because the deductive relations between sentences and so the propositions which they are express are so complicated that it needs all the rules contained in a dictionary and grammar of the language to express them. These rules are independent rules and do not follow from a few more general rules. Consider how few of the words which occur in a dictionary can be defined adequately by other words in the dictionary, and so the same must hold for the concepts which they express; and consider in how many different ways describable by the grammar of the language words can be put together so as to form sentences with different kinds of meaning, and so the same must hold for the propositions which they express.

So any mind/brain theory which sought to explain how prior brain events cause the beliefs, desires, etc. which they do would consist of laws relating brain events with numerically measurable values of transmission of electric charge in various circuits, to conscious (and non-conscious) beliefs, desires, intentions, etc. with a content individuated by sentences of a language (varying slightly for each person), and also sensations. The contents of the mental events do not differ from each other in any numerically measurable way, nor do they have any intrinsic order (except in the respect that some entail others). Those concepts which are not designated by words fully defined by other words—and that is most concepts—are not functions of each other. And they can be combined in innumerable different ways which are not functions of each other, to form the propositions which are the contents of thoughts, intentions, etc. So it looks as if the best we could hope for is an enormously long list of separate laws (differing slightly for each person) relating brain events and mental events without these laws being derivable from a few more general laws.[6]

Could we not at least have an "atomic" theory which would relate particular brain events involving only a few neurons to particular aspects of a conscious state—particular beliefs, occurrent thoughts, etc., the content of which was describable by a single sentence (of a given subject's language), in such a way that we could at least predict that a belief with exactly the same content would be formed when the same few neurons fired again in the same sequence at the same rate (if ever that happened)? The "language of thought" hypothesis[7] (LOT), which takes seriously the analogy of the brain to a computer which manipulates symbols, seems to involve some version of an atomic theory. It claims that there are rules relating brain events and beliefs of these kinds, albeit a very large and complicated set of them. It holds that different concepts and different logical relations which they can have to each other are correlated with different features in the brain. For example, it holds that there are features of the brain which are correlated with the concepts of "man," "mortal," and "Socrates," and that there is a relation R which these features can sometimes have to each other. When someone believes that Socrates is mortal, R holds in their brain between the "Socrates"-feature and the "mortal" feature; when someone believes that Socrates is a man, R holds between the "Socrates"-feature and the "man"-feature; and when someone believes that all men are mortal, R holds between the "man"-feature and the "mortal"-feature. (The holding of this relation might perhaps consist in the features being connected by some regular pattern of signals between them.) The main argument given for LOT is that unless our brain worked like this, the operation of the brain couldn't explain how we reason from "all men are mortal" and "Socrates is a man" to "Socrates is mortal," since our reasoning depends on our ability to recognize

6. Donald Davidson (1980) is well known for arguing that "there are no strict psychophysical laws" (op. cit., 222). However he uses this thesis in defense of his theory of "anomalous monism," that all events are physical, some events are also mental, and so physical-mental causal interaction (which we both recognize) is lawlike causal interaction of two physical events. But, contrary to Davidson, I am assuming (for reasons stated briefly at the beginning of this paper) that there are events of two distinct types, physical and mental; and so I reject Davidson's resulting theory.

7. Originally put forward by Fodor (1979).

the relevant concepts as separate concepts connected in a certain particular way. Beliefs, and so presumably other propositional events, the theory claims, correspond to "sentences in the head."

I argued earlier however that no belief can be held without being sustained by certain other beliefs—for logical reasons; which other beliefs a given belief is thought of as entailing determines in part which belief the latter belief is. Now consider two beliefs, whose content is expressed in English by "this is square" and "this has four sides"; someone couldn't hold the first belief without holding the second. So these two beliefs cannot always be correlated with different brain events, since in that case a neuroscientist could eliminate the brain event correlated to the latter belief without eliminating the brain event correlated to the former belief. On the other hand these two beliefs cannot always be correlated with the same brain event since someone can have the belief "this has four sides" without having the belief "this is square." It follows that any individual propositional event, such as the belief "this has four sides" must be correlated in any particular brain with more than one brain event; and by similar arguments it can be shown that it must be correlated with several other brain events. That leads to the view that individual propositional events only occur as part of a total mental state, including many propositional and other mental events, and it is this whole mental state which is correlated with a whole brain state without there being correlations between separate parts of the mental and brain states. This view is that of connectionism,[8] the rival theory to LOT. Mind/brain relations are holistic. Only if connectionists hold, as they often do, that mental events are identical with (or supervene logically on) individual brain events, is it an objection to connectionism that brain events do not have a structure corresponding to that of a human language. But given my initial assumption that mental events are not identical to or supervene (metaphysically) on brain events, mental events can have a sentential structure without brain events having this. So, given connectionism, a mind/brain theory could at best only predict the occurrence of some conscious event in the context of a large mental state (consisting of many beliefs, desires, etc., some of them conscious) and of a large brain state (events involving vast numbers of neurons).

Further, the influence of mental events depends on their strength; and (apart from occurrent thoughts) they all have different strengths. One person's sensation of the taste of curry is stronger than another person's. One person's

8. For a selection of papers on both sides of the language-of-thought/connectionism debate see Parts II and III of Lycan and Prinz (2008).

belief that humans are causing global warming is stronger than another person's (that is, the first person believes this proposition to be more probable than does the second person). Yet while subjects can sometimes put sensations in order of strength on the basis of their subjective experience, what they cannot do—despite 150 years of work on "psychophysics"[9]—is to ascribe to them numerical degrees of strength in any objective way. There is no sense in supposing that a sensation feels "twice as strong" as another one. And, despite 80 years of work on "subjective probability," the same applies to beliefs[10] and other propositional events. Yet differences in the strength of mental events affect behavior in a rational way. Someone is more likely (despite counter-influences) to stop eating curry, the stronger is the taste of the curry which she dislikes. Someone is more likely (despite counter-influences) to choose to travel by bus rather than by car because of a belief that humans are causing global warming and a belief that it is good to prevent this, the stronger are those beliefs. Yet in order to measure the influence of sensations, beliefs, etc. on intentions in a situation where there are many conflicting influences, we need a measure of their absolute strength which can play its role in an equation connecting these; and subjects cannot provide that from introspection. The alternative is to try to infer the absolute strength from the brain events which cause the mental events. Neuroscience might discover that greater frequency of certain kinds of brain event causes the beliefs caused by those brain events to be stronger. But for prediction of their effects in all circumstances we would need to know how much stronger were the resultant beliefs. So we would need a theory by means of which to calculate this, which gave results compatible with subjects' reports about the relative strengths of their beliefs. But the brain circuits, rates of firing, etc. which sustain beliefs in different subjects are so

9. See Laming (2004): "Most people have no idea what 'half as loud' means. In conclusion, there is no way to measure sensation that is distinct from measurement of the physical stimulus."

10. There is a long tradition beginning with the work of F. P. Ramsey, of attempting to measure someone's degree of belief in a proposition (the "subjective probability" which they ascribe to it) by the lowest odds at which they believe that they would be prepared to bet that it was true. If someone is, they believe, prepared to bet $N that q is true at odds of 3–1 (i.e would win $3N if q turned out true, but lose their $N if q turned out false) but not at any lower odds (e.g 2–1), that—it was claimed—showed that they ascribe to q a probability of 1/4 (because then in their view what they would win multiplied by the probability of their winning would equal what they would lose multiplied by the probability of their losing). But that method of assessing subjective probability will give different answers varying with the amount to be bet—someone might be willing to bet $10 at 3–1 but $100 only at odds of more than 4–1; and people have all sorts of reasons for betting or not betting other than to win money.

different from each other that it is difficult to see how there could be a general formula connecting some feature of brain events with the absolute strength of the mental events which they sustain. The most we could get is a long list of the kinds of brain activity which increase or decrease the strength of which kinds of mental events.

So the part of a mind/brain theory which predicts human intentions and so human actions would consist of an enormous number of particular laws relating brain events to subsequent sensations, thoughts, beliefs, and desires (some of them conscious), and these (together with other brain events) to subsequent intentions, having this kind of shape:

> Brain events (B_1, B_2 . . . B_j) + Sensations (M_1 . . . M_e) + Thoughts (M_f . . . M_i) + Beliefs (including value beliefs) (M_j . . . M_k) + Desires (M_k . . . M_1) → Intention (M_n) + Beliefs (about how to execute the intention) (M_p . . . M_q) + Brain events → bodily movements.

The arrow designates "causes." The B's describe events in individual neurons, and each law would involve large numbers of these; the M's describe particular mental events with a content describable by a short sentence, and (to the extent to which we could measure this) with a strength. The strength of an intention measures how hard the agent will try to do the intended action.

There are cases where mental events alone determine a person's resulting intention, and in those cases, we can no doubt often predict that intention (and if an action is one easy to perform, the exact strength of the intention will make no difference to what the agent actually does). These are the cases where a person has a strongest desire to do a certain action and no value belief that it is not the best action, and where he has a strongest value belief and no relevant contrary desire, and the agent believes that he is able to do the action. In these cases the agent will form the intention to act on the strongest desire or value belief. But it doesn't include the crucial case where someone's desires conflict with their value beliefs, and so mental events cannot alone determine which intention the person will form. If a person's intention is determined in that situation of "difficult moral decision," brain events would have to play a role. The intention would be determined for each person by one of an enormous number of different laws relating total brain states to total mental states, including large total conscious states. So we could not work out what a person will do on one occasion when she had one set of brain events, beliefs, and desires, on the basis of what she (or someone else) did on a previous occasion when she had a different set differing only in respect of one relevant belief. For there would be no general rule about the effect of just that one change of belief on different belief and desire sets; the effect of the change would be different according to what was the earlier set, and what were the brain states correlated with it. But no human being ever has the same total brain state and mental state at any two times or the same total brain state and mental state as any other human does at any time, and—I suggest—it is most improbable that any human being considering a difficult moral decision will ever have the same conscious state, let alone the same brain state in the respects which give rise to consciousness and determine its transitions, as at another time or as any other human ever. For making a difficult moral decision involves taking into account many different conflicting beliefs and desires. The believed circumstances of each such decision will be different, and (consciously or unconsciously) an agent will be much influenced by her previous moral reflections and decisions.

Consider someone deciding how to vote at a national election. She will have beliefs about the moral worth of the different policies of each party, and the probability of each party executing its policies; she will desire to vote for this candidate and against that candidate for various reasons (liking or disliking them for different reasons); she will desire to vote in the same way as (or in a different way from) her parents, and so on. But each voter will have slightly different beliefs and desires of these kinds. So because each voter's total conscious state would never have occurred previously, there could not be any evidence supporting a component law of the mind/brain theory to predict what would happen this time. A very similar conscious state might have occurred previously (in the same or a different voter), supporting a detailed law about the effects of that similar conscious state. But that suggested law (weakly supported by one piece of evidence) would (because of the slight difference in the conscious state) only predict what would happen this time with a degree of probability surely less than a half. Add to this the point that almost certainly the part of the overall brain state which determines the strength of the different events constituting the conscious state, and how rationally subjects will react to them, will almost certainly be different on the different occasions. And so in summary it is immensely improbable that a deterministic psychophysical theory of human behavior could ever satisfy the simplicity criterion for a well-justified scientific theory. And a further reason why it is immensely improbable that such a theory could be well justified is provided by the difficulties described earlier involved in getting some of the evidence required to support any such theory. I conclude that it is immensely improbable that a prediction about which difficult moral decision someone would make, and so which resulting action they would do, could ever be supported by enough evidence to make it probably true. Human brains and human mental life are just too complex for humans to understand completely.

My arguments for my earlier conclusion that there could never be a well-justified deterministic epiphenomenalist theory of human behavior showed, I claimed, that it is impossible that there could be such a theory. But my claim with regard to deterministic psychophysical theory is only that it is "immensely improbable" that there could be a well-justified such theory. This is because this latter claim depends on what I have argued to be an immensely probable contingent truth that no scientist will ever be able to find enough subjects having at a given time sufficiently similar brain events over a large brain area and a large enough number of sufficiently similar mental events, so as to be able to check whether those events are always followed by the same intentions (of the same strength). If this could be done, my claim that they will not always be followed by the same intentions could itself be checked, and—it is logically possible—be confirmed or refuted.

My claim, which I have argued is immensely probable, nevertheless has a crucial consequence that those brain events which cause the movements which constitute human actions will—very probably—never be totally predictable. But even if it should turn out that the behavior of other physical systems is totally predictable, it should not be too surprising that the brains (of humans and perhaps higher animals) are different, since the brain must be totally unlike any other physical system in that it causes innumerable mental events. Yet, even if it is unpredictable which intention we will form and how strong it will prove, what reason do we have for supposing that that intention (with its particular strength) is not caused (in a way too complicated to predict) by brain events? After all, I have acknowledged, our intentions often are caused—when they are caused by a strongest desire and we have no contrary value belief, and when they are caused by a strongest value belief when we have no contrary desire.

My answer is that it is in just those circumstances where desires and moral beliefs are in opposition to each other, or we have both equally strong competing desires and competing value beliefs and only in those circumstances, that we are conscious of deciding between competing alternatives. We then believe that it is up to us what to do, and we make a decision. Otherwise we allow ourselves to do as our desires and value beliefs dictate, which is so often just to conform to habit. The principle of credulity in its most general form says that things are probably the way they seem to be in the absence of counter-evidence.[11] So we should believe that in these circumstances where we believe that we are making a choice without being caused to choose as we do, we are indeed doing just this. In other cases it does not seem to us that we are choosing without being caused to choose as we do, and so we should not believe that we are then making an uncaused choice. Most of the time we do what we feel inclined to do (that is, what we desire to do) and have no value beliefs that we ought not to do this. We perform innumerable intentional actions as we go through our daily routines (of dressing, breakfasting, going to work, etc.) because that's what we desire to do and we desire to do these things because we have got into the habit of doing them. Only rarely during the day do we decide between alternative actions (ones which are not determined by our mental events, our existing desires and beliefs with their relative strengths); and among those decisions, decisions between doing what we most desire to do and doing what we believe we ought to do are even rarer. And the phenomenology of deciding between rival possible actions is very different from the phenomenology of doing the everyday things we do intentionally. So we should expect the underlying brain processes to be similarly different, and that when we are making decisions between rival possible actions, and it seems to us that we are deciding without being caused how to decide, that we should believe that that is how it is. Anyone who denies this would have to defend a more limited principle of credulity claiming that it is a priori that only for beliefs of a certain kind should we believe that things are as they seem to be, and show that that does not cover beliefs about our decisions being uncaused. I do not myself think that such a defense can be sustained.

REFERENCES

Davidson, D. (1980) "Mental Events." In his *Essays on Actions and Events*. Oxford University Press.

Fodor, J. A. (1979) *The Language of Thought*. Cambridge, Mass.: Harvard University Press.

Gray, J. (2004) *Consciousness: Creeping Up on the Hard Problem*. Oxford: Oxford University Press.

Haggard, P. (2011) "Does Brain Science Change Our View of Free Will?" In R. Swinburne, ed., *Free Will and Modern Science*, published for the British Academy by Oxford University Press.

11. For a defense of the most general form of the Principle of Credulity see Swinburne (2013), 42–44; and for its application to the present issue see op. cit., 201–202.

Laming, D. R. J. (2004) "Psychophysics." In Richard L. Gregory, ed., *The Oxford Companion to the Mind*, second edition, 771–73. Oxford: Oxford University Press.

Libet, B. (2004) *Mind Time*. Cambridge, Mass.: Harvard University Press.

Lycan, W. G., and J. J. Prinz, eds. (2008) *Mind and Cognition: An Anthology*, 3rd edition. Oxford: Blackwell Publishing.

Robinson, R. (2009) "Exploring the 'Global Workspace' of Consciousness." PLoS Biol 7 (3): doi: 10.1371/journal.pbio.1000066.

Shinkareva, S. V., R. A. Mason, V. L. Malave, W. Wang, T. M. Mitchell, and M. A. Just. (2008) "Using fMRI Brain Activation to Identify Cognitive States Associated with Perception of Tools and Dwellings." PLoS ONE 3(1): e1394.doi 10.1371/journal .pone.0001394.

Swinburne, R. (2011) "Dualism and the Determination of Action." In R. Swinburne, ed., *Free Will and Modern Science*, published for the British Academy by Oxford University Press.

Swinburne, R. (2013) *Mind, Brain, and Free Will*. Oxford: Oxford University Press.

CHAPTER 8

On the Import of the Impossibility

Daniel Speak

The distinctively systematic nature of Richard Swinburne's work is both admirable and a real hassle. With respect to its admirability, we should not ignore just how very difficult it is to achieve the kind of wide and deep integration of argument characteristic of his work. Furthermore, I am convinced that such integration also stands to reveal (and, indeed, has revealed) interrelations and dependencies between ideas that would otherwise remain hidden from us. However, Swinburne's systematicity presents commentators like myself with a special challenge. I am painfully aware that Swinburne's argument here is, as usual, embedded in a much larger argumentative context the understanding of which might very well render local challenges otiose. Imagine someone who is largely in the dark regarding the complex inter-workings of mechanical watches. When this person is shown a particular intricately crafted bit of gearing pulled from the guts of a watch, he may very well be puzzled about how it contributes to time-keeping. In my own case, at least, I worry that the concerns I am about to raise might indeed be of this ignorant sort. To the degree that they are, I invite Professor Swinburne to treat them as requests to illuminate his wider project here and the connection between that project and this one.

With the honorifics and hedgings behind us, I will be raising two concerns with the argument Swinburne has offered us here, both of which simply presuppose that his central claims go through. First, I will object to a phenomenological claim that his wider argument depends upon. Second, I will contend that his substantive conclusion does little to weaken the traditional threat to human free will posed by determinism.

It is important to see that Swinburne takes himself to be vindicating (or contributing to the vindication of) a substantive and controversial view about human free will. He describes this view as one according to which "we often have freedom to perform intentional actions, not caused to do so by prior causes." He is in the business, then, of defending the credibility of the view known in the standard parlance as "libertarianism." The libertarian makes a two-pronged claim, notice; first, that we enjoy free will and, second, that we would not enjoy this free will if determinism were true. That is, the libertarian is committed to both

> (F) Human beings (many normal adult instances, at least) sometimes act freely
>
> and
>
> (I) Acting freely is incompatible with the truth of the thesis of determinism.

Given these commitments, you can see why a defender of libertarianism, like Swinburne, would be eager to undermine any claims to the effect that determinism is true. After all, if determinism is true and the libertarian remains committed to (I), then she must give up (F).[1]

There is no point in hiding my own sympathies for libertarianism; which is to say that I join Swinburne in the cause of defending both (F) and (I). I am also prepared to accept (and not just for the sake of argument but from substantive philosophical agreement) the broadly Reidian commonsense epistemology enshrined in his "principle of credulity." This principle tells us that we are epistemically justified in believing that things are as they seem to be, in the absence of defeaters. Our seemings, that is, provide us with prima facie justification for belief in accordance with them.

My sympathies with Swinburne go even further. I find the broad form of argument for libertarianism that he is advancing here very promising. The form is this. Start with how things seem to us. It seems to us that we act freely. Since our seemings give us prima facie justification for believing, we are justified in believing in our free will unless there are compelling defeaters for this belief. All that remains to do, then, is to face down those supposed defeaters, showing, in each case, that they do not rise to a level sufficient to undermine

1. Peter van Inwagen has somewhat famously admitted that, though he is a libertarian, he would give up on (I) rather than (F) upon discovering that determinism is true. See *An Essay on Free Will* (Oxford: Oxford University Press, 1986).

the justification initially established by how things seem to us. In the main, I agree that the makings are here for a very powerful defense of libertarianism.

Why am I hesitating to go all-in with Swinburne on this argument? It is because I am skeptical about the phenomenological claim at the heart of his version of this argument. On his view, it seems to us that "it is often up to us, uncaused by prior causes, how we will behave." It's the bit between the commas that I am not prepared to report as a feature of my experience of myself as an agent. This isn't to say that I reject a phenomenological grounding for belief in free will. Indeed, I think it is clear that we often do experience ourselves as free to do other than what we have in fact done.[2] That is, I am inclined to accept that it seems to us, especially in characteristically deliberative moments of choice, that we have alternative possibilities. In fact, at least some experimental data confirms that this experience is the norm. In a recent series of studies, Deery, Bedke, and Nichols found that more than 90% of survey participants reported feeling free to choose among options in the decision circumstances with which they were presented.[3] Still, it is one thing to feel as if I have alternative possibilities—to feel as if I can do any of the things over which my deliberations are ranging—and another thing to feel as if my action is disconnected from the prior system of causes.

In fairness to Swinburne, Deery, Bedke, and Nichols also report substantial findings in favor of the phenomenology on which his argument depends (though these findings are not as robust as those supporting the general phenomenology of freedom). That is, they report that subjects making deliberative decisions tend to describe the experience of their own agency in these circumstances as incompatible with the thesis of determinism. Still, I have my doubts about these results. There are powerful (to my mind) *arguments* for the incompatibility of the ability to do otherwise with determinism; and these arguments do (I believe) rest on very intuitive grounds that it is not at all hard to draw out of us. It would be very easy to confuse (1) the quick *inference* from these intuitive grounds for incompatibilism with (2) its seeming that one's

2. Strictly speaking, an experience of one's own agency as uncaused by prior causes would seem to provide initial justification not just for the rejection of the thesis of determinism but also for the rejection of the thesis of universal causation—a thesis often enough confused with determinism. To reject determinism is only to reject the claim that every event has a *determining* cause; it is not necessarily to reject the thesis that every event has some cause, perhaps a probabilistic one. I am therefore taking Swinburne's use of "uncaused by" to be equivalent to "undetermined by."

3. "Phenomenal Abilities: Incompatibilism and the Experience of Agency," in *Oxford Studies in Agency and Responsibility* (Oxford: Oxford University Press, 2013), 126–50.

choice was free in the incompatibilist sense. Frankly, this is what I suspect is going on in the study in question. Participants report its seeming to them that they have alternative possibilities when faced with a particular decision. Then they are presented with the thesis of determinism and, once it is understood, asked to assess the compatibility of the veridicality of their experience of freedom with it. A quick and dirty argument for the incompatibility of determinism and the freedom to do otherwise becomes operative at some level of their consciousness; and they, therefore, report that their feeling of freedom cannot be consistent with determinism. But this would not be quite the same as its seeming to them directly that they make their choice independently of the deterministic causal nexus.

The content of this complex seeming—upon which Swinburne's argument depends—strikes me as too far beyond the reach of the faculties that could reliably produce veridical judgments of this kind. By analogy, it is as if it seemed to me not only that there is a mug on the table but also that the mug's being on the table is incompatible with Berkeleyan idealism; or as if it seemed to me not only that 2 + 2 = 4 but also that if Platonism about numbers is false, then my initial seeming would be misleading. Perhaps there are good reasons for accepting these controversial conjunctive claims (I honestly don't know), but it is hard to imagine that the way things seem to us could get us to these conclusions in one phenomenological step.[4] In addition, Richard Holton has offered what is to my mind a fairly powerful error theory for complex incompatibilistic phenomenological reports of these kinds. He accepts (as do I) that it often seems to us that we could have done something other than what we did, even with the beliefs and desires that we had at the time of action. That is, he grants that it sometimes seems to us that we are not determined *by our prior mental states*. And, indeed, he concludes that we are justified in believing this. But we err (though in a way that is easy to

4. One could go either of two ways with the judgments I am making here. On the one hand, one might say that those who report the Swinburnean seemings are simply making a phenomenological mistake. Things do not seem to them as they report. On the other hand, one might say that there may be seemings of this kind but that such unusually complex seemings cannot do the epistemic work Swinburne needs them to do; seemings of this sort do not necessarily provide us with prima facie justification for believing their content. Taking this approach would entail, given endorsement of something like his principle of credulity, eventually developing a principled way of distinguishing between the basic-justification-generating seemings and their neutered kin. I am somewhat inclined to favor the first approach, both because I do not think I find myself with the phenomenology Swinburne describes and because it permits a more attractively unified account of the epistemology of seemings. But I could be talked into the second approach.

understand) in thinking that, in these cases, it seems to us that we are not determined by *anything*.[5]

I conclude, then, that we will need an *argument*[6] to get us from the phenomenology we actually have (as of having alternative possibilities) to the libertarian thesis; and that, contra Swinburne, the libertarian will not be able to move directly from supposed incompatibilist seemings to her favored position merely by parrying would-be defeaters.

Let's return, now, to the title of Swinburne's paper: "The Impossibility of Proving that Human Behavior Is Determined." This title suggests what philosophers, speaking in their admittedly technical jargon, are likely to call a sexy thesis. Setting aside the controversial and ambiguous concept of proof that this appearance of sexiness may be turning upon, there is no question that an argument purporting to undermine that chronic bugbear "determinism" is bound to get the attention of philosophers. But when Swinburne announces his formal conclusion in the first paragraph of his paper, the thesis does not seem quite as provocative. There he tells us that the conclusion his argument establishes is "that it is immensely improbable that there could ever be a well-justified deterministic theory of how humans are caused to perform all the intentional actions which they perform." And the improbability, he tells us, is going to be due to the fact that "our very criteria for a well-justified scientific theory make it almost impossible for a theory of this kind to be well justified." The concerns I will now raise about Swinburne's project here have to do with my inability to see just what its successful execution could tell us about any interesting version of the claim that human behavior is determined. My strategy will be, then, largely to grant Swinburne his conclusion but go on to wonder if anything important about the thesis of determinism can follow from it.

It is will be useful to ask what particular thesis of determinism Swinburne has in mind. One version of the thesis that is likely to jump immediately to mind is the one ordinarily deployed, for example, in debates about free will and moral responsibility. As determinism is typically understood in these contexts, it is the thesis that the laws of nature, together with the facts about the world

5. Richard Holton, *Willing, Wanting, Waiting* (Oxford: Oxford University Press, 2009), 170.

6. Fortunately, we have at least one—the so-called consequence argument—if not more. For details of the consequence argument see my "The Consequence Argument Revisited" in *The Oxford Handbook of Free Will*, 2nd ed (Oxford: Oxford University Press, 2011), 115-30. For wider reflection on arguments for incompatibilism, see Kadri Vihvelin's contribution on this topic to the *Stanford Encyclopedia of Philosophy*: http://plato.stanford.edu/entries/incompatibilism-arguments/.

at some distant point in the past, circumscribe a unique future. Given the laws and given the past, there is only one way for the future to unfold. Formalizing this just a bit we can take this thesis to be:

> SD (Standard Determinism): The world is governed by (or is under the sway of) standard determinism if and only if, given a specified way things are at a time t, the way things go thereafter is fixed as a matter of natural law.[7]

Is this the thesis of determinism that Swinburne has in mind in his title? Probably not. Though standard determinism comes pre-loaded with the philosophical import the history of the free will debate has conferred upon it, Swinburne appears to have something less general in mind. What he seems to be concerned about is a thesis according to which physical states in the brain are causally linked with overt actions (typically by way of the causal mediation of mental states). Maybe the thesis Swinburne is after, then, is:

> PD (Psychophysical Determinism): The world is governed by (or is under the sway of) psychophysical determinism if and only if, given a specified way things are at a time with respect to the brain states of S at t, what mental states S will be in and what actions S will perform thereafter are fixed as a matter of natural law.

So I have now put before us two deterministic theses, one that is recognized as of general philosophical significance and another presented as my best effort to crystalize what Swinburne may actually have in mind. What I will try to show now is that Swinburne's conclusion won't do much to threaten either of these theses.

Would it show us that these determinisms are false, for example? Surely not. What Swinburne attempts to demonstrate is that a deterministic theory of human action will either be unable to have predictive power in virtue of its adherence to epiphenomenalism or (very likely) be unable to unify the necessary psychophysics under a simple set of laws. But either or both of SD and PD could be true even if Swinburne's argument goes through on both of these points. The failure of predicatibility won't show that deterministic epiphenomenalism is false. Neither will our incapacity to discover simple unifying laws show that deterministic psychophysicalism is false.

7. Borrowed, with modification, from Carl Hoefer, SEP article on Causal Determinism: http://plato.stanford.edu/entries/determinism-causal/.

But even if Swinburne's argument can't show us that SD and PD are false, can't it show us that we are not epistemically justified in accepting them? I think not. The *best* Swinburne's argument could do, I think, is to establish that no theory like SD or PD could be well justified on *scientific grounds*. It's those pesky criteria for *scientific* justification that are going unmet according to Swinburne. But whether belief in SD or PD is broadly *epistemically* justified is another matter—unless one is tempted by the view that a theory can be epistemically justified only if it is scientifically justified; but you shouldn't think that. Certainly, Swinburne doesn't think this. As he tells us, he takes epistemic justification to be a matter of a theory's being "made probable by the total evidence."

There seems to be no reason to think that the total evidence must be within the domain of science. Many theories just don't fall within the domain of the sciences in such a way as to be getting their epistemic justification from scientific justification. For example, our failure to find scientific justification for, say, a eudaimonistic moral theory surely doesn't license the conclusion that the theory is epistemically unjustified. The epistemic justification for a moral theory just may have nothing (or very little) to do with science. But even when a theory falls within the domain of the sciences it is nevertheless false that our epistemic justification for accepting it need be principally a matter of the theory's purely scientific credibility. Long before Big-Bang cosmology added scientific credence to the claim that the universe had a beginning in time, there were various philosophical arguments to the same conclusion. I can't see any reason to think that people aware of these arguments couldn't be epistemically justified in believing that the universe has not always existed, even in ignorance of the cosmological evidence. Similarly, astute observers of human behavior probably didn't need the rigorous results of contemporary social psychology to be justified in believing that we are subject to the phenomenon of confirmation bias. So I don't see how an argument demonstrating that a theory could never be scientifically well justified would, all by itself, also constitute a case against the epistemic credibility of the theory. Theories premised on deterministic theses like SD and PD may be able to get their epistemic justification from something other than their status as well-justified scientific theories. Thus, I don't see how Swinburne's argument could show us that belief in SD or PD is epistemically unjustified, even if it succeeds in showing us that no SD or PD theory could get the scientific stamp of approval.

Perhaps what we should conclude, on the basis of Swinburne's arguments, is that anyone who hopes to undermine the epistemic credibility of our belief in libertarian free will by appeal to the scientific legitimacy of a broad determinism bears a heavier argumentative burden than she might have originally thought. Insofar as this kind of legitimacy presupposes that we have a scientifically well-justified theory of determinism with respect to human behavior, the skeptical argument will have to show either that epiphenomenalism is not stultifying or that a psychophysical theory can plausibly be unified by a sufficiently simple set of laws. And I grant that Swinburne has thrown up some rather serious obstacles to anyone's showing these things.

Still, to my mind the most probative critics of libertarianism have not put much (if any) weight on a scientific demonstration of human determinism. This is no doubt due, in part, to the fact that deterministic theories of foundational physics are largely out of fashion. But it is also due to the fact that a number of powerful but purely (or essentially) philosophical arguments cut quite deeply to the root of libertarianism without depending on very much by way of empirical support. I have in mind here the family of luck or chance arguments against libertarianism that purport to show that indeterminism would either undermine the kind of control we want in free action or would not contribute anything to this control over and above what can be had by a determined agent.[8]

To be clear, I accept neither SD nor PD; indeed I reject them both—and hold out some glimmer of hope that I am epistemically justified in my commitment to libertarianism. However, I suspect that my commitment can't get much of whatever epistemic justification it has from Swinburne's argument, both because it rests on the wrong phenomenological evidence and because it places inordinate weight on scientific justification. As I said at the outset, however, I have been quite deeply impressed by the systematic depth and explanatory power of Swinburne's fuller corpus. So I would not be surprised to discover that the parts of the entire watch I have been picking at here work much better together than my local criticisms suggest. I will be happy to learn more about time-keeping and watch-making from a truly masterful craftsman.

8. Even Peter van Inwagen, a stalwart libertarian, has been pushed into "Mysterianism" by concerns of this sort. For a penetrating treatment of luck arguments, see Mele, *Free Will and Luck* (New York: Oxford University Press, 2006). My considered judgments about luck arguments can be found in "Libertarianism, Luck, and Gift," *The Modern Schoolman* (now *Res Philosophica*) 88(1/2) (2012): 29–49.

CHAPTER 9

A Rejoinder to Speak

Richard Swinburne

Thanks very much to Dan Speak for his very kind opening remarks, and for the license which it gives me to make a couple of references to my own writings. His paper raises two main issues. The first issue concerns my empirical claim that it seems to most of us that we often make decisions without those decisions being fully caused by some other event. I am glad of the reference to the study by Deery, Bedke, and Nichols which reports "substantial findings" to the effect that "subjects making deliberate decisions tend to describe the experience of their own agency in these circumstances as incompatible with the thesis of determinism." Hence my use of the principle of credulity to claim that—in the absence of counter-evidence (that is, a defeater)—we who have such experiences should believe that not all our decisions, and so not all our intentional actions, are fully caused. I should have added that the Principle of Testimony should lead those who do not have experiences of apparently making uncaused decisions and who learn that many others do have such experiences, also to believe—in the absence of a defeater—that the decisions of many other people are not always fully caused. Given these principles Speak cannot just claim that the subjects studied in this report are "simply making a phenomenological mistake," without providing some argument to show this.

The main argument that Speak provides for his claim is Holton's assertion that what is really going on when some of us claim to have such experiences is that it seems to us that we are not determined by our prior mental states, and that we mistakenly claim that it seems to us that we are not determined by anything. But what we are concerned with is the causation or non-causation of our intentional actions; and an intentional action just is one done because we desire to do it or believe it good to do it. To desire to do an action is to feel an inclination to do it either for no further reason or because we believe that it will forward some goal which we feel an inclination to bring about for no further reason. To believe it good to do it entails feeling an inclination to do it because it is good to do. An action wouldn't be an intentional action unless it was done in order to fulfill some desire or moral belief. If I eat some chocolate, although I have no desire to do so or any belief that it is good to do so, my putting the chocolate in my mouth cannot constitute an intentional action—it would be an unintended bodily movement. And desires and value beliefs are the sole factors which influence our actions, as we can see by the fact that any one desire or value belief will determine our action unless it is in conflict with other desires or value beliefs. If my only desire is to eat the chocolate and I have no value belief that it would be bad to do so, inevitably I will eat the chocolate. Of course brain events influence (and, as I acknowledged, often determine) our intentional actions; but they do so by causing our mental events, that is causing our desires (e.g. to eat the chocolate) and/or value beliefs (e.g. that it would improve my health to eat the chocolate), which in turn influence us to do the action. So Holton has misdescribed our situation; there are no events other than mental events which directly influence our decisions and so our intentional actions. If we are mistaken in "supposing that we could have done something other than we did," this must be because we are misjudging the strength of some desire or inclination resulting from a value belief.[1] It may seem to me that I am choosing on which of two desires of equal strength to act, when really one desire is stronger than the other and that causes me to make the choice I do. Or it may seem to me that I am resisting the strong desire to eat the chocolate and acting on a moral belief which gives rise only to a weaker inclination to act, but really the desire is weaker or the inclination resulting from the value belief is stronger than I believe. That of course, I allow, could happen. But the strength of a desire or the influence of a belief is something we feel; I feel just how difficult it is to resist the temptation to eat the chocolate. Its strength is a property of a mental event to which we have privileged access (but not infallible access)—just as, to take an important analogy, I feel the force of a weight which I am holding; I can make a rough assessment of its strength by the effort which I need to exert in order to continue to hold it. And it is because it does often seem to us that the strengths of our desires and

1. I write of the "strength" of an "inclination" resulting from a value belief, and not of the "strength" of the value belief, because by "the strength" of a belief may be meant how probable the believer believes it to be. But one may be fairly confident that some value belief is true without having any strong inclination to act on it. By contrast the "strength" of a desire is simply the strength of the inclination to satisfy it.

inclinations resulting from value beliefs are not such as to determine what we will do, that in the absence of a defeater it is probable that (that is, we are justified in believing that) our choice between them is free.

Speak's other argument for his claim is that "the content of this complex seeming" that we are not determined by any event in forming our intentions, "[is] too far beyond the reach of the faculties that could reliably produce veridical judgments of this kind" (112). Now if Speak has a justified belief (B_2) of the latter kind, then that would be a defeater to the justification of the belief (B_1) about "the content of our complex seeming." But presumably Speak does not hold B_2 (the belief about the reach of our faculties) as a basic belief, and so he needs an argument for it, and I do not see that he has provided one.

The second issue which Speak raises concerns the worth of my conclusion that "psychophysical determinism" (PD) cannot be established on scientific grounds. There is of course a distinction between PD and SD ("Scientific Determinism"); but the falsity of PD entails the falsity of SD, and so if are are not justified in believing PD (as I argue), then we are not justified in believing SD. I do not assume that all deterministic causation is causation in accord with laws of nature. There may exist "singular causation"; one particular substance may cause some effect, without there being a law of nature to the effect that all similar substances in similar circumstances cause similar effects. So I prefer to formulate PD simply as "every mental event has a necessary and sufficient cause." Now it is true that there are a priori arguments for this claim, normally phrased as arguments for the Principle of Sufficient Reason. But one has to be selective in the arguments one discusses in a short paper, and—perhaps erroneously—it has always seemed to me that such arguments are highly implausible.[2] Such a bold and apparently metaphysically contingent claim about the nature of the world as is PD, would seem to need an a posteriori argument. And the only a posteriori way of showing (i.e. making it epistemically probable) that PD holds is by showing that some detailed scientific theory which entails PD is probably true (and showing this would show that there was no singular causation). Hence the relevance of my arguments to show that very probably it couldn't ever be shown that such a theory is true; and so that we should believe that things are often as they seem to be with respect to our decisions not being fully caused. "The family of luck or chance arguments against

2. I do give an argument for rejecting the popular a priori argument in favor of the similar principle of the "Causal Closure of the Physical," that since we cannot understand how the mental influences the physical, it probably does not do so, in *Mind, Brain, and Free Will* (Oxford University Press, 2013), 104–5.

libertarianism" is not relevant here. Such arguments are relevant only to the topics of whether indeterminism is a necessary condition for "free will" (in a technical sense) or moral responsibility, neither of which topics are discussed in my paper in this volume. But of course I do use the conclusion of this paper, which summarizes arguments in my book *Mind, Brain, and Free Will,* to argue in that book for a libertarian account of free will.

CHAPTER 10

Neuroscience and the Human Person

Kevin Corcoran and Kevin Sharpe

We don't believe that there are nonphysical souls in the natural world that we inhabit, the world within which we live and move and have our being. Therefore, we don't believe that we are or have such nonphysical souls as parts. We hold that human persons are wholly physical entities exhaustively composed of physical particles (the sorts of things whose job it is for physics to investigate).[1] You might call this the Madonna Metaphysic of human persons: *we are material girls and boys living in a material world.* But here's the amazing thing, the physical stuff that wholly composes us is chock-full of astonishing potentialities, such as the potential to produce the Technicolor phenomenology of consciousness from the spectacularly complex network of one hundred billion nerve cells and their several hundred trillion synaptic connections in the wet-ware of the human brain.

Material Beings in a Material World

Ours is a world, a *natural*, *material* world overflowing with wonders. Consider marsupial wolves (those are wolves with a pouch like a kangaroo!) and carnivorous plants (*flesh*-eating plants!). Or, even more wondrous, consider *consciousness*. We *could be* exactly like computers, elaborate machines with wholly material components that interact with each other in such ways as to produce very interesting behaviors. Everything about computers and other

1. Note that we don't claim all persons are physical entities, nor do we make any claim regarding which type of physical entity we are (at least not here).

machines is *third-person* observable, *objectively* existing and *measurable*. And yet when it comes to us there is an ineliminable *subjectivity*. There's something it's like to *feel* pain and pleasure, to *taste* an orange, to *smell* lavender, to *hear* a beautiful song, to *see* a sunset. Unlike computers and combustion engines, our experiences of such things are irreducibly subjective in that they have a qualitative, or phenomenal, character that is fully comprehensible only from a single type of perspective—the first-person, experiential perspective of having the experience in question (Nagel 1974). In other words, unlike computers and combustion engines, we are *conscious* creatures. And like marsupial wolves and carnivorous plants, the existence of consciousness in the natural world is astonishing and wonderful!

Of course, we're not the *only* creatures that enjoy consciousness; your dog does too. As does your cat. And lots of even physically simpler creatures as well. Their consciousness, though, is less complex given their less complex brains. And this brings us to the main point: while the "why" that the universe should contain such creatures as ourselves seems to us at least to more easily fit within a *theistic* understanding of the universe, the "how" that it does seems increasingly to yield to naturalistic explanation. The neurosciences have made incredible strides in recent decades in explaining a wide variety of extremely puzzling phenomena. From how someone could feel water trickling down a nonexistent arm to how a person could "guess" with near perfect accuracy the location and direction of motion of an item in a blind field of vision, the neurosciences promise to unravel longstanding perplexities regarding human cognition.

Our goal in this paper is to give a number of actual examples from neuroscience and to say why, as physicalists about human persons, we believe that it is physicalism, not dualism, that best fits the neurobiological data. In the next section we illustrate this by considering three cases in which certain remarkable features of consciousness are explainable in terms of neuroscience. In the third section we argue that the current (and very likely continued) explanatory power of neuroscience makes the hypothesis that human persons are (or have as parts) nonphysical souls less plausible than materialism. Our reasoning here is *not* that these cases or any future discoveries in neuroscience, and the cognitive sciences in general, will produce data that is *inconsistent* with dualism. We do not believe that will ever be the case. Even the phenomenon of *divided consciousness* that results from commissurotomy (Nagel 1971; Sperry 1984) can be *made to fit* the dualist hypothesis. But while dualism can be made to fit the data, the phenomenon of divided consciousness certainly fits more seamlessly with a *physicalist* picture of the natural world and consciousness than it does a *dualist* picture. Moreover, the phenomenon itself is certainly not what one might *expect* were dualism in fact true. Our reasoning, based on cases like those discussed in the next section, is just that *given* the progress and successes at explaining various facets and features of consciousness already achieved, and the future progress and successes we can expect in these fields, dualism becomes a less and less plausible thesis when it comes to an account or explanation of consciousness. We conclude by explaining why we don't think that the mystery of consciousness (and it is a mystery) favors dualism over physicalism.

Three Examples from Neuroscience

Our goal is to show that physicalism is a better fit with the deliverances of neuroscience than dualism. To that end, we focus on three widely discussed cases from neuroscience: extreme amnesia (both retrograde and anterograde), blindsight, and phantom limbs. Each case illustrates the extent to which key features of consciousness are dependent on and explained in terms of neural anatomy and physiology. Each case offers a vivid illustration of how minor damage to (or the non-normal functioning of) a specific part of the brain can result in a highly selective loss or alteration of consciousness and, as Ramachandran notes, the fact that small lesions in a specific part of the brain result in highly selective loss of one specific function while preserving other functions is a "good indication that the affected part of the brain is somehow involved in mediating the impaired function." (2004, 4) Given the preponderance of known cases, the picture of consciousness emerging from the neurosciences is one of a fine-grained, systematic dependence on neural structure that does not fit naturally a dualist understanding of human persons. Before pursuing that argument, we turn to our cases.

Case 1: The Real Life Memento Man

Clive Wearing is a 74-year-old former composer and musician who, in March 1985, was struck with one of the worst cases of amnesia ever recorded. Not only is his retrograde amnesia (the inability to recall previous formed memories) so bad that he has lost nearly all memory of his previous life, he has also completely lost the ability to lay down new, conscious memories (anterograde amnesia). For nearly the past thirty years, Wearing has been unable to remember anything for more than a few seconds. Some memories are gone within six to seven seconds, while others are retained for nearly a minute. In her memoir, Wearing's wife, Deborah, described his subjective world as consisting

> of a moment with no past to anchor it and no future to look ahead to . . . Clive is unaware there have been other days prior to the one in which he finds himself. He only ever has knowledge of being conscious for a couple of minutes.[2]

and in stressing the momentary nature of Wearing's conscious awareness, she writes that he

> did not seem to be able to retain any impression of anything for more than a blink. Indeed, if he did blink, his eyelid parted to reveal a new scene. The view before the blink was utterly forgotten. Each blink, each glance away and back, brought him an entirely new view.[3]

From his perspective, Wearing is in a perpetual state of "just waking up." Whether his wife has been gone for ten minutes or ten years, it doesn't matter: when she enters his room he embraces her ecstatically, believing that he is seeing her for the first time after a long separation. Several minutes into a game of solitaire, a game he loves, he will have no recollection that it was he who dealt and played the cards lying before him. Even when he records copious notes for himself on the progression of the game, he will still insist that, although the notes are indeed in his handwriting, he did not write them. He has no idea how the notes got there or who may have dealt the cards.[4]

Imagine that your whole conscious life were lived out on a mental treadmill; no matter how far you run it is always the same well-worn path you travel. That's the character of Clive Wearing's conscious life—his sense of being a continuous self stretches back no farther than just a few minutes. Lacking any self-conscious awareness of persisting from one moment to the next, Wearing is forever trapped in a series of disconnected present moments utterly devoid of a

2. Quoted in McMahan (2002), 77.

3. Quoted in Sacks (2007).

4. The horror of Wearing's condition is captured by his extensive journal entries. Running hundreds of pages, they are all variations on "I am awake," "I am conscious," "This time I am properly conscious" with each entry cancelled out by a subsequent assertion that he is, contrary to previous claims, finally conscious. As Sacks notes, Wearing has some awareness of his condition, which he describes as "like being dead."

past and a future. Lacking any durable sense of being a continuing self, Wearing fails to possess the subjective continuity of experience that unifies one's experiences into a coherent and meaningful autobiography (Glannon 2011, 2013).

What is the cause of Clive Wearing's severe and unusual form of amnesia? His amnesia is the result of a viral infection (herpes encephalitis) that insinuated itself into his brain, completely destroying his hippocampus, a part of the medial temporal lobe responsible for storing *conscious*, episodic memories. Interestingly, the infection did not affect the regions responsible for procedural, working, and emotional memory, three types of unconscious memory that allow Wearing to continue playing the piano and relate to his wife despite his condition (Glannon 2011; Sacks 2007). That consciousness can be altered or even eliminated by altering or destroying certain regions of the brain demonstrates the degree to which our conscious lives are radically physically based. That the capacity for episodic memory can be nearly destroyed while preserving the capacity for various types of unconscious memory demonstrates the fine-grained nature of this dependence.

Case 2: Blindsight

The second case we consider is that of *blindsight*.[5] This is a fascinating condition that renders patients who suffer from it able to "see" without *consciously* seeing. A patient suffering from blindsight can be shown (say) a spot of light in their "blind" field of "vision" and asked "what is it you see?" They will answer "nothing." Which is exactly what we would expect. But if asked to point to the spot of light, they can do it. If the object is moving up or down, left or right, *in the blind field* they can tell you with near perfect accuracy which direction the "unseen" object is moving. Similarly, patients suffering from blindsight can reach for objects, state whether a stick is oriented vertically or horizontally, and even catch a ball thrown towards them—all in their blind field of vision. Most astonishing, they do this with remarkable accuracy even while insisting that they are merely guessing.[6] But how that be? How can someone "see" without seeing?

5. Here and in the following case, we rely on Ramachandran's work, especially his (1998) and (2004).

6. See Weiskrantz (1986) for a detailed discussion of the empirical issues. Weiskrantz summaries research conducted since 1986 in the second edition. Accessible discussions can also be found in Ramachandran and Blakeslee (1998), Ramachandran (2004), Ramachandran (2012). Block (1988), Dennett (1991), and Tye (1995) offer varying assessments of the impact of blindsight on a philosophical theory of consciousness.

The answer lies in the neuroanatomy of vision (Ramachandran and Blakeslee 1998; Ramachandran 2004). It's long been known that damage to the primary visual cortex (a part of the occipital lobe, a region in the back of the brain devoted to conscious visual processing) results in blindness. For example, damage to the right primary visual cortex results in blindness in the left field of vision. This damage inhibits the functionality of the visual pathway running from the retina, through the thalamus to the primary visual cortex and from the primary visual cortex to a cluster of thirty or so highly specialized visual processing areas, e.g., V4 (devoted to color perception) and MT (devoted to perception of motion). As this pathway specializes in processing aspects of conscious visual perception, you need it in order to *consciously* see something. But there is a second, evolutionarily older, visual pathway that subserves a different aspect of vision and runs from the retina to the superior colliculus in the brain stem and from there to the parietal lobe (a higher cortical area concerned with spatial representation and spatial navigation). This older pathway is involved in reflexive behavior and orienting toward something important in your visual field (perhaps something that threatens your continued existence). This second pathway is found in birds and reptiles (non-human animals which some believe do not enjoy consciousness). It is the higher centers of bird, reptile, and human brains that substantially differ, and that accounts for why the one (humans) and (likely) not the other (reptiles and birds) enjoys consciousness.

In blindsight, part of the newer pathway, the primary visual cortex, is damaged. Therefore, blindsight patients do not *consciously* see anything. But the older pathway, the one that subserves the "fight or flight" reflex and that's responsible for object location and orientation in a visual field, remains intact. An object in the blind field of vision activates this older pathway allowing the patient to locate and respond to it. Since the older pathway is not conscious, it can process visual stimuli without the blindsighted individual being consciously aware of those stimuli. It is in virtue of this evolutionarily older pathway that blindsight patients are able to non-consciously "see" the direction of objects they do not "see" consciously.[7]

7. In case you were wondering, damage to the older pathway (in particular the right parietal lobe) results in *neglect*, which is something like the converse of blindsight. Ramachandran (2004) describes it as a kind of indifference to objects in the left visual field. Patients suffering from neglect no longer move their eyes to objects in the left visual field, nor do they reach for or point to objects there. They will only eat food on the right side of their plate and shave the right side of their face (Ramachandran 2004, 33).

Case 3: Phantom Limb Phenomena

In the past ten to fifteen years, there has been a lot of talk about *neural plasticity*. During most of the last century, the consensus was that brain structure was pretty much set and immutable after some specified critical period of childhood development. More recent research, however, shows that while the brain is not endlessly plastic, it is plastic within limits or boundaries. Within certain circumscribed boundaries, our brain can, indeed, be "re-wired." In fact, experience can change not just brain *structure* or anatomy but also the functional *organization* or physiology of the brain. Connections or neural pathways within the brain are removed or preserved almost entirely based on use or non-use. Not only that, but neighboring neurons that fire together or simultaneously, often fuse to make a new pathway within the network. Likewise, neighboring neurons that do not fire together form independent neural routes.

A vivid example of brain plasticity is found in phantom limb patients. These are patients who have lost a limb but continue to feel the presence of their missing limb and experience pains, itches, and other sorts of sensory stimulation in it. For example, one patient who was missing a right arm continued to feel it itch whenever he shaved the left side of his face. Other patients feel cold sensations in their phantom limb when an ice cube touches their face and still others feel water trickle down their missing arm when a drop of water trickles down their face (Ramachandran and Blakeslee 1998). But how is this possible? How can someone feel an itch in their right arm when they don't have a right arm? How can someone feel water trickle down their right arm when, again, they don't have a right arm? How can touching a person's cheek result in a sensation in a limb that's been missing for a decade?

In a series of experiments performed during brain surgeries using only local anesthesia, Wilder Penfield discovered that stimulating the post-central gyrus, a narrow vertical region of cortex in the parietal lobe, produces sensations in different parts of the body (Ramachandran and Blakeslee 1998). Penfield discovered that this strip of cortex contains an entire neural map, called the Penfield homunculus, of our whole body. As it turns out, the location of our right arm on this map is adjacent to that of the face. When the patient loses a limb, the cortical region corresponding to the right arm region of the map no longer receives stimulation as the limb is missing and is no longer sending it signals. The neurons in this understimulated cortical region are so "hungry for sensory input" that they begin overreaching their borders and extending their way into the adjacent region, that of the face, where they receive signals and stimulation. These signals are then interpreted as being sent from the hand as well as the face. Thus, sensory stimulation originating in the face results in the stimulation of both the facial and hand regions of the Penfield map and this is why when the patient shaves (or stimulates that area) he also feels it as an itch on his phantom arm.[8] Neural plasticity makes limited neural remapping possible and this remapping explains the felt location of sensations as if they are occurring in a missing limb.[9]

Against the Soul

As we noted at the outset, dualism is logically consistent with the empirical findings in the neurosciences discussed above; for example, it is logically consistent with the fact that severe atrophying of the hippocampus results in the near total loss of continuity of conscious memory. Yet we maintain that in at least two ways materialism is a better fit with these findings and this makes dualism less plausible as a theory of human persons than materialism. The argument of this section is that there's a tension between dualism and both the neural dependence of consciousness and the seeming irrelevance of a nonphysical soul in explaining certain features of our conscious mental life. Given this tension, the neurological data supports materialism over dualism. Other things being equal, then, we should prefer a materialist account of human persons to dualism.

Suppose that the dualist is right and the subject of conscious experience (in both its cognitive and phenomenal aspects) is a nonphysical substance devoid of any mereological structure. Then while we would expect a fairly high degree of some kinds of dependence (e.g., dependence of the soul on the brain for sensory stimuli), we would not expect to find such a radical, causal dependence of our conscious lives on the physical, which is exactly what we do find. The point is best appreciated by considering the fine-grained dependence that our examples illustrate. While conscious experience may seem to be a seamless unity, our examples reveal a fairly high degree of struc-

8. Ramachandran discovered a map of a patient's entire hand on his face as well as a second map of the hand on the patient's arm a few inches above the amputation line. The second map is also a result of neural remapping, as the hand region of the Penfield map is adjacent to both the facial and upper arm regions. See Ramachandran and Blakeslee 1998, 29.

9. Remapping alone doesn't explain other phantom limb phenomenon, such as the seeming voluntary control some patients have over the movement of their phantom limbs or the painful paralysis other patients experience. See Ramachandran and Blakeslee 1998, 45–58, for a discussion of the neurological explanation of these aspects of the experience of phantom limbs.

tural complexity in which distinct aspects of experience are implemented in anatomically distinct neural structures. For example, blindsight reveals that visual processing involves two pathways, only one of which is conscious, that control different aspects of visual perception. The fact that damage to a specific part of the brain, in this case the primary visual cortex, results in a highly selective visual impairment, rather than the total loss of all capacity for visual processing, suggests that different parts of the visual system depend on distinct neural structures. This, in conjunction with the other cases, suggests an overall picture in which consciousness and cognition rest on a structurally complex architecture that maps onto a neural structure that is at least equally complex, in which each element of our mental architecture is mapped onto a different neural structure on which it depends.

We would not expect to find this sort of systematic, fine-grained dependence of consciousness and experience on patterns of neural activity if dualism were true. Why wouldn't we expect the kinds of dependencies revealed by neuroscience? If the dualist were correct, then not only would all conscious experience take place within a nonphysical subject, but additionally the kind of neural activity mapped out by the neurosciences should be explanatorily irrelevant to its occurrence and character. This supposed explanatory irrelevance of the physical for the features of consciousness is the driving force of a typical anti-materialist argument, the "inadequacy of materialism" objection. Here's Leibniz's famous statement of that argument:

> We must admit that perception, and whatever depends on it, cannot be explained on mechanical principles, i.e. by shapes and movements. If we pretend that there is a machine whose structure makes it think, sense and have perceptions, then we can conceive of it enlarged, but keeping to the same proportions, so that we might go inside it as into a mill. Suppose that we do: then if we inspect the interior we shall find there nothing but parts which push one another, and never anything which could explain a perception. Thus, perception must be sought in simple substance, not in what is composite or in machines.[10]

10. (Leibniz 1989). Alvin Plantinga offers a contemporary version of the argument in his papers "Against Materialism" and "Materialism and Christian Belief." Putting the point in terms of intentional content, he argues (in a neo-Leibnizian tone) that "we can examine this neuronal event as carefully as we please; we can measure the number of neurons it contains, their connections, their rates of fire, the strength of the electrical impulses involved, the potential across the synapses—we can measure all this with as much precision as you could possibly desire; we can consider its electro-chemical, neurophysiological properties in the most

But if complex patterns of neural firings were explanatorily irrelevant in a way that demanded a nonphysical subject of conscious experience, then—in the absence of strong reasons to contrary—we'd expect conscious experience to be nomologically independent of such neural activities. But conscious experience is not nomologically independent of neural activity. So in the absence of strong reasons to expect otherwise, the fine-grained, neurobiological dependence of consciousness make physicalism a better fit with what we know from the neurosciences.

So far we've focused on how our examples motivate a kind of dependence of consciousness on brain activity that is in tension with dualism, but the cases motivate another aspect of the case for materialism (or against dualism, if you prefer). The cases illustrate how certain remarkable features of consciousness are explainable in terms of neuroscience and so explaining the curious features of consciousness, for example, Clive Wearing's conscious life, is achieved without any need to invoke a non-physical soul. Many other features of consciousness too, from the ability to discriminate and react to environmental stimulae and the ability to access our own internal conscious states, to the focus of attention and the difference between wakefulness and sleep, to the very existence of human emotions, *all* are in fact *explainable* in terms of brain structures and neural activity. In other words, science explains these features of consciousness without invoking a non-physical soul. So there is, at least with respect to all of these aspects of conscious experience, no explanatory work for a non-physical soul to do. The steady march of progress and explanatory successes already achieved in neuroscience and its cognate disciplines, coupled with the *continued* progress and successes we can expect in the future, leaves less and less room for a non-physical soul. The ongoing success of the neurosciences is squeezing the soul out of the explanatory picture.

Consider again the phenomenon of phantom limbs. Touching the cheek of a phantom limb patient causes a sensation in the missing limb. As we saw earlier, this is explained in terms of a facial tactile stimulation sending a sensory message to adjacent areas in the Penfield map. The felt location of a sensation is explained by stimulation of the part of the sensory cortex corresponding to that location in the Penfield map. Similar explanations are given for other features of conscious experience, e.g., the type of sensation experienced (i.e., whether it's an itch, a vibration, or the feeling of a trickle of water) and its intensity—all without positing a nonphysical soul. The lesson seems to be that

exquisite detail; but nowhere, here, will you find so much as a hint of content. Indeed, none of this seems even vaguely relevant to its having content" (2007, 109).

transformations in a nonphysical soul play no role in explaining these features of consciousness. The fact that more and more aspects of consciousness are being explained in terms of neurophysiology is galvanizing physicalists and providing them with ever more optimism that experience itself will one day yield to explanation, explanation wholly in terms of principles and laws that are consistent with everything else we know about the natural world, and the workings of the brain. Neurology, therefore, threatens to screen off any contribution the soul may make.

There is a further consideration we would like to call attention to, and that is just how materialism about human persons fits what we know about the slow, gradual emergence and development of increasingly complex living things, as well as what we know about the gradual development of biological organismic life and consciousness itself. We know, for example, that new conscious capacities emerge as brain structure develops in complexity. The slow, gradual development of increasingly complex conscious capacities fits the picture we get from nature. If what dualists say about the soul is true—that it's a non-physical, partless entity and that *it* is the bearer of psychological properties and states of human consciousness—then, it seems difficult, if not impossible, to account for the *gradual* development of conscious capacities, as it's hard to see how a *partless* thing can develop. In other words, it would seem that the soul that is *you* must have had the capacity to engage in the solving of differential equations from its earliest days as the soul of the embryo that became your body. But yet we know that the neural structure of an embryo lacks the kind of complexity necessary to underwrite the sort of cognitive sophistication one needs to think about, let alone solve, differential equations. At the very least, we see this as an additional challenge to dualism.

We've said enough to see that dualism is a less plausible thesis than materialism when it comes to an explanation of consciousness. In fact, we've said enough to make it doubtful that the soul has any role to play in an explanation of consciousness and this grounds an argument from expectation to the explanatory *irrelevance* of a non-physical soul. *If* dualism were true, we would not *expect* to discover the thoroughgoing and deep causal dependencies of consciousness and experience on brain activities and states we do in fact find. The more we study, the more we discover the underlying neural (i.e., physical) dependence and (physical) causal explanations of consciousness. Therefore, the more we learn about the neural correlates of consciousness, the more explanatorily irrelevant a non-physical soul becomes.

Should we accept a dualist account of human persons? Not if the above argument is correct. The inclusion of a theoretical entity, like the soul, is justified solely on the basis of that entity's role in the explanation of a set of phenomena. Does including the entity in the theory ground successful predications the theory would otherwise miss? Does including the entity make it possible to explain a range of otherwise unexplainable phenomena? If not, then positing the entity is unjustified. Since the only reason we have to believe in a theoretical entity is that it does necessary explanatory work, we're warranted in accepting the existence of a theoretical entity only if it does the required explanatory work it's invoked to do (other things being equal). If the postulated entity is unable to do the explanatory work or if the resulting theory fails to explain the target phenomena at least as well as a rival theory, we're not warranted in accepting the entity. Therefore, the explanatory irrelevance of the soul implies that we're not warranted in accepting the existence of the soul and hence, in the absence of other evidence, we should accept materialism.

The Mystery of Consciousness

While we are able to explain many features of consciousness in physical terms, i.e., in terms of neural structures and activity, it must be confessed that we are at present unable to explain how consciousness emerges from patterns of neural activity. Indeed the aspects of consciousness that seem the most resistant to naturalistic explanation, namely the subjective and phenomenal character of consciousness, threaten to make the mystery of consciousness intractable. With his characteristic flair, McGinn states the problem like this:

> How is it possible for conscious states to depend upon brain states? How can technicolour phenomenology arise from soggy grey matter? . . . Somehow we feel the water of the brain is turned into the wine of consciousness, but we draw a total blank on the nature of this conversion. (1993, 1–2)

Does our concession that we are not yet able to explain just *how* consciousness emerges from the workings of the human brain weaken our claim that it is physicalism that best fits the deliverances of neuroscience? We don't think so. Although it's understandable how one might be led to think otherwise. For one might reason as follows:

1. There is no naturalistic explanation for the felt qualities of experience, like pleasure and pain, flavors, and smells.

2. The primary qualities of physical objects (like brains themselves) are quite obviously physical, third-person observable, and measurable.
3. Felt qualities of experience, like pleasure and pain, flavors, smells, and color experience are precisely *not obviously* physical or third-person observable and are in fact *very difficult* to fit into a naturalistic or physicalist framework.
4. Therefore, the felt qualities of experience are not wholly physical (nor perhaps even partly physical).

Again, we frankly admit that there is now no adequate physical theory that explains just *how* consciousness arises from the complicated network of wet-ware that is the human brain. Consciousness is a veritable mystery. The problem is that we fail to see how *dualism* takes the mystery out of consciousness. If anything, it seems to multiply mystery by adding to the mystery of consciousness the mystery of a non-physical substance that enjoys consciousness. Is it really any easier to see how a non-physical soul could be conscious than it is to see how a physical organism could? We don't think so at all.

So suppose, like us, you are a traditional theist. Is there any reason *you* should be sanguine about explaining consciousness in natural, physical terms? We think there is. One need not embrace *atheistic* naturalism in order to believe that it is in virtue of some *natural* property of brains that organisms are conscious and, in fact, we think our theistic commitments make it more likely that a naturalistic explanation is possible. Since the natural world has yielded in so many ways to scientific explanation over the past several hundred years, it seems only plausible to believe that God created the world—the *natural* world—with its own integrity and such that it operates according to regularities that can be grasped and understood. Since it is plausible to believe that God created the natural world, and all that it contains, with its own integrity, it is also reasonable to believe that consciousness itself—a feature encountered in the natural world—has a *natural* explanation. One need not be a *metaphysical* naturalist to believe *that*.

It may be helpful here to distinguish *metaphysical* naturalism from both *methodological* naturalism and what, in the past, one of us referred to as *chastened* naturalism.[11] *Metaphysical* naturalism amounts to the claim that the natural world is all there is and is exhaustive of reality. *Methodological* naturalism, on the other hand, amounts to a presupposition of the practice of science. It says that scientific explanations must exclude reference

11. Corcoran (2006).

to supernatural entities. If science is in the business of discovering *natural* causes, this ought not to surprise or offend. *Methodological* naturalism, as we understand it, is compatible with a robust theism insofar as it does not rule out explanations that appeal to God. It simply would not count such explanations as *scientific* explanations. *Chastened* naturalism recognizes the enormous contribution science has made to our understanding of the natural world and takes the natural world to possess its own integrity and to exemplify regularities that can be understood without reference to supernatural entities. What makes it *chastened* naturalism is its refusal to make the "metaphysical" turn and to claim that the natural world is all there is and, therefore, that the sciences are the *only* source of genuine knowledge. Chastened naturalism is compatible with there being religious experience and Divine revelation. Such experience and revelation provides for religious *knowledge*, which is genuine knowledge even if not visible to the practice of science and by definition not *scientific* knowledge. Therefore, to grant that consciousness has a natural explanation does not require that we sacrifice our theistic commitments. Indeed, it is our theistic commitments that ground the hope we expressed in the previous section that future science will produce a theory that accommodates consciousness and shows just how it relates it to everything else in the natural world.

Conclusion

Are the deliverances of the neurosciences consistent with the view that human persons *are* or *have* an immaterial soul? Yes, they are. But they fit much more seamlessly with a physicalist understanding of human nature and the world. The explanatory successes enjoyed by neuroscience demonstrate the explanatory irrelevance of the soul as well as consciousness' thoroughgoing dependence on brain activity. Given the explanatory irrelevance of the soul, we should accept materialism—lacking any additional evidence. Is it possible to explain the sheer fact of consciousness in purely physical, neurobiological terms? Not yet. Isn't the existence of *consciousness* an absolute mystery in a wholly *physical* world? Indeed it is. But yet even here, we have suggested that as theists, we have good reason to think that it is indeed possible to naturalistically explain consciousness and hence the mystery of consciousness doesn't provide evidence for dualism over materialism. The existence of consciousness in a wholly physical world is an undeniable mystery. Granted. But the natural world is an astonishing place! It has thrown up such things as flesh-eating plants, marsupial wolves, Buddhist monks who can actually increase their body temperature just by meditating, and, as we've suggested, it's even produced consciousness (even if we don't yet understand the mechanism by which this happens). Introducing a non-physical soul does nothing to remove the mystery of consciousness. If anything, it multiplies mysteries beyond necessity. We conclude, then, that materialism is a better fit with what we know about consciousness and its neural basis than is dualism.

REFERENCES

Block, Ned (1995). "On a confusion about a function of consciousness," *Behavioral and Brain Sciences* 18, 227–47.

Corcoran, Kevin (2006). *Rethinking Human Nature: A Christian Materialist Alternative to the Soul.* Grand Rapids: Baker Academic.

Dennett, Daniel (1991). *Consciousness Explained.* New York: Back Bay Books.

Nagel, Thomas (1971). "Brain Bisection and the Unity of Consciousness," *Synthese*, 396–413 (repr. in *Mortal Questions*).

Glannon, Walter (2011). *Brain, Body, and Mind: Neuroethics with a Face.* Oxford: Oxford University Press.

Glannon, Walter (2013). "Brain Injury and Survival." In *The Metaphysics and Ethics of Death: New Essays*, ed. James Stacey Taylor, 245-66. Oxford: Oxford University Press.

Leibniz, G. W. (1989). "Monadology." In *Philosophical Essays*, eds. Roger Ariew and Daniel Garber, 213-24. Indianapolis: Hackett Publishing Company.

McGinn, Colin (1993). "Can We Solve the Mind-Body Problem?" In *The Problem of Consciousness: Essays toward a Resolution*, 1-22. Cambridge, MA: Blackwell.

McMahan, Jeff (2002). *The Ethics of Killing: Problems at the Margins of Life.* Oxford: Oxford University Press.

Nagel, Thomas (1974). "What is it like to be a bat?" *Philosophical Review*, 435–50 (repr. in *Mortal Questions*).

Plantinga, Alvin (2006). "Against Materialism," *Faith and Philosophy* 23, 3–32.

Plantinga, Alvin (2007). "Materialism and Christian Belief." In *Persons: Human and Divine,* ed. Peter van Inwagen and Dean Zimmerman, 99-141. Oxford: Oxford University Press.

Ramachandran, V. S., and Sandra Blakeslee (1998). *Phantoms in the Brain: Probing the Mysteries of the Human Mind.* New York: William Morrow and Company.

Ramachandran, V. S. (2004). *A Brief Tour of Consciousness: From Impostor Poodles to Purple Numbers.* New York: Pi Press.

Ramachandran, V. S. (2012). *The Tell-Tale Brain: A Neuroscientist's Quest for What Makes Us Human.* New York: W. W. Norton and Company.

Sacks, Oliver (2007). "The Abyss: Music and Amnesia." *The New Yorker*, September 24, 2007, 100–111.

Sperry, Roger (1984). "Consciousness, personal identity, and the divided brain." *Neuropsychologia* 22, 661–73.

Tye, Michael (1995). *Ten Problems of Consciousness.* Cambridge, MA: Bradford Books.

Weiskrantz, Lawrence (1986). *Blindsight: A Case Study and Implications.* Oxford: Oxford University Press.

CHAPTER 11

Saving Our Souls from Materialism

Eric LaRock and Robin Collins

In "Neuroscience and the Human Person," Corcoran and Sharpe lay down two important target phenomena, both of which concern deep ontological matters: (1) what is the nature of the human person and (2) what is the nature of subjective experience? They suggest that these target phenomena have distinct levels of physical explanation in the hard scientific fields of physics and neuroscience, respectively. Yet, after all of their musings over objective neural structures and functions, we discover that Corcoran and Sharpe ultimately plunk down a *physicalist promissory note* about the nature of subjective experience, owing to the fact that subjective experience continues to resist a purely physical explanation. Corcoran and Sharpe's commitment to physicalism about subjective experience is, therefore, an extrascientific belief not warranted by the currently available evidence, and in fact, we will argue, contrary to the main preferences of science—namely, being true to the data of experience and simplicity.

Although Corcoran and Sharpe admit that they (currently) cannot provide a physicalist explanation of the nature of subjective experience (even to the slightest extent), they nonetheless assume throughout their chapter to be in a theoretical position to assess whether dualism fits the neurobiological data better than physicalism. Logically speaking, one cannot compare the explanatory power of two theories unless one knows what those theories involve as core theoretical explanatory entities. So, it is bewildering to us that Corcoran and Sharpe go about trying to provide an explanatory assessment of dualism versus physicalism about the nature of subjective experience.

In what follows, we refute the three key claims on which Corcoran and Sharpe base their argument against dualism: (1) the claim that dualism implies that "we would not expect to find such a radical, causal dependence of our conscious lives on the physical, which is what we do find"; (2) the claim that dualism implies "mysteries beyond necessity" (and hence that dualism is, theoretically speaking, less simple than physicalism); and finally, (3) the claim that dualism implies that a metaphysical simple (e.g., a human soul) is incapable of undergoing a process of development. We conclude by arguing that based on the underlying preferences of scientific thought, dualism is currently the most scientifically feasible account on offer with respect to subjective experience.

Soul-Brain Dependence

Corcoran and Sharpe's primary objection to dualism rests upon the assumption that if dualism were true, then we would not expect to discover that our conscious lives causally depend on the physical: "Then while we would expect to find a fairly high degree of some kinds of dependence (e.g., dependence of the soul on the brain for sensory stimuli), we would not expect to find such a radical, causal dependence of our conscious lives on the physical, which is exactly what we do find" (128). How might one respond? Along with William Lycan, one might begin by posing the following rhetorical question: what noteworthy dualist has ever asserted, or even suggested, that mind is dependent on brain for nothing more than "sensory stimuli" and perhaps other non-phenomenal (informationally sensitive) events? Not even Descartes would deny that mental states causally depend on neural states, a noteworthy exception of which might be free will (Lycan 2009, 2013). Descartes, in fact, conducted experiments on human cadavers in order to achieve a better understanding of the causal relation between mind and brain and "knew very well that the mental depended in a very detailed way upon the brain" (Lycan 2013, 536). Presumably, this is why Descartes argued that the immediate cause of our mental states is our neural states (Meditation VI, in Cooney, 23).

Moreover, most contemporary dualists hold to a naturalistic approach, which could be called *naturalistic dualism*.[1] For the naturalistic dualist, the term "soul" might only refer to (a) irreducible mental properties that are causally dependent on neural properties (i.e., property dualism), or to (b) an irreducible entity that is generated by, and thus causally dependent on, neural properties (i.e., emergent dualism).[2] William Hasker articulates option (b) as

1. This phrase was introduced by David Chalmers (1995) to name his preferred brand of dualism. I use it here because it clearly applies (in different senses) to other contemporary brands of dualism.

2. Option (a) traces all the way back to Aristotle (see Caston 2006; LaRock 2008), while

follows: "the human mind [or soul] is produced by the human brain and is not a separate element 'added to' the brain from the outside" (1999, 189). Option (b) insists that the human brain is the "natural seat" of the human soul: without the human brain, there could be no human soul that undergoes phenomenal and non-phenomenal (informationally sensitive) events. Moreover, because the human brain is the "natural seat" of the human soul, the human soul derives certain properties from the human brain, such as being located in space and being functionally related to the natural world. Hence, options (a) and (b) actually entail the neural dependence of our conscious lives on the physical.[3]

Perhaps what Corcoran and Sharpe have in mind when they use the phrase "nonphysical soul" is a popular ("folk-psychological") theistic approach to soul. However, not every theistic approach is equivalent, and some formulations entail soul-brain dependence in a very detailed way. For example, consider option (c): God simply wires the human soul (an irreducible entity that has subjective and non-subjective properties) to the human brain, so to speak; a consequence of that wiring process is that the human soul is dependent on the human brain in a very detailed way in this life (e.g., see Collins 2011). Why would God make our souls highly dependent on our brains in this life? If, for example, God's purposes were for embodied conscious agents to be highly vulnerable to each other and the environment, then God would make the soul highly dependent on the brain in this life.

In sum, what options (a)-(c) hold in common is that the human soul is highly dependent on the human brain in a very detailed way. A broader theoretical implication of options (a)-(c) is that we would expect to discover highly detailed physical correlates upon which our phenomenal and non-phenomenal (informationally sensitive) events depend. Not surprisingly, some dualists these days are, in fact, interested in discovering those highly detailed physical correlates for the sake of developing a testable theory.[4] Thus, whatever Corcoran and Sharpe might mean by a "nonphysical soul" in their chapter, one thing is clear about the issue of neural dependence: over the past 2400 years

---

option (b) is advocated by several contemporary philosophers (e.g., see Hasker 1999; Lowe 2008; Zimmerman 2010, 2011; LaRock 2013a).

3. Moreover, option (b) possesses the explanatory power needed to address Jaegwon Kim's famous pairing relations objection to Cartesian dualism. Also, entity dualism entails property dualism, but the reverse does not follow.

4. For example, many of the authors in the book *The Soul Hypothesis: Investigations into the Existence of the Soul* (New York: Continuum, 2010) are interested in developing such a testable theory: for example, Mark Baker, 2011, 73–98; William Hasker, 2011, 202–21; and Robin Collins, 222–46; see also LaRock 2007, 2013a.

very few, if any, noteworthy dualists have denied that "soul" causally depends in a very detailed way on the physical.

Corcoran and Sharpe might push back on grounds that, so far, our response to the neural dependence objection to dualism has not addressed any of the specific cases they cite, such as those cases involving amnesia, blindsight, and phantom limb syndrome. They claim that these cases reveal "remarkable features of consciousness" that "are dependent on and explained in terms of neural anatomy and physiology." We think their "remarkable features of consciousness" boil down to easy problems of consciousness (which are really just problems about objective physical structures and functions).[5] For example, *amnesia* concerns problems about information encoding, storage, and access, but not the harder problem of subjective experience. When a computer begins to lose its capacity to encode, store, and access information, we do not thereby conclude that it has begun to lose its subjective experience. Presumably, it never had subjective experience. So why would we ever conclude that human persons are subjects of experience on the basis of encoding, storing, and accessing information? Perhaps we would not, unless we've already conflated the hard problem with one or more of the easy problems of consciousness.[6] Also, none of the specific data surrounding Clive Wearing entail that Wearing lacks a subjective point of view. It's just that his experience of being a subject is truncated in time because the objective physical structures responsible for encoding, storing, and accessing information have undergone damage. Wearing still knows what it is like to be a subject of experience, if only over brief periods of time.[7]

5. See Chalmers (1995, 1996, 2010). For a list of many more such articles, see "New Dualism Archive: A Philosophical Archive for the Constructive Study of Dualism" at http://www.newdualism.org/online-articles.htm.

6. That Corcoran and Sharpe conflate the hard problem of subjective experience with one or more of the easy problems of consciousness is also strongly suggested when they claim that several "other features of consciousness too, from the ability to discriminate and react to environmental stimulae and the ability to access our own internal conscious states, to the focus of attention . . . *all* are in fact *explainable* in terms of brain structures and neural activity." Take note that many contemporary dualists expect that the "other features of consciousness" which Corcoran and Sharpe list in the preceding quotation will eventually succumb to purely neuroscientific and/or computational explanations because these "other features of consciousness" all concern questions about objective physical structures and functions. Many contemporary dualists merely *deny* that telling a story about objective physical structures and functions suffices for an account of the subjective point of view intrinsic to experience (e.g., see Chalmers 1995, 2010).

7. Another way to put the point involves Ned Block's well-known distinction between

In the case of blindsight, one could draw a distinction between *informational sensitivity* versus *phenomenal (or experiential) sensitivity* (see Flanagan 1992; Holt 2003). Informational sensitivity refers to a system's capacity to encode and react to information in the natural world. Informational sensitivity, however, does not require phenomenal sensitivity. Something as simple as a motion detector on a security system is informationally sensitive. Our brains, too, have evolved several specialized subsystems that are informationally sensitive to the stimuli they discriminate, including the capacity to encode motion and other features of objects. However, a subject cannot be phenomenally sensitive to motion (or to other stimuli) without being informationally sensitive. The relation is asymmetric: phenomenal sensitivity requires informational sensitivity, but the reverse does not hold (Holt 2003; see also Chalmers 1995, 2010; LaRock 2008, 2013b). This suggests that while blindsight patients are still informationally sensitive to stimuli, they're just not phenomenally sensitive to the stimuli they discriminate. As Jason Holt observes:

> With respect to blind field stimuli, patients are clearly informationally sensitive. Remember, their shots in the dark betray excellent marksmanship. Their visual systems take in and deploy much information about unseen stimuli. Patients are not, however, experientially sensitive to the stimuli they discriminate. (2003, 34)

These data map elegantly onto recent soul hypotheses, such as options (b) and (c) above: human souls undergo both phenomenal and non-phenomenal (informationally sensitive) events; thus some of what we do (as embodied souls) is likely influenced by the non-phenomenal (informationally sensitive) events that we undergo via our brains.[8]

---

access consciousness and phenomenal consciousness: Wearing has undergone a breakdown of access consciousness, not phenomenal consciousness. In fact, Corcoran and Sharpe do not deny that Wearing has a subjective point of view (or, as they say, "From his perspective . . ."). Wearing, in other words, *knows what it is like* to undergo amnesia.

8. Due to space constraints, we've chosen to set phantom limb syndrome on the side. It should be noted that Corcoran and Sharpe make several contentious claims in this context regarding neural plasticity. We find it ironic that they appeal to neural plasticity to secure evidential grounds for physicalism when a subset of the recent data surrounding neural plasticity fits elegantly within the dualist hypothesis concerning agent-directed neuroplasticity (see, e.g., Schwartz and Begely 2002; LaRock 2013a, 2013b).

Simplicity of Dualism versus Physicalism

Corcoran and Sharpe assume that introducing a "soul does nothing to remove the mystery of consciousness. If anything, it multiplies mysteries beyond necessity." The first point that needs to be made here is that dualists do not purport to *explain* consciousness or intentionality in the sense of reducing it to some other set of properties; this is an all too common caricature of what motivates dualists. Rather, against the physicalist, they argue that consciousness and intentionality cannot be reduced to physical or other kinds of properties and hence must be taken as irreducible properties. If this is right, this leaves the materialist with some non-physicalist form of materialism. This is where the problem posed by the existence of an experiencer comes into play: besides consciousness itself, there is something that is conscious, a something we will call the "experiencer." Apart from denying the existence of an experiencer, a materialist has no choice but to identify it with some material composite. But then difficult questions arise regarding what determines whether a particular material object is part of the experiencer or not. For example, in the case of humans, is a dead skin cell part of the experiencer? Is the silicone implant in the brain part of the experiencer? Is the artificial limb part of the experiencer, and if so, when does it become part of the experiencer? Are the good bacteria in the gut (which play a crucial role in metabolism and hence function like a bodily organ) part of the experiencer? And so forth. One might reply that the experiencer is just the body. This, however, only pushes the question back one step—e.g., whether an artificial limb belongs to the body. Further, it also runs into difficulties in other cases, such as Siamese twins who share the same organs from the neck on down: it is obvious in such a case both that there are two persons, and that, just as a two-headed worm only has one body, there is only one body (with two heads).[9]

Since some set of laws must determine which atoms compose the experiencer and which do not, and given the huge diversity of possibilities for an atom's relation to the experiencer (being part of a hair cell, an artificial limb, a bacteria in the gut, and so forth), these laws would have to be enormously complex. Notice here that this case is fundamentally different from other composite objects, such as someone's car. If asked whether the hubcaps or bike rack are part of the car, one can simply reply that there is no answer to the question since it is a matter of human linguistic convention what aggregate of material

9. Although there are no Siamese twins that are this fused together, there is no reason why this could not happen. The closest is the case of Brittany and Abbey Hensel who share the same organs below the stomach.

we call a car. In contrast, it cannot be a matter of linguistic convention which aggregates are experiencing the world.

Claiming that it is sometimes vague whether some atom belongs to the experiencer, or saying that there is a large number of experiencers with different sets of overlapping parts, does not solve this problem. One would still need an enormously complex set of laws to determine when an atom was merely vaguely part of an experiencer or, of all the enormous number of physical aggregates, which ones are experiencers.

In contrast, since the typical entity dualist holds that the experiencer is a metaphysical simple (an entity not composed of other entities), they do not need to hypothesize any such enormously complex set of new laws to account for the experiencer. Further, the category of a metaphysical simple is already part of fundamental physics, whereas convention-independent composites are not. For example, an electron is considered a non-composite particle. In these ways, entity dualists are much more in keeping with the scientific preference for simplicity.[10]

Another way of putting the point is that under the entity dualist view, after one has given a complete biological, chemical, and physical description of the particles and their interrelationships in the region the body occupies, there is no relevant physical fact left out. For those materialists who accept the existence of an experiencer, however, there is a further relevant physical fact: namely, some of the particles *compose* the experiencer and some do not. This not only leads to the need to hypothesize an enormously complex set of laws (as explained above), but also to a plethora of vagueness problems (see also Zimmerman 2010; 2011).

To evade these problems, Corcoran and Sharpe could deny the existence of an experiencer. Such a response, however, is contrary to one of the most obvious facts of experience (and the seemingly true principle that there is no experience without something to experience it). Since the true spirit of science is to account for the data of experience, not to deny one's experience because of some prior philosophical commitment, this reply would be just the opposite of the scientific approach that Corcoran and Sharpe claim to take. We can

10. One might worry that entity dualists run into the need to hypothesize such complex laws to explain the correlations between brain states and mental states. In response, we first note that non-physicalist versions of materialism run into the same problem (and arguably, even physicalism does—see Robert Adams 1987, 259–60). Second, via offering an explicit possible model of soul-brain interaction, Collins (2011) has argued in detail that the postulate of an immaterial simple could potentially greatly simplify such laws in a way similar to how the postulate of atoms greatly simplified the laws of chemistry.

conclude, therefore, that everything else being equal, entity dualism accords much better with the central preferences of science—being true to the data of experience and simplicity—than the materialist view.

Developing Our Souls

Corcoran and Sharpe also assume that a metaphysical simple cannot develop: "If what dualists say about the soul is true—that it's a non-physical, partless entity and that *it* is the bearer of psychological properties and states of human consciousness—then, it seems difficult, if not impossible, to account for the *gradual* development of conscious capacities, as it's hard to see how a *partless* thing can develop." Corcoran and Sharpe are assuming that development *per se* requires a change in the position of the parts. In its most general sense, however, development is merely a change in an entity's properties, and they offer no argument for thinking that the properties of a metaphysical simple could not change. In fact we know from physics that some of the properties of non-composite particles, such as an electron or neutrino, do change: for example, a very fast moving electron will have a greater mass (by special relativity) than a slow moving electron, and neutrinos change their flavor in flight through what is known as neutrino oscillations. Further, superstrings are widely regarded as non-composite, yet they can change from one complex quantum vibrational state to another. Hence metaphysical simples can develop.

Finally, under the hypothesis of entity dualism, an important aspect of the development of the capacities of human beings in this life consists of the development of the instrument—the brain—that the soul uses. It is like a computer one relies on that every day gets improved software; this would give one the capacity to do more and more sophisticated things as one got better and better software.

Physicalist Progress?

Before concluding, we should say something about the so-called (physicalist) progress of neuroscience to which Corcoran and Sharpe appeal, and how it has made *no progress* on either the hard problem of consciousness or the unity of subjective experience. As noted above, it is the hard problem—along with problems of intentionality and the experience of the unity of consciousness—that motivates dualists to reject physicalism; and it is the problem of the existence of an experiencer—which is closely connected with the unity of consciousness—

that motivates dualists to reject non-physicalist versions of materialism. So, the progress Corcoran and Sharpe appeal to is irrelevant; in fact, since these are just the features of humans that dualists would expect neuroscience to be unable to account for, the *lack of progress* on these problems supports dualism over materialism. While neuroscience has made progress on explaining how widely distributed neuronal processes function to encode, store, and access information, it has yet to make any progress on either the hard problem of consciousness or the unity of subjective experience (Chalmers 1995, 2010; LaRock 2006, 2007, 2010, 2012, 2013a). Further, Mark Baker (2011) has argued that neuroscience has failed to make progress in just those areas of language use where such failure would be expected under dualism. If materialism were true, why would neuroscience fail to make progress in those areas that would be expected under dualism, but not in other areas? So, just as the failure to find Big Foot after much searching is evidence against the existence of Big Foot, so is the failure of neuroscience to account for these features of experience evidence against materialism. In fact, on a more general level, the discoveries of science that humans are ultimately made of a myriad of atoms in complex relations with each other has made the enormously complex set of laws problem mentioned previously much more acute, and thus has made it much more difficult to believe in the materialist account of the experiencer. Hence, the situation is just the opposite of what materialists assert: the rise of the scientific picture of reality has in a fundamental way given us more reason to believe in entity dualism, not materialism.

Since the scientific attitude prefers that the simplest theories take into account all the available data—such as consciousness and the unity of subjective experience—we suggest that dualism is currently the most scientifically feasible account on offer with respect to subjective experience.

REFERENCES

Adams, Robert Merrihew. "Colors, Flavors and God," in Robert Adams, *The Virtue of Faith and Other Essays in Philosophical Theology*. Oxford: Oxford University Press, 1987, 243–62.

Baker, Mark. "Brains and Souls; Grammar and Speaking," in *The Soul Hypothesis: Investigations into the Existence of the Soul*. New York: Continuum, 2010, 73–98.

Block, Ned. "Troubles with Functionalism," in *Perception and Cognition: Issues in the Foundation of Psychology*. Minneapolis: University of Minnesota Press, 1978, 261–325.

Caston, Victor. "Aristotle's Psychology," in *A Companion to Ancient Philosophy*. Oxford: Wiley-Blackwell, 2006, 316–46.

Chalmers, David. *The Character of Consciousness*. Oxford: Oxford University Press, 2010.

Chalmers, David. *The Conscious Mind: In Search of a Fundamental Theory*. Oxford: Oxford University Press, 1996.

Chalmers, David. "Facing Up to the Hard Problem of Consciousness," *Journal of Consciousness Studies*, 1995, Volume 2: 200–19.

Collins, Robin. "A Scientific Case for the Soul," in *The Soul Hypothesis: Investigations into the Existence of the Soul*. New York: Continuum, 2010, 222–46.

Cooney, Brian. *The Place of Mind*. Belmont, CA: Wadsworth, 2000.

Descartes, Rene. "Meditation VI," in *The Place of Mind*, ed. Brian Cooney. Belmont, CA: Wadsworth, 2000.

Flanagan, Owen. *Consciousness Reconsidered*. Cambridge, MA: MIT Press, 1992.

Hasker, William. "Souls Beastly and Human," in *The Soul Hypothesis: Investigations into the Existence of the Soul*: New York: Continuum, 2010, 202–21.

Hasker, William. *The Emergent Self*. Ithaca: Cornell University Press, 1999.

Holt, Jason. *Blindsight and the Nature of Consciousness*. Orchard Park, NY: Broadview Press, 2003.

LaRock, Eric. "From Biological Naturalism to Emergent Subject Dualism," *Philosophia Christi*, 2013a, Volume 15: 97–118.

LaRock, Eric. "Aristotle and Agent-Directed Neuroplasticity," *International Philosophical Quarterly*, 2013b, Volume 53: 385–408.

LaRock, Eric. "An Empirical Case against Central State Materialism," *Philosophia Christi*, 2012, Volume 14: 409–28.

LaRock, Eric. "Cognition and Consciousness: Kantian Affinities with Contemporary Vision Research," *Kant-Studien*, 2010, Volume 101: 445–64.

LaRock, Eric. "Is Consciousness *Really* a Brain Process?" *International Philosophical Quarterly*, 2008, Volume 48: 201–29.

LaRock, Eric. "Disambiguation, Binding, and the Unity of Consciousness," *Theory and Psychology*, 2007, Volume 17: 747–77.

LaRock, Eric. "Why Neural Synchrony Fails to Explain the Unity of Consciousness," *Behavior and Philosophy*, 2006, Volume 34: 39–58.

Lowe, E. J. *Personal Agency*. Oxford: Oxford University Press, 2008.

Lycan, William. "Is Property Dualism Better Off Than Substance Dualism?" *Philosophical Studies*, 2013, Volume 164: 533–42.

Lycan, William. "Giving Dualism Its Due," *Australasian Journal of Philosophy*, 2009, Volume 87: 551–63.

Jeffrey Schwartz and Susan Begley. *The Mind and the Brain: Neuroplasticity and the Power of Mental Force*. New York: Harper Perennial, 2002.

Zimmerman, Dean. "From Experience to Experiencer," in *The Soul Hypothesis*, ed. Mark Baker and Stewart Goetz. New York: Continuum Press, 2011, 168–96.

Zimmerman, Dean. "From Property Dualism to Substance Dualism," *Proceedings of the Aristotelian Society Supplementary*, 2010, Volume LXXXIV: 119–50.

CHAPTER 12

Saving Materialism from a "Souler" Eclipse

Kevin Corcoran and Kevin Sharpe

The Dependence Objection

In "Neuroscience and the Human Person," we argued that were dualism true, we would not expect to find the radical, *fine-grained* causal dependence of consciousness on the physical structures revealed by the neurosciences. In their response, LaRock and Collins repeatedly insist that no dualist has ever denied that mental states are dependent on brain states. This is true, but it's the *fine-grained* causal dependence that we believe is at issue. And while it's true that no dualist has ever denied that mental states are dependent on brain states, it's beside the point in the current context. What's at issue in this context are the *predictive resources* of dualism. Our argument was that were dualism correct, we'd expect to find a much greater degree of mind/brain *independence* than what we do in fact find; and given this expectation, there's a tension between what we find in the neurosciences and what dualists say about the nature of the mind and mentality.

It's at just this point that LaRock and Collins remind us that traditional Cartesian dualism is not the only brand of dualism on offer and that alternative formulations may have greater predictive and explanatory resources. On one such alternative, naturalistic "entity dualism," the soul is "an irreducible entity that is generated by, and thus causally dependent on, neural properties." Since this conception of the soul "entail[s] the neural dependence of our conscious lives on the physical," it leads us to expect exactly the sort of dependence revealed by neuroscience.

We wish to make two points here. First, when it comes to Hasker's emergent dualism, which LaRock and Collins cite in this regard, while the soul is dependent on the brain for its *emergence* it's not dependent on the brain for its *continued existence* and functioning. For, as Hasker has it, the immaterial souls that we are can continue to exist *in the absence of* material brains. So while the soul may be causally dependent on the brain, that causal dependence is only contingent. And this seems to us very odd indeed. But even if emergent dualism is a significant advance over the standard Cartesian varieties of dualism, and goes some distance toward undermining earlier versions of the argument from neural dependence, we don't think it's adequate to the neurobiological data. Naturalistic entity or emergent dualism may well lead us to expect *general* patterns of dependence not underwritten by Cartesian dualism, but it doesn't lead us to expect the sort of *fine-grained* dependence exemplified by (say) visual systems like ours in which aspects of conscious visual experience (e.g., color perception) depend on highly specialized neural structures (e.g., the V4 area of the visual cortex).

Similarly, coupling naturalistic entity dualism with theism will not do the trick either. It may well be that the value of vulnerability would give God a reason to "hard-wire" the soul to the brain. Yet as there are many different ways for God to achieve the goods associated with embodiment—vulnerability included—without matching fine-grained aspects of conscious experience with highly specialized neural structures devoted to those aspects of experience, the conjunction of naturalistic entity dualism and theism fails to predict the specific patterns of dependence we appeal to in our case for materialism. For this theistic strategy to work, dualists need independent reason to think that God has chosen to secure *these* particular goods in *this* particular way, but no such story has been forthcoming.

LaRock and Collins also fault us for not offering a physicalist explanation of subjectivity and phenomenal consciousness. But, as we've made clear, we think that *reductive* explanations of this sort are bound to fail. On this point, we are in total agreement with LaRock and Collins. While we agree that the neurosciences have made no progress toward solving the "hard problem of consciousness," this counts against materialism only if materialism *per se* requires *reductive* physicalism. Since, as LaRock and Collins agree, materialism doesn't require reductive physicalism, the hard problem of consciousness doesn't support dualism over materialism. Yet, once we've got the right sort of physical explanation of consciousness clearly in mind, not only is it clear that the neurosciences have made amazing progress in explaining consciousness, it's also clear that this progress offers *prima facie* support for materialism. To see that this support is not defeated by challenges to materialism and, therefore, that the total balance of evidence supports materialism, we turn to LaRock and Collins' case against a materialist account of the subject of experience.

The Experiencer Objection

LaRock and Collins claim that materialism has a problem accounting for a subject of experience. Or worse, we're left with "some non-physical form of materialism."

> *"Apart from denying the existence of an experiencer, a materialist has no choice but to identify it with some material composite. But then difficult questions arise regarding what determines whether a particular material object is part of the experiencer or not."*

There are two ways to respond to this objection. Neither, we admit, is without difficulties. But show us a view in the philosophy of mind, science, or neuroscience without problems and difficulties and we'll show you a view that has zero detractors. In any case, the first way to respond is to point out that, according to the constitution view of human persons, while human persons are wholly physical objects constituted by human animals (i.e., their bodies) they are nevertheless numerically distinct from those animals. And it is the human *person* (constituted by his or her composite human body) that is the subject of experience. The second way to respond to the objection is to defend the claim that the subject of experience, i.e., the *experiencer*, just is the human organism, all of whose parts (i.e., all the simples caught up in its life) are part of the experiencer, i.e., part of him or herself. In other words, if, along with van Inwagen, a materialist believes that the only composite material things there are are organisms and the simples that sometimes compose them, then one can say that the subject of experience just is the organism that one is. Since organisms don't have parts that are themselves composites (the only composite material objects there are are organisms) there isn't much of a problem identifying which parts of the organism are parts of the experiencer. *All* are. Are there problems of vagueness and the like in the neighborhood? Of course there are. Are there problems attending naturalistic entity dualism? Of course there are. We enumerated some of them above.

The Problem of Dicephalus Twins

Then there is the problem posed by the reality of dicephalus twins. If we claim that human persons are *identical to* organisms, then we are committed to the claim that wherever there is *one* human person or experiencer, there is exactly *one* organism identical to that experiencer and wherever there is a human organism (assuming that organism underwrites subjective, first person experience) there is *one and only one* experiencer identical to it. Dicephalus twins, therefore, pose problems for an organismic view of human persons. This is so because each twin is a subject of experience and is related to the organism in the same way. There appears to be no plausible way to hold that one is the organism and the other isn't. But given the transitivity of identity, two experiencers cannot be identical to a *single* organism without being identical to each other. Since no *two* experiencers can be identical to each other, it appears that neither is identical to the organism.

This is indeed a problem for an organismic view of human persons. But there are problems facing emergent entity dualism every bit as serious. For example, emergent entity dualists like Hasker chide Cartesian dualists for viewing the soul as "fundamentally totally different from the body and bear[ing] no necessary relation to it." Now one would expect that emergent entity dualism contrasts with this feature of Cartesian dualism. But as we saw earlier, it doesn't. Although the *emergent* soul is *causally* dependent on the complexly configured network of neural circuitry in the brain for its *emergence,* it bears no metaphysically necessary (i.e., essential) relation to that neural network. After all, Hasker believes the soul can, with God's help, exist in a disembodied state between death and resurrection. That's odd. There are also problems concerning "re-embodied souls" in naturalistic entity dualism's account of the afterlife. Unfortunately, we lack the space to explore these issues here.

The bottom line is simply this: the neurosciences have made amazing progress in explaining consciousness. And we have made it clear just what kind of physical explanation we mean. This progress offers *prima facie* support for materialism.

CHAPTER 13

Neuroscience and the Hard Problem of Consciousness

Eric LaRock

There are many scientific problems associated with the phenomenon of consciousness. Some problems seem relatively easy, yet some are quite hard.[1] If we draw a distinction between hard and easy problems, we can avoid conflating the hard problem with one (or more) of the easy problems. According to David Chalmers, a problem of consciousness counts as easy when it is entirely vulnerable to the explanatory methods of mechanistic neuroscience and computational science. Those methods cash out explanations in terms of cognitive functions and their related structures: "The easy problems are easy precisely because they concern the explanation of cognitive abilities and functions. To explain a cognitive function, we need only specify a mechanism that can perform the function."[2] Some of the easy problems include the ability to distinguish (i.e., select, mark, or label) competing information states, categorize and integrate information, access information, focus attention, control behavior deliberately, and report the contents of internal states to others.[3] For example, consider a problem about distinguishing between competing information states of the features of two (or more) objects: if my brain processes (or fires in response to) information about the distinct shape and color features of a red circle and a blue square at the same time, there must be some mechanism (or cognitive process) that functions to select (mark or label) the color red as

1. I say *relatively* easy because not every person agrees that all of the problems that Chalmers categorizes as easy are actually easy. For example, see E. J. Lowe, "There are no easy problems of consciousness," *Journal of Consciousness Studies* 2 (3) (1995), 266–71.

2. David Chalmers, "Facing Up to the Hard Problem of Consciousness," in *The Place of Mind*, ed. Brian Cooney (Belmont: Wadsworth, 2000), 384.

3. Chalmers, "Hard Problem of Consciousness," 383.

belonging to the circle instead of the square; otherwise, I might see the circle as blue and the square as red. As Nobel laureate Francis Crick observes, "In other words, if awareness corresponded merely to rapid (or sustained) firing, the brain might easily confuse the attributes of different objects."[4] Crick is referring to the feature ambiguity problem. A solution to this (easy) problem would involve discovering a mechanism that functions to select (mark or label) the features of two (or more) objects when competition arises in the cortical hierarchy.[5] Although the problems surrounding the integration of information and the deliberate control of behavior might not be that easy, Chalmers thinks that further research on them will likely yield purely functional and structural explanations.[6]

Even so, it is not clear that a solution to any (or all) of the easy problems would entail a solution to the hard problem of consciousness. The hard problem of consciousness is the "Holy Grail"[7] of scientific approaches to consciousness. The hard problem is the problem of phenomenal consciousness

4. Francis Crick, *The Astonishing Hypothesis* (New York: Charles Scribner's Sons, 1994), 210. Please note that the terms *feature*, *property*, and *attribute* are used interchangeably by researchers who work on the scientific problems surrounding binding and disambiguation.

5. However, simply telling a story about how our cognitive system selects an object's features when competition arises in the cortical hierarchy does not address a more difficult question about the unity of consciousness. Even if we discover a mechanism that selectively activates the correct set of features distributed within and across the visual hierarchy, we have yet to explain how those features, once selectively activated, are bound together to form a single unified object of consciousness. Thus, binding the *correct* set of features together entails selection, but selection *per se* does not entail binding. See my "Why Neural Synchrony Fails to Explain the Unity of Visual Consciousness," *Behavior and Philosophy* 34 (2006), 39–58; "Disambiguation, Binding, and the Unity of Visual Consciousness," *Theory & Psychology* 17 (2007), 747–77.

6. The problem of information integration is not exactly easy. For example, recent experiments conducted by Semir Zeki (Zeki, "The Disunity of Consciousness," *Trends in Cognitive Sciences* 7 [2003], 214–18) have shown that very few, if any, connections exist between certain subsystems of specific modalities of the brain: for example, color (V4) and motion (V5) processing sites of the visual cortex have very sparse, *if any*, connections between them and operate at time scales asynchronous to each other; in fact, there is a temporal gap as much as 80 ms between the processing events of V4 and V5 in response to a colored object in motion. Since functional connectivity between V4 and V5 is most probably absent at both temporal and spatial scales, it is difficult to see how merely appealing to the relevant structures and functions is going to suffice when trying to explain the kind of information integration required for a unified experience of, say, a cardinal in flight (or any experienced property-unified object in motion).

7. Christof Koch, *Consciousness: Confessions of a Romantic Reductionist* (Cambridge: MIT Press, 2012), 121.

(or experiencing subjects).[8] What is meant by phenomenal consciousness is essentially tied to a subjective individual point of view.[9] As Chalmers observes: "When we think and perceive, there is a whir of information-processing, but there is also a subjective aspect."[10] For example, there is something it is like for a subject to feel joy, undergo chronic pain and nausea, touch a supple surface, smell cinnamon sticks, taste chocolate, and hear Jason Becker's melodious guitar sound off in the distance. These are all phenomenal states and what unites them is a subject. A subject is the common locus of its phenomenal states in virtue of being the one that undergoes them.[11] The problem of phenomenal consciousness is truly a hard problem because it is not clear that a subjective individual point of view could ever be accounted for in terms of objective, physical structures and functions alone. No matter how fine-grained the analysis becomes, one thing is sure: out of objective, physical structures and functions, you only get more objective, physical structures and functions. Whether it concerns facts about axons, dendrites, cell types, neural transmitters, oscillations, or ions, you will only be learning facts about the objective domain. But an objective, physical domain does not encompass all facts. There is a subjective domain, too.

Philosophers are not alone in proclaiming the hard problem of consciousness in the current theoretical landscape. The hard problem is also being broadcast by well-known neuroscientists. Christof Koch, Cal-Tech neuroscientist and Chief Scientific Officer of the Allen Institute for Brain Science, has reflected upon the hard problem for over two decades and confesses that every recent attempt to solve it through the explanatory methods of mechanistic, computational, and quantum science has failed:

8. David Chalmers, *The Character of Consciousness* (Oxford: Oxford University Press, 2010); Thomas Nagel, *Mind and Cosmos* (Oxford: Oxford University Press, 2012); Michael Tye, "Philosophical Problems of Consciousness," in M. Velmans and S. Schneider, eds., *The Blackwell Companion to Consciousness* (Oxford: Blackwell, 2007), 23–35; Dean Zimmerman, "From Property Dualism to Substance Dualism," *Proceedings of the Aristotelian Society Supplementary,* Volume LXXXIV (2010), 119–50.

9. Thomas Nagel, *Mind and Cosmos,* 44. For the sake of clarification and, at times, economy, I will use the term *subject* interchangeably with the phrase *subjective individual point of view.*

10. Chalmers, "Problem of Consciousness," 383.

11. See also my "From Biological Naturalism to Emergent Subject Dualism," *Philosophia Christi* 15 (2013), 97–118; Roderick Chisholm, "On the Observability of the Self," *Philosophy and Phenomenological Research* 30 (1969); E. J. Lowe, *Personal Agency* (Oxford: Oxford University Press, 2008); Dean Zimmerman, "From Property Dualism to Substance Dualism," 119–50. See also Nagel, *Mind and Cosmos.*

> Global availability, strange loops, attractor networks, this neurotransmitter or that brain region have all been nominated for the essence of consciousness. The more unconventional proposals invoke quantum mechanical entanglement or other exotic physics. But no matter what features prove critical, what is it about these particular ones that explains subjectivity? Francis [Crick] and I toyed with the idea that consciousness must engage feedback circuits within the cortex, but what is it about feedback that gives rise to phenomenology, to feelings? A room thermostat also has feedback: When the ambient air temperature reaches a predetermined value, cooling is switched off. Does it have a modicum of consciousness? How is this fundamentally different from believing that rubbing a brass lamp will make a djinn appear?[12]

Indeed, after examining a legion of physical structures and functions that are purported to be the special correlates of phenomenal consciousness, there appears to be a further unanswered question: why does a subjective individual point of view accompany those (or any) objective, physical structures and functions in the first place?[13] When it comes to experience, an explanation about cognitive functions and their related structures fails to do justice to the phenomenon. As Chalmers observes: "What makes the hard problem hard and almost unique is that it goes beyond problems about the performance of functions."[14]

Philosophers and scientists who are concerned about the hard problem of consciousness seek to understand (or explain) the nature of phenomenal consciousness. This issue inspires a fundamental question. Is phenomenal consciousness reducible to physical processes? Those who provide an affirmative response to this question hold to *reductive physicalism* in the philosophy and science of consciousness (hereafter, RP). RP claims that phenomenal consciousness is entirely physical. For example, Francis Crick once argued that subjects and the phenomenal states they undergo (e.g., the experience of sorrow and joy, as well as the experience of a feature-unified object) are "in fact no more than the behavior of a vast assembly of nerve cells and their associated molecules."[15] If RP

12. Koch, *Consciousness*, 114.

13. Chalmers, "Problem of Consciousness," 385.

14. Chalmers, "Problem of Consciousness," 385.

15. Crick, *The Astonishing Hypothesis*, 3. As Crick observes, "The Astonishing Hypothesis is that 'You,' your joys and your sorrows, your memories and your ambitions, your sense of personal identity and free will, are in fact no more than the behavior of a vast assembly of nerve cells and their associated molecules. As Lewis Carroll's Alice might have phrased it: You're nothing but a pack of neurons" (3).

is true, then all facts about phenomenal consciousness boil down to facts about structure and function. Conversely, if there is even a single fact about phenomenal consciousness that is not a physical fact, then reductive physicalism is false.

I doubt that RP can deliver adequate explanatory goods when it comes to phenomenal consciousness. My thinking in this chapter unfolds as follows. I discuss why (causal) reductive functionalism (of the sort advocated by David Armstrong and David Lewis) and purely neural mechanistic approaches still fail to explain phenomenal consciousness. After laying down an empirical case against RP on grounds of the unity of experience, I then argue that the reality of an inverse zombie provides a new objection to Daniel Dennett's reductive physicalist approach to consciousness. Dennett's approach boils down to a brand of reductive functionalism, in that it seeks to explain first-person phenomenology in terms of third-person reports, or what Dennett calls heterophenomenology. I suggest that the reality of an inverse zombie counts as an empirically based defeater to Dennett's heterophenomenology. I conclude that some facts about consciousness (viz., experiencing subjects) are irreducible to the physical world and, hence, RP is false (or is most probably false).

The Hard Problem and Reductive Functionalism

What is functionalism and why does it fail to explain phenomenal consciousness? Functionalism arose on the philosophical scene, in part, as a critical reaction to behaviorism and the type-type identity hypothesis. Let's start our discussion by reflecting on a core theoretical claim made by B. F. Skinner, a pioneering advocate of the radical behaviorist movement: "We may take feeling to be *simply* responding to stimuli."[16] Skinner thought that once psychology discovered a more detailed understanding of the relations between stimuli and responses through behavior-based experiments involving operant conditioning, there would be no need to postulate mental causes.[17] Skinner's assumption was that once you had explained the whole range of our behavioral lives, you would have explained the whole range of our mental lives. The upshot was that mind could be explained in terms of behavior without remainder. David Armstrong articulates a pithy summary of the philosophical upshot of radical behaviorism: "Thought is not an inner process that lies behind, and brings

16. B. F. Skinner, "About Behaviorism," in *Problems in Mind*, ed. Jack Crumley (Mountain View, CA: Mayfield, 2000), 62 (emphasis added).

17. Jerry Fodor, "The Mind-Body Problem," in *Problems in Mind*, 118–19.

about, the words I speak and write: it is my speaking and writing. The mind is not an inner arena, it is outward act."[18] The trouble facing radical behaviorism is that it denies our ordinary experience of mental processes going on within us, even though "there is no behavior occurring that could possibly be treated as expressions of those processes."[19] For example, one can have a thought about eating a steak without actually eating a steak. And there are occasions when we deliberate over possible courses of behavior but ultimately decide to refrain from behaving. If I perceive a black bear in the Pennsylvania woods and believe that black bears are potentially threatening to my well-being, I might conclude that remaining still is the best option to take. Thus, mental events can (and do at times) relate causally even when there is no behavioral output.

Type-type identity advocates swung in the other direction; rather than seeking to explain mind in terms of observable behavior alone, they argued that mind can be reduced to the very stuff that fictitious zombies "love" to feed upon, brains! Under the type-type identity hypothesis, mind is nothing over and above brain. Early proponents of the type-type identity view claimed, for example, that pain is nothing but c-fiber stimulation in the somatosensory cortex. Arguments from analogy were offered in defense of the type-type identity hypothesis: heat is to molecular motion as pain is to c-fiber stimulation.[20] Upon logical reflection, one might ask whether the identification of pain with c-fiber stimulation is actually analogous to the identification of heat with molecular motion. For one thing, pain is essentially pain because it is *felt as pain*. But is heat essentially heat because it is *felt as heat*? No, science tells us that heat *is* nothing over and above molecular motion. The *felt* quality of heat is not part of the scientific definition of heat. Thus, the scientific definition that "heat is molecular motion" is not a conscious-dependent state of affairs: heat could exist without being *felt as heat*. As Saul Kripke observes, "what seemed really possible is that molecular motion should have existed without being *felt as heat*, that is, it might have existed without producing the sensation *S*, the sensation of heat."[21] If we follow Kripke's train of thought, an important question surfaces. Is there a state of affairs in which "c-fiber stimulation" could exist without being felt as pain? Not according to the identity theorist, for being felt as pain *just is* "c-fiber stimulation." However, if the identity analogue were

18. Armstrong, "The Nature of Mind," in *The Place of Mind*, ed. Brian Cooney (Belmont: Wadsworth, 2000), 138.

19. Armstrong, "Nature of Mind," 138.

20. For a pithy summary of the type-type identity hypothesis and its typical analogues, see Saul Kripke, *Naming and Necessity* (Cambridge, MA: Harvard University Press, 1980), 144-55.

21. Kripke, *Naming and Necessity*, 151.

possible, then "c-fiber stimulation" could exist without being felt as pain, "since for it to exist without being *felt as pain* is for it to exist without there *being any pain*."[22] But such a state of affairs would lead the proponent of the type-type identity hypothesis to a contradiction; for it would deny what it seeks to affirm, namely, a necessary identity between pain and its corresponding material type, i.e., "c-fiber stimulation."[23] Now, no empirically informed proponent of nonreductive physicalism or dualism would deny that pain has a causal basis in our neurophysiology. The problem is that "the identity theorist does not hold that the physical state merely *produces* the mental state, rather he wishes the two to be identical and thus *a fortiori* necessarily co-occurrent."[24] Having examined some foundational explanatory failures of the type-type identity hypothesis and radical behaviorism, let us now turn to functionalism.

Functionalism tries to make concessions on both fronts without accepting their explanatory costs. How so? Functionalism holds that mental states are defined not simply in terms of behavior or simply in terms of a specific material type, but rather in terms of causal relations. One could formalize a functionalist construal of any mental state as follows: the defining characteristic of any mental state M is the set of causal relations that M has with respect to inputs, other mental states, and behavioral outputs.[25] Consider an ordinary example. I'm tending my garden. I feel a sudden change in the ambient air: it goes from cool to warm and then suddenly the sky darkens around me. When I look up and *perceive* certain cloud formations, I form the *belief* that a tornado is likely going to occur; since I *desire* to live, I form the *intention* to run to the cellar, and so I run to the cellar. In this example, my perception, belief, desire, and intention function to produce behavior. Unlike radical behaviorism, mental states are not explained in terms of behavior alone, but relate causally between inputs, further mental states, and outputs. In contrast to the type-type identity hypothesis, functionalists do not hold that mental states can be identified exclusively with a single type of matter (e.g., the physicochemical stuff that composes our brains), but instead maintain that mental states can be realized by any suitably organized system. For example, David Lewis argues

22. Kripke, *Naming and Necessity,* 151.

23. As Kripke puts it, "Such a situation would be in flat contradiction with the supposed necessary identity of pain and the corresponding physical state, and the analogue holds for any physical state which might be identified with a corresponding mental state" (151).

24. Kripke, *Naming and Necessity,* 151.

25. See Jerry Fodor, "The Mind-Body Problem," 118–23; also, David Lewis, "Mad Pain and Martian Pain," in Crumley, ed., *Problems in Mind*, 110–17; also Paul Churchland, *Matter and Consciousness* (Cambridge, MA: MIT Press, 1996), 36–38.

that it is conceivable that pain could be realized by exotic material systems, such as the inflation of cavities in a Martian's feet: "When you pinch his skin you cause no firing of c-fibers—he has none—but, rather, you cause the inflation of many smallish cavities in his feet. When these cavities are inflated, he is in pain."[26] Lewis ultimately defines pain or any other mental state as a "a state apt for being caused in certain ways by stimuli plus other mental states and apt for combining with certain other mental states to jointly cause certain behavior."[27] This definition is broad enough to include human, alien, and other species-specific instances of pain because the concept of pain picks out a certain causal role and, at the same time, abstracts away from (or remains neutral about) the kind of stuff that composes it. Whereas a specific neuronal event (e.g., "c-fiber firing") occupies pain's causal role in our own case, inflating cavities occupies pain's causal role in the Martian's case. Thus, it is not the type of stuff that is essential to a mind on the functionalist account, but the way the stuff is organized. Against Kripke's essentialist view of mental and physical states, Lewis claims that the concept of pain is not a rigid concept: the term pain "is a nonrigid designator. It is a contingent matter what state the concept and the word apply to."[28] Under this assumption, the relation between pain and its physical realization base is not a necessary relation and therefore pain could be realized by any suitably organized substrate. It might be useful to clarify the preceding assumption with the use of possible worlds: if in this world (w1) pain can be realized by a specific neural state *gamma*, and in some other possible world (w2) pain can be realized by some other physical state *alpha*, then the relation between pain and its physical correlate is not a necessary relation. The physical realization base of pain need not be the same across possible worlds. Or, as Lewis observes, "the concept and name of pain contingently apply to some neural state at this world, but do not apply to it at another."[29]

Why is a functionalist approach to phenomenal consciousness not adequate? Let's begin with some logically based counterexamples before moving on to empirically based ones. First of all, functional explanations are logically compatible with the absence of experience. Even if mental states could be realized by different types of matter, an explanatory gap problem about experience is still implicit within the functionalist hypothesis. As Paul Churchland observes, by defining mental states in terms of (extrinsic) causal relations

26. Lewis, "Mad Pain and Martian Pain," 110.
27. Lewis, "Mad Pain and Martian Pain," 112.
28. Lewis, "Mad Pain and Martian Pain," 112.
29. Lewis, "Mad Pain and Martian Pain," 112.

alone, functionalism logically excludes the intrinsic, qualitative character of experience itself.[30] This suggests that, in principle, reductive functionalism may not be fit for the explanatory task when it comes to experience. David Armstrong, in fact, makes this sober confession about reductive functionalism, the very view that he and Lewis advocate:

> Now can we say that to be conscious, to have experiences, is simply for something to go on within us apt for the causing of certain sorts of behavior? Such an account does not seem to do any justice to the phenomena. And so it seems that our account of the mind, like Behaviorism, will fail to do justice to the first-person case.[31]

A purely objective (or third-person), causal reductive type of explanation can get along just fine without ever mentioning a subjective (or first-person) point of view. However, a subjective point of view is intrinsic to experience. Thus one might rightly wonder how Armstrong and other reductive functionalists can account for subjective (or first-person) mental phenomena within a purely objective (or third-person), causal reductive account.

Another counterexample is rooted in the possibility of a subjective individual who has an inverted color spectrum disorder.[32] For example, imagine a being that is functionally identical to you but whose conscious experience of color is inverted. Your functional duplicate suffers from a condition called *inverted spectrum disorder*, and goes by the name of Sean. When you visually experience a red apple, for instance, your color phenomenology is of redness and your report is in terms of redness. Your experience and report are veridical. Oddly enough, when Sean visually experiences a red apple, Sean's color phenomenology is of greenness but the report is in terms of redness. Like you, Sean has learned the meanings of color words through typical matching procedures in early development and applies them to objects in the usual ways. While there is no difference at the functional level between you and Sean (i.e., with respect to inputs, reports, and behaviors in general), there is nevertheless a difference at the conscious level. It follows that Sean's experience and report are *not* veridical, but there is no way to know this on the basis of functional

30. Churchland, *Matter and Consciousness*, 38; also Chalmers, *The Conscious Mind* (Oxford: Oxford University Press, 1996).

31. Armstrong, "Nature of Mind," 142.

32. Ned Block and Jerry Fodor, "What Psychological States Are Not," *Philosophical Review* 83 (1972): 151–81; also Robert Van Gulick, "Functionalism and Qualia," in Velmans and Schneider, eds., *The Blackwell Companion to Consciousness*, 381–95.

analysis alone. Hence, a functional analysis fails to provide an adequate account of phenomenal consciousness.[33]

Critics might claim that the inverted spectrum argument is possible only because it abstracts away from particular neurobiological considerations. This is not necessarily true. Even if we accept, for the sake of argument, that the functional role of color phenomenology is correlated with and performed by a particular form of neural activity, such as 40 hertz oscillations[34] in V4, there would be no way to detect a difference between you and Sean on this basis alone; that is because the purported functional role of color phenomenology would be the *same* for you and Sean.

This consequence raises a general problem of phenomenology for those who claim that phenomenal consciousness can be accounted for in terms of a particular form of neural activity. How could the same *particular* form of neural activity explain *various* states of phenomenal consciousness, such as the experiential quality of red, the feeling of an itch, the sensation of freshly cut grass, and the subjective character of pain? Notice, an appeal to specialized *areas* could not account for phenomenal *difference*, if what allegedly correlates with the variety of phenomenal features across those specialized areas is the *same* form of neural activity (e.g., 40 hertz oscillations). How can phenomenal difference arise from the same form of neural activity? This problem applies to any theory that seeks to explain phenomenal consciousness in terms of a particular form of neural activity.[35]

Does that mean that Lewis, Armstrong, and other reductive functionalists have conceded defeat? No. Lewis and Armstrong were pivotal to the rise of reductive functionalism, and hence to the idea that phenomenal consciousness must reduce to various abilities (e.g., the abilities to distinguish or recognize objects). For example, Lewis claims that "knowing what it's like is the possession of abilities: abilities to recognize, abilities to imagine, abilities to predict one's behavior by means of imaginative experiments."[36] Can phenomenal consciousness be explained adequately in terms of abilities, such as the ability to recognize? I think Lewis's claim can be questioned on empirical grounds. For instance, recent neuropsychological evidence has shown that persons with

33. See also Tye, "Philosophical Problems," 23–35.

34. I chose "40 hertz oscillations" because it has been a dominantly proposed mechanism of consciousness in the neuroscientific literature.

35. See also my "Philosophical Implications of Awareness During General Anesthesia," in *Consciousness, Awareness, and Anesthesia*, ed. George Mashour (New York: Cambridge University Press, 2010).

36. Lewis, "Mad Pain and Martian Pain," 116.

associative agnosia disorder cannot recognize objects, but can nevertheless visually experience them.[37] The following is an example of an elderly man diagnosed with this type of agnosia:

> A sixty-year old man . . . woke from a sleep unable to find his clothes, though they lay ready for him close by. As soon as his wife put the garments into his hands, he recognized them, dressed himself correctly, and went out. In the streets he found he could not recognize people—not even his own daughter. He could see things, but not tell what they were.[38]

Although he could not recognize objects, he could visually experience them. This suggests that phenomenal consciousness cannot be adequately explained in terms of certain abilities, such as the ability to recognize. Therefore, Lewis's attempt to solve the problem of phenomenal consciousness in terms of abilities is less than convincing. One might also say, in light of Chalmers's distinction between hard versus easy problems, that the scope of Lewis's purported solution to the problem of phenomenal consciousness is, at best, consistent with a solution to one of the easy problems of consciousness (e.g., the problem of recognition); but no solution to an easy problem entails a solution to the hard problem. Hence, what Lewis sets out to explain and what he actually explains are not the same.

David Armstrong also takes a reductive functionalist approach to experience. Armstrong proposes that experience is ultimately a higher-order neuronal function of perception: experience refers to nothing but a "self-scanning mechanism in the central nervous system."[39] The idea is that some part (or process) of the central nervous system scans another part (or process). Armstrong claims that this mechanism is essentially a selective neuronal mechanism that enables an animal with perceptual capacities to distinguish between the properties of objects of any given visual scene, such as the kind of selective behavior that would be required to distinguish between a green object and a red object: "We can think of the animal's [conscious] perception as a state within the animal apt . . . for selective behavior between the red-and green-lighted pathways."[40]

37. See Martha Farah, *Visual Agnosia: Disorders of Object Recognition and What They Tell Us about Normal Vision* (Cambridge: MIT Press, 1990); also Stephen Kosslyn and Olivier Koenig, *Wet Mind: The New Cognitive Neuroscience* (New York: Free Press, 1995).

38. Michael Critchley, *The Parietal Lobes* (London: Edward Arnold, 1953), 289.

39. Armstrong, "Nature of Mind," 143.

40. Armstrong, "Nature of Mind," 143.

Though Armstrong only formulates a logical sketch of experience that is compatible with reductive functionalism, one could charitably fill in the details with recent findings in neuroscience about the role that neuronal mechanisms of selective behavior play in distinguishing the properties of two or more objects that comprise a visual scene. For example, if a visual scene were comprised of a red square (RS) and a green triangle (GT), the neuronal mechanisms of selective behavior would somehow have to assign properties to the correct objects. This form of selective neuronal behavior could not merely be understood in terms of synchronous neuronal firing; for if the neurons that fire in response to RS and GT were to fire at the same time, the brain might confuse the properties of those objects, such that the square would be seen as green and the triangle as red. Thus many contemporary neuroscientists argue that the neuronal mechanisms of selective behavior (usually dubbed *selective attention*)[41] function at distinct times to select (mark or label) properties as belonging to the correct objects when competition arises in the cortical hierarchy. Armstrong, of course, has a metaphysical axe to grind and makes an even stronger claim than some contemporary neuroscientists: first-person (or subjective) experience is nothing but a self-scanning mechanism in the central nervous system. And thus, for Armstrong, the implication is that experience is nothing but the neuronal mechanisms of selective behavior (i.e., selective attention).[42]

If Armstrong's reductive functionalist view of experience (or any recent view that reduces experience to the functions of attention) is even close to being plausible, then there could be no experiential state that emerges independent of the neuronal mechanisms of selective attention, for Armstrong (and company) identifies experience with such neuronal mechanisms. Some of the experimental work of Anne Treisman on the neuronal mechanisms of selective attention will prove useful in addressing this issue. In one experimental set-up, individuals were briefly shown two colored letters at the same time: a green T and a red O. The experimenters found that when the neuronal mechanisms of selective attention were prevented by means of a brief presentation of the letters, individuals would

41. To be clear, I use the phrases "neuronal mechanisms of selective behavior" and "neuronal mechanisms of selective attention" interchangeably, since they seem to map onto Armstrong's views regarding the nature of experience.

42. It is worth pointing out that this position is not peculiar to Armstrong. William Lycan claims that "consciousness is the functioning of internal attention mechanisms" which select and relay (that is, scan) information about ongoing perceptual processes. See William Lycan, "Consciousness as Internal Monitoring," in *The Nature of Consciousness*, ed. Ned Block, Owen Flanagan, and Guven Guzeldere (Cambridge, MA: MIT Press, 1977), 755. Lycan, in fact, sees himself as advocating a view that is consistent with Armstrong's view.

nonetheless experience false binding (also known as "misbinding"):[43] the individuals reported seeing "a red T when a green T and a red O" were presented at the same time.[44] Consequently, red, rather than green, was bound to T and the result was an experience of false binding. Thus false binding (or "misbinding") occurs when some properties of competing objects are bound together.

Several inferences can be drawn from the above study. First, experience is not reducible to the neuronal mechanisms of selective attention on grounds that experiential states can emerge independent of those mechanisms. Second, binding properties to form a unified object of experience can occur without the activation of the neuronal mechanisms of selective attention. Third, object-property binding *per se* is not reducible to activities carried out by the neuronal mechanisms of selective attention. All of the above evidence suggests that experience and the neuronal mechanisms of selective attention are distinct and thus experience could *not* merely be a self-scanning mechanism in the central nervous system. Hence, Armstrong's reductive functionalist conjecture about the nature of experience appears to be false (or is most probably false) on empirical grounds.

What functional role do the mechanisms of selective attention perform with respect to our cognitive lives? They perform the role of disambiguating the properties of objects when competition arises in the cortical hierarchy.[45] Thus what Armstrong proposes for an account of the metaphysics of experience boils down to an epistemic capability: the neuronal mechanisms of selective attention function to disambiguate properties of objects when competition occurs in the cortical hierarchy. This cognitive function enhances survival value. For example, my cognitive capacity to disambiguate a lion's structure from its movements against the backdrop of swaying golden grass is crucial to my survival. While this cognitive capacity enhances my survival value, it does not explain the harder problem about consciousness. Armstrong's proposed theory of experience, therefore, offers at most an explanation of an easy problem of consciousness.[46]

43. In this study, false binding (or misbinding) occurred when the properties that were bound together (and experienced as a unity) were not from the same object. Under ordinary circumstances object property binding usually reflects properties of the same object. See my "Disambiguation," 747-77.

44. Anne Treisman, "Consciousness and perceptual binding," in *The Unity of Consciousness: Binding, Integration, and Dissociation*, ed. Axel Cleeremans (Oxford: Oxford University Press, 2003), 99.

45. LaRock, "Disambiguation," 747–77.

46. For a more thorough empirically based critique of Armstrong's reductive function-

The Hard Problem and Reductive Mechanistic Explanation

Are there compelling logical and empirical reasons against a reductive mechanistic explanation of phenomenal consciousness? First, we might consider the explanatory scope of a purely mechanistic approach. For example, what is the mechanism that underlies brittleness in a piece of glass? And how does that mechanism explain brittleness? As Michael Tye observes, brittleness is caused by "the irregular alignment of crystals" and, as a result of this type of alignment, the forces that hold the crystals together are weak.[47] That is why brittle pieces of glass shatter easily. Now if phenomenal states are to neural mechanisms as brittleness is to its lower-level mechanisms, then we should be able to explain phenomenal states by simply identifying their underlying mechanisms. What makes the usual mechanistic explanations in science effective is that higher level properties can be explained in terms of their lower level mechanisms *without remainder*. However, it is difficult to see how any *objective* mechanism (by itself) could explain the *subjective* character of phenomenal states: even if we understood all of the fine-grained structures and chemical changes associated with the mechanisms of our brains, "we still seem to be left with something that cries out for a further explanation, namely, why and how *this* collection of neural and/or chemical changes produces *that* subjective feeling, or any subjective feeling at all."[48] Similarly, the well-known neurofunctionalist, Jesse Prinz, has expressed doubts about whether there could be a satisfactory (reductive physicalist) answer to a question about *why* a particular "brain state [is] experienced as red rather than green."[49]

The explanatory gap that RP faces in its quest to ascertain the nature of phenomenal consciousness inspires further related questions. What could underlie the incompleteness of a purely mechanistic approach to experience? Those committed to a purely mechanistic approach implicitly assume that appearance is not essential to reality, and thus providing an account of experience will only require identifying the underlying mechanisms of experience.[50] Undoubtedly, the preceding *appearance versus reality* distinction has led to a

---

alism, see my "An Empirical Case against Central State Materialism," *Philosophia Christi* 14 (2012), 409–26.

47. Tye, "Philosophical Problems," 26–27.

48. Tye, "Philosophical Problems," 27.

49. Jesse Prinz, "The Intermediate Level Theory of Consciousness" in Velmans and Schneider, eds., *The Blackwell Companion to Consciousness*, 252.

50. For the nascent conceptual roots of the appearance-reality distinction, see the early Greek philosopher Democritus.

powerful method of explanation in the hard sciences and has achieved success in certain cases. For example, in the "water-H_2O case" it is possible to exclude the way water *appears* to a conscious subject without also excluding something essential to the definition of H_2O. However, the "experience-neurons case" is *not* like the "water-H_2O case" because the reality of experience is essentially tied to the way things appear (to a subject). As Searle remarks, "*Where appearance is concerned we cannot make the appearance-reality distinction because the appearance is the reality.*"[51] Searle is not alone on this score. Nagel poses a rhetorical question to advocates of reductive physicalism about this very issue: "Does it make sense, in other words, to ask what my experiences are *really* like, as opposed to how they appear to me?"[52] Nagel and Searle are suggesting that there could be no appearance without a subjective individual point of view. The paradox of a purely mechanistic approach to experience is that it excludes itself from addressing the way things *appear* (to a subject). Appearance (and thus experience) is a target that lies outside the scope of a purely (reductive) mechanistic explanation. Is this an "in-principle" (i.e., methodological) defeater of reductive physicalism?

Reductive mechanistic explanation (RME) not only leaves out appearance, but the existence of a subjective individual point of view that makes an appearance (including sensations or qualia) possible. Consider the following pithy reflection of Nagel on this score: "What has to be explained is not just the lacing of organic life with a tincture of qualia but the coming into existence of subjective individual points of view—a type of existence logically distinct from anything describable by the physical sciences alone."[53] Appearances do not float freely; they are tied to a subjective individual point of view. Since appearances depend on a subjective individual point of view, and RME leaves out (or excludes) appearances, RME leaves out (or excludes) a subjective individual point of view.[54]

Is it possible to strengthen the argument against RME on empirical grounds? I think so. One way to bolster our case involves showing why recent attempts to explain the unity of experience on neural mechanistic grounds alone fall short of a satisfying account.

51. John Searle, *The Rediscovery of Mind* (Cambridge, MA: MIT Press, 1992), 122.

52. Nagel, "What Is It Like to Be a Bat?" 329.

53. Nagel, *Mind and Cosmos*, 44.

54. Moreover, the framework of RME logically excludes what is metaphysically required for any explanatory practice, a subjective individual point of view. However, any theory of experience worth its salt will have to provide theoretical space for a subjective individual point of view, since that datum is intrinsic to experience.

Neuronal Mechanisms and the Unity of Experience

I take a subjective individual point of view to be a (metaphysically primitive, physically irreducible) kind of unity, i.e., subject unity. I have argued elsewhere that providing an account of subject unity would involve explaining the singularity intrinsic to every conscious experience and how that singularity relates to the unity of experience across modalities of the brain.[55] In what follows, I raise empirically-based doubts that RP can deliver the explanatory goods when it comes to the unity of experience and, more specifically, object unity, diachronic object unity, and subject unity.

Advocates of RP must face up to the problem of objectual unity, also called the object feature binding problem. I will now clarify and delve into the scientific motivation behind this problem, and show how it applies to RP. Contemporary neurobiology indicates that visual consciousness relies upon the specialized activity of neuronal assemblies distributed throughout the visual hierarchy.[56] For example, as one gazes upon a California black oak tree, the oak's retinotopic pattern is rapidly laid out on the surface area of V1.[57] Neurons in V1 and V2 respond to primitive visual features, such as edges and contours, in a variety of orientations.[58] Once a relatively stable figure of the oak has been established and segregated from its background in these lower areas, attentional mechanisms select (and relay) information about the oak downstream for further processing in specialized areas of the ventral and dorsal pathways, also known as the *what* and *where* systems.[59] The ventral system's neuronal pathway projects from the occipital lobe to the inferior temporal lobe (IT); separate neuronal subassemblies distributed throughout the ventral system play the functional roles of processing information about an object's figure, color, and texture. Neurons in V3 respond to figure and neurons in V4 respond to color. The dorsal system's neuronal pathway projects from the occipital lobe to the parietal lobe (7a); it performs the functional role of processing information about an object's location and size. The middle temporal and middle superior temporal lobes (MT and

55. See my "From Biological Naturalism to Emergent Subject Dualism."

56. D. Felleman and D. Van Essen, "Distributed Hierarchical Processing in the Primate Cerebral Cortex," *Cerebral Cortex* 1 (1991), 1–47.

57. V in V1 stands for visual area.

58. D. Grosof, R. Shapely, and M. Hawken, "Macaque V1 Neurons Can Signal Illusory Contours," *Nature* 365 (1993), 550–52.

59. M. Mishkin, L. Ungerleider, and K. Maco, "Object Vision and Spatial Vision: Two Cortical Pathways," *Trends in Neurosciences* 6 (1983), 414–17.

MST) process movements associated with individual objects or collections of objects against stable or relatively stable background conditions. Thus, visually perceiving an oak's features on a blustery day would at least involve the relevant firing patterns of neuronal subassemblies in areas V1–4, IT, 7a, MT and MST.[60]

Neuropsychological evidence provides further confirmation to this distributed view of visual feature processing. For example, damage to neurons in V4 produces achromatopsia, i.e., color blindness; damage to neurons in IT produces associative agnosia, i.e., the inability to identify shapes; and damage to neurons in MT produces akinetopsia, i.e., motion blindness.[61] At the same time, there are very few, if any, direct neural connections between specific visual areas, such as those that represent color and motion.[62] Moreover, various studies implicate the dorsal system as underlying our spatial attention capacity and the ability to discriminate within and between objects.[63] Thus, what we currently know about the visual system is that it relies upon several specialized subsystems distributed throughout the visual hierarchy. Although this functional specialization has enabled the brain to process information efficiently, it also implies several vision-related binding problems, including the object feature binding problem. As Bayne and Chalmers observe:

> The notion of objectual unity is closely tied to a central issue in cognitive psychology and neurophysiology. When I look at a red square, the color and the shape may be represented in different parts of my visual system. But somehow these separate pieces of information are brought together so that I experience a single red square. . . . This phenomenon is often referred to as binding, and the question of how it is achieved is often referred to as the binding problem.[64]

60. See also Kosslyn and Koenig, *Wet Mind*, 52–127.

61. J. Meadows, "Disturbed Perception of Colours Associated with Localized Cerebral Lesions," *Brain* 97 (1974), 615–32. J. Zihl, D. von Cramon and N. Mai, "Selective Disturbance of Movement Vision after Bilateral Brain Damage," *Brain* 106 (1983), 313–40.

62. Zeki, "The Disunity of Consciousness," 214–18.

63. M. Posner and S. Petersen, "The Attention System in the Human Brain," *Annual Review of Neuroscience* 13 (1990), 25–42. L. Robertson, "What Can Spatial Deficits Teach Us about Feature Binding and Spatial Maps?," *Visual Cognition* 6 (1999), 409–30. R. Elgy, J. Driver, and R. Rafal, "Shifting Visual Attention between Objects and Locations: Evidence from Normal and Parietal Lesion Subjects," *Journal of Experimental Psychology* 123 (1994), 161–77.

64. T. Bayne and D. Chalmers, "What Is the Unity of Consciousness?" in *The Unity of Consciousness: Binding, Integration, and Dissociation*, ed. A. Cleeremans (Oxford: Oxford University Press, 2003), 25.

Now, here's the rub against RP. RP maintains that all higher-level mental features are explained in terms of their respective lower-level neural processes. Thus, under RP's hypothesis, a color feature is reducible to activity in V4, a motion feature is reducible to activity in V5, a figure feature is reducible to activity in V3, and so forth. By implication, the distinct features of an object are reducible to activities in their respective geographically separate neuronal areas, and thus it is not clear how RP could account for objectual unity.[65] This is truly a difficult problem of experience *for* RP.

Couldn't an advocate of RP maintain that objectual unity is explained in terms of the synchronization of neurons? The implication is that consciously experiencing an object's features as a unity occurs because the underlying neurons of those features, though distributed in geographically separate areas, respond at the same time. An analogy might prove helpful: a synchronized assembly of neurons could be conceived as analogous to a group of violinists who play their respective notes in perfect timing throughout a musical score. As the conductor signals to the individual players to play more quickly, the individual players speed up together, exhibiting a dynamic phase-locking bond of synchronous activity. The underlying neurons of an object's features are said to be activated at the same time and in phase (at about 35–75 hertz), and this mode of neural activity ostensibly accounts for the experience of objectual unity. This dominant proposal is usually referred to as the binding by synchrony (BBS) hypothesis or the hypothesis of neuronal synchrony in the gamma range (NSGR).[66]

However, there are significant empirical problems for the BBS hypothesis. Experimental research indicates that neural synchrony "is notoriously difficult to measure with stationary stimuli."[67] In fact, the experimentation of Tovee and Rolls has shown that neuronal activity in IT of alert monkeys revealed *no* evidence of synchrony when the cells in IT were activated by stimuli that were sta-

65. In other words, because the stimulus features of an object do, in fact, generate activity in separate areas of the visual cortex, it is difficult to see how—*from within the explanatory confines of RP*—a feature unified object arises in consciousness.

66. See Crick, *The Astonishing Hypothesis*, 245; C. Tallon-Baudry and O. Bertrand, "Oscillatory Gamma Activity in Humans and Its Role in Object Representation," *Trends in Cognitive Sciences* 3 (1999), 151–62; C. von der Malsburg, "The Binding Problem of Neural Networks," in *The Mind-Brain Continuum: Sensory Processes,* ed. R. Llinas and P. Churchland (Cambridge, MA: MIT Press, 1996), 131–46. For my purposes here, I focus my discussion on this dominantly proposed mechanism of binding.

67. J. Hummel and I. Biederman, "Dynamic Binding in a Neural Network for Shape Recognition," *Psychological Review* 99 (1992), 509.

tionary.[68] This has dramatic consequences for the neural synchrony hypothesis. It is difficult to see how neural synchrony could be an adequate binding mechanism since *some* of the objects we perceive in both natural and artificial environments (e.g., mountains, boulders, houses, etc.) are *stationary*. Moreover, recent evidence derived from studies on primate visual cortex show that motion detection is not correlated with neural synchrony. For example, Thiele and Stoner constructed an experiment that employed perceptually coherent plaid patterns and two types of non-coherent plaid patterns to test the BBS hypothesis. By exposing these distinctive patterns to alert monkeys, they could test the predictive value of BBS. If BBS is plausible, the coherent plaids should elicit synchronization in the neuronal area that encodes motion of awake, fixating primates. However, the experimental results indicate that, contrary to the BBS prediction, the "synchrony elicited by our coherent plaids was statistically indistinguishable from that of non-coherent plaids."[69] These particular objections imply that neuronal synchrony falls short of a *complete account* of objectual unity on grounds that it can explain neither *stationary* nor *moving* objects. And since the capacity for a conscious subject to extract motion from structure is evolutionarily important (e.g., consider a gazelle's ability to extract the structure of a lion that is quietly approaching through tall, golden grass), the BBS hypothesis is problematical on grounds of biological evolution as well.

Furthermore, the neuroscientific research that is commonly used to support the BBS hypothesis has been derived from both anesthetized and awake animals.[70] This would suggest that neuronal synchrony occurs in response to visually presented objects in the brains of both unconscious and conscious animals. Consequently, we cannot maintain that neuronal synchrony is the *special* correlate of the experience of objectual unity.

Couldn't an advocate of RP reply to the preceding objection as follows? Some animal studies use lighter forms of anesthesia, which probably do *not* produce a complete loss of experience. This experimental result implies that we should not reject neuronal synchrony in the gamma range (NSGR) as the

68. M. Tovee and E. Rolls, "The Functional Nature of Neuronal Oscillations," *Trends in Neurosciences* 15 (1992), 387.

69. A. Thiele and G. Stoner, "Neuronal Synchrony Does Not Correlate with Motion Coherence in Cortical Area MT," *Nature* 421 (2003), 367; also G. Mashour, "Consciousness Unbound: Toward a Paradigm of General Anesthesia," *Anesthesiology* 100 (2004), 428–33; see also my "Disambiguation," 747-77.

70. See Crick, *The Astonishing Hypothesis,* 15; also O. Imas, K. Ropella, J. Wood, and A. Hudetz, "Halothane Augments Event-Related Gamma Oscillations in Rat Visual Cortex," *Neuroscience* 123 (2004), 269–78.

special correlate of feature binding on grounds that experience is still present, though to a lesser degree, in lighter anesthesia cases. Nonetheless, there are animal studies that use deeper forms of anesthesia, which do produce a loss of experience; and yet the same kind of neuronal activity (i.e., NSGR) that correlates with the animal's waking (experiential) life also correlates with the animal's anaesthetic-induced loss of experience.[71] Therefore, NSGR cannot be the special neural correlate of binding in experience. Furthermore, this deeper form of anesthesia does not prevent the transmission of information from striate cortex to higher levels of the visual cortex. Moreover, very recent experiments show that NSGR increases while the animal is unconscious.[72] Although the brain is functioning as if the animal were undergoing experience (for example, evoked NSGR is still possible), the animal is nevertheless not undergoing experience. It follows that NSGR cannot be the special neural correlate of the animal's visual (and perhaps other sensory modes of) experience. This raises deeper metaphysical questions about what is being rendered unconscious. It cannot be the animal's brain for those who advocate NSGR as the special correlate of experience, for NSGR is present in both waking states and anaesthetic-induced unconscious states. Could it be that what is being rendered unconscious is the subject, instead of the brain to which the subject relates?[73]

Recent evidence also indicates that neuronal synchrony correlates strongly with preattentive awareness, that is, unconscious activity in the *primary visual cortex* (or V1).[74] Neuronal synchrony has also been observed in the hippocampus, a primitive neural structure that plays unconscious roles in receiving and sending information to several subsystems and in the formation and storage of new information in those subsystems.[75] This raises an important question. How

71. See also Imas et al., "Halothane Augments Event-Related Gamma Oscillations in Rat Visual Cortex."

72. See Logan Voss, Cecilia Bass, Linnea Hansson, Duan Li and James Sleigh, "Investigation into the effect of general anaesthetic etomidate on local neuronal synchrony in the mouse neocortical slice," *Brain Research* 1526 (2013), 65–70. See also A. Hudetz, "Suppressing Consciousness: Mechanisms of General Anesthesia," *Seminars in Anesthesia, Perioperative Medicine and Pain* 25 (2006), 196–204. Hudetz points out that gamma activity can actually increase in the anesthetized state.

73. See also my "Cognition and Consciousness: Kantian Affinities with Contemporary Vision Research," *Kant-Studien* 101 (2010), 445-64.

74. G. Rols, C. Tallon-Baudry, P. Girard, O. Bertrand, J. Bullier, "Cortical Mapping of Gamma Oscillations in Areas V1 and V4 of the Macaque Monkey," *Visual Neuroscience* 18, 527–40; also C. Gray, "The Temporal Correlation Hypothesis of Visual Feature Integration: Still Alive and Well," *Neuron* 24 (1999), 31–47.

75. L. Colgin, T. Denninger, M. Fyhn, T. Hafting, T. Bonnevie, O. Jensen, M. Moser,

is it possible for neuronal synchrony to be the special neural correlate of binding in experience if such neuronal activity also correlates with unconscious activity in the primary visual cortex and the hippocampus?[76] Similarly, Chalmers doubts that neural synchrony could be the special correlate of binding in experience on grounds that it is arguable that "binding also take[s] place in the processing of unconscious information."[77] All of this suggests that neuronal synchrony is *too widespread* to count as the special neural correlate of experience.

Another empirically based problem for RP is that the type of neuronal activity that allegedly correlates with an object's stimulus features probably cannot account for the experience of *diachronic object unity* because of the fleeting nature of such neuronal activity. Some recent experimental data indicates that the experience of a feature-unified object *persists* beyond the subpopulation of cells that fire in response to the object's stimulus features. For example, O'Reilly, Busby, and Soto observed that once an object is removed from a subject's visual field, and the neuronal events that correlate with that object's stimulus features ceases firing, there is no indication that those neuronal events were bound together over time and yet we can undergo "enduring" experiences of bound features; "so somehow this problem needs to be addressed."[78] O'Reilly and colleagues are referring to our capacity to experience a feature-unified object *over* time, or diachronic object unity (i.e., DOU). DOU refers to the *enduring character* of object experience that ordinarily accompanies our waking and dreaming lives. Because DOU *persists beyond* the subpopulation of cells that fire in response to an object's respective features, DOU is *not* reducible to the activation of such neurons. This empirical result has

---

E. Moser, "Frequency of Gamma Oscillations Routes Flow of Information in the Hippocampus," *Nature* 462 (2009), 353–57; also Kosslyn and Koenig, *Wet Mind*, 342–49. More recent experiments suggest that the hippocampus might carry out its unconscious roles by alternating between gamma and theta oscillations. See j. Lisman and O. Jensen, "The Theta-Gamma Neural Code," *Neuron* 77 (2013), 1002–16.

76. For more on why the primary visual cortex could not be the neural correlate of visual consciousness, see F. Crick and C. Koch, "Are We Aware of Neural Activity in Primary Visual Cortex?," *Nature* 375 (1995): 121–23; J. Prinz, "A Neurofunctional Theory of Visual Consciousness," *Consciousness and Cognition* 9 (2000), 243–59.

77. Chalmers, "Problem of Consciousness," 387.

78. Randall O'Reilly, Richard Busby, and Rudolfo Soto, "Three Forms of Binding and Their Neural Substrates: Alternatives to Temporal Synchrony," in *The Unity of Consciousness*, ed. A. Cleeremans (Oxford: Oxford University Press, 2003), 171.

an important metaphysical implication: some of the properties of experience (e.g., DOU) are unlikely to be captured by the net of neural reductionism.[79]

One might suppose that advocates of RP could reply with the following short-term working memory (hereafter, WM) objection. WM probably functions to temporarily store visual and other modes of information for several seconds at a time. Thus, WM might underlie the continuity of experience in some important sense. The research of Patricia Goldman-Rakic supports this claim. Goldman-Rakic discovered that an important function of prefrontal neurons involves temporarily storing the locations of objects within one's visual field. Carrying out basic behavioral tasks would seem to depend upon temporarily stored spatial information, such as the location of an object.[80] For example, the spatial information temporarily stored by WM could be what underlies the individual's ability to guide the relevant motor outputs over time: reaching for the red ball to my left rather than the blue ball to my right requires access to the relevant locational information. Recent evidence shows that the neural correlate of this spatial mode of WM is related to the association areas of the dorsal prefrontal cortex, which can be subdivided into three distinct regions of the principal sulcus: the cortical area surrounding the sulcus, as well as the cortical areas ventral and dorsal to the sulcus. Researchers have utilized delayed response tasks to corroborate these claims. One such task involved showing a morsel of food to a monkey; then, after a brief delay, the monkey was allowed to reach for the food. Researchers found that prefrontal neurons fire selectively in response to an object's location and then continue to fire *during* the delay period of such tasks. Other experiments on monkey cortex show that a small lesion to the principal sulcus causes a deficit in WM.[81] By implication, *behavioral continuity* depends on access to the relevant spatial information temporarily stored by WM. Apart from temporarily storing locational information, it would seem that WM would have to play a role in transiently storing information about an object's shape and color for the purposes of object recognition. The cortical region that is *ventral* to the principal sulcus is the likely region where WM functions to transiently store information about an object's "what" features, e.g., its color, shape, texture. And the cortical region that is *dorsal* to the principal sulcus is the likely region where WM functions to tran-

79. See also my "Is Consciousness Really a Brain Process?," *International Philosophical Quarterly* 48 (2008), 201-29.

80. Patricia Goldman-Rakic, "Circuitry of Primate Prefrontal Cortex and Regulation of Behavior by Representational Memory," in *Handbook for Physiology*, ed. Fred Plum and Vernon B. Mountcastle (Bethesda, MD: American Physiological Society, 1987).

81. Eric Kandel, James Schwartz, and Thomas Jessell, *Principles of Neural Science* (New York: McGraw Hill, 2000), 356–61.

siently store information about an object's "where" features, e.g., its location and size. These data suggest that WM is modular, in the sense that separate neuronal areas selectively respond to and temporarily store information about an object's *what* and *where* features.[82] Having looked at some of the *neural correlates* of WM, we might also discuss briefly the *cellular mechanisms* of WM. Eric Kandel's research on the sea slug, *Aplysia*, is illuminating in this respect because it suggests that "the duration of short-term memory storage depends on the length of time a synapse is weakened or strengthened."[83] Kandel recognizes, however, that WM is not located "at a single specialized site," but involves the synapses of thousands of neurons distributed throughout the relevant specialized cortical areas.[84]

Nevertheless, these empirical data raise an important binding question: why would binding problems not arise at the level of WM, if the cellular mechanisms that underlie WM are distributed throughout each cortex? The implicit challenges that confront a purely (reductive) physicalistic approach to WM with respect to objectual unity over time should not be underestimated. For example, how does WM bind an object's *what* and *where* features, if the cellular mechanisms that correlate with WM are distributed in separate neuronal regions? Will not the spatial spread of the neural events that correlate with WM thwart the unification process? Somehow the separate pieces of information regarding an object's features are bound together so that I experience a single, feature-unified object *over time*, despite the limitations of WM. Based upon these data, one could infer that explaining how an object's separate features are *temporarily stored* (or transiently sustained) by WM is one thing; while explaining how the distributed operations of WM could bind such features into a *unified* object over time (i.e., diachronic object unity) is another matter. Which is to say: temporary storage does not entail DOU. Even if WM is necessary for DOU, it is *not* also sufficient for it.[85]

Some advocates of neuronal synchrony (mistakenly) suppose that their account implies an "elegant solution" to the problem of objectual unity because

82. Kandel, Schwartz, and Jessell, *Principles of Neural Science*.

83. Eric Kandel, *In Search of Memory* (New York: W. W. Norton and Company, 2006), 204–05.

84. Kandel, *In Search of Memory*, 204. Kandel is not alone in making the observation that WM is distributed across specialized areas of the brain. For example, Crick and Koch also maintain: "Both iconic and working memory are likely to be distributed throughout the appropriate cortical areas, with auditory events transiently stored in auditory cortices, visual events in the visual cortices, and so on." See Francis Crick and Christof Koch, "Towards a Neurobiological Theory of Consciousness," *Seminars in the Neurosciences* 2 (1990), 270.

85. See my "Disambiguation," 747–77; see also my "Is Consciousness Really a Brain Process?," 201–29.

temporal synchrony could "selectively tag" the responses of neurons that code for the same object when competition occurs and hence "demarcate their responses from those of neurons activated by other objects."[86] Nevertheless, how the brain selectively tags the correct features (when two or more objects are present in a subject's visual field) is *distinct* from how the features of an object are brought together as a single, unified object. It is, therefore, a mistake to run the questions of feature *selection* and feature *binding* together. To further clarify and motivate this point, an illustration may be helpful. Imagine a grid of lights, such that each light is labeled to represent an individual feature of an object. To simplify matters, the total number of objects that can be represented by the grid is five. The labels that represent an object's features at any given moment are distributed throughout the grid-like system; the label for "red" is above the label for "circle" and the label for "motion" is above and to the right of the label for "red," and so forth. Since an object's features are represented (via labels) in a distributed fashion, we need a mechanism to selectively tag (or disambiguate) an object's respective group of features when competing object features light up at the same time. One way to know which features belong to their respective objects is by means of a selecting (or "tagging" or "marking") mechanism. In the case of the grid, an electrical switch causes ("selects") the correct coalition of labeled lights to turn on (or "fire" more brilliantly than competing sets of lights) at a distinct time. Notice, however, that *simply because we have a mechanism that selectively activates (i.e., "tags") the correct set of features distributed throughout the grid-like system, we have yet to explain how those features, once selectively activated, are bound together to form a single unitary object as opposed to an unconnected group of features.* Thus, binding the *correct* set of features together (when competition occurs in the cortical neural network) entails selective tagging (or feature disambiguation), but selective tagging (or feature disambiguation) per se does not entail binding. One can imagine, though, that some advocates of neuronal synchrony might reply that all they mean by feature binding is feature selection. However, just explaining feature selection when competition arises in the cortical hierarchy does not explain the more difficult question about a feature-unified object of experience.[87]

A further fundamental reason why tagging theories fail to explain a feature-unified object of experience is that those theories are motivated by and essentially linked to considerations drawn from an extrinsic laboratory perspective.

86. Andreas Engel, "Temporal Binding and the Neural Correlates of Consciousness," in *The Unity of Consciousness*, ed. A. Cleeremans (Oxford: Oxford University Press, 2003), 134.

87. For details of this objection, see my "Neural Synchrony," 39–58; "Disambiguation," 747–77; and "Cognition and Consciousness," 445–64.

As cognitive scientist Frank Van der Velde observes, neuroscientists can make observations of neuronal synchrony occurring in different areas of the visual cortex, but this type of observation is ultimately an "observation from an extrinsic (laboratory) perspective."[88] After having discovered the local information processing areas of the visual cortex (and synchrony of activation in those areas), some researchers might conclude that a theory of global information processing (e.g., an account of objectual unity) has been achieved. But this inference would be mistaken on grounds that the situation is essentially different from *inside* the brain: "from the perspective of a neuron buried deep within the cortex, the situation is different. It has only an intrinsic perspective, which does not allow it to 'look beyond its horizon.'"[89] Van der Velde concludes that solving the object feature binding problem is akin to solving a global information problem, and thus a solution to the former problem would involve a processing approach that extends "beyond the local information obtainable within each of the different brain areas involved."[90] Indeed, if the scope of a neuron's perspective is inextricably tied to the scope of its specialization area (e.g., V4 for color and V5 for motion), then that perspective will not be able to take up a global point of view. A feature-unified object of experience requires a global point of view. Any theory about a feature-unified object of experience that fails to account for such a view should be rejected. Synchrony of activation and other tagging theories are logically compatible with the absence of a global point of view and consequently should be rejected. An analogy: if five chefs are located in separate kitchens and each chef is consciously aware of only *part* of the same recipe, it does not follow that any one chef is consciously aware of the recipe as a whole—*even if all of the chefs are consciously aware of their respective recipe parts at the same time.* What is the philosophical upshot here? It would not matter whether the proposed neuronal firings were pitched in terms of alpha waves, beta waves, gamma waves, theta waves, firing in bursts, et cetera. The same problems would arise for RP, owing to the fact that information pieces about an object's features bear a distributed relation to the processing hierarchy. Which is to say: temporal correlation (or selective tagging) is not sufficient for objectual unity.

Finally, RP must confront the problem of *subject unity* (or the problem of explaining the singularity intrinsic to every conscious experience and how that singularity relates to the unity of experience across modalities of the brain). For

88. Frank Van der Velde, "Binding and Consciousness from an Intrinsic Perspective," *Theory & Psychology* 17 (2007), 793.

89. Van der Velde, "Binding and Consciousness," 793.

90. Van der Velde, "Binding and Consciousness," 793.

example, in addition to the sensory objects of experience, there is also a subject (i.e., a point of view or "singularity") in relation to the sensory objects of experience. Subjects have sensory objects of experience; they are not the sensory objects of experience. For example, I hear Jason Becker's melodious guitar sound off in the distance (an object of audition) while seeing a red ball rolling down a hill (an object of vision). I have these two objects as part of my total experience. Thus a further question arises for any theory that purports to offer an explanation of experience, and that is a question about *subject unity*: let us hold that, for any two (or more) objects (or features) of experience that correlate with different modalities of the brain, those objects (or features) count as subject unified only if they are possessed by the same subject at any given time.[91] As with the problem of objectual unity, there are empirically based worries that motivate the problem of subject unity for RP: how could a *distributed* account of objects (or features) within and across different modalities of the brain explain subject unity?[92]

Zombies and the Hard Problem

The persistent failures of purely functional and neural mechanistic approaches to the hard problem of phenomenal consciousness imply that RP is consistent with a philosophical zombie world. A philosophical zombie is materially, functionally, and behaviorally identical to a sentient individual (e.g., a sentient human being). There is an important difference between sentient human beings and zombies though: zombies have no subjective individual point of view. Chalmers maintains that the very conceivability of a philosophical zombie implies a refutation of RP, in the sense that there is no logical entailment from facts about structures, functions, and behaviors to the reality of conscious experience. How can something that is essentially subjective (or first-person) in character ever be explained in objective (or third-person) terms alone? While RP is compatible with a zombie world, *we* are not zombies. So, RP cannot be the complete story about *us*.[93] One could formalize the gist of Chalmers's argument as follows:

91. See my "From Bilogical Naturalism to Emergent Subject Dualism"; see also Bayne and Chalmers, "The Unity of Consciousness," in *The Unity of Consciousness*, ed. A. Cleeremans (Oxford: Oxford University Press, 2003).

92. See also my "From Biological Naturalism to Emergent Subject Dualism." In the aforementioned, I show why this problem is especially acute for weaker versions of emergence and, by logical extension, those committed to non-reductive physicalism about phenomenal properties.

93. There is an important question about whether conceivability entails possibility,

(1) If RP is true, then phenomenal consciousness is entailed by structure and function alone.
(2) Phenomenal consciousness is not entailed by structure and function alone.
(3) Therefore, RP is not true.

We've already examined several lines of empirical evidence for premise 2. After considering those lines of evidence, one might be inclined to say that the conceivability of a philosophical zombie provides further (logical) support to premise 2.[94] It is important to emphasize that the central requirement of this zombie demonstration is *only* conceptual coherence. As Joseph Levine observes, "since zombies have to be literally impossible on the materialist view, their conceivability is an embarrassment to the position. How can what's impossible—a situation that is inherently contradictory—be conceivable? It must be that the situation is not really impossible."[95]

However, for those adopting an empirical approach to the problem of consciousness, a philosophical zombie might not be the most appealing concept. That does not mean that a zombie concept might not be useful to the empirical sciences in some sense. For example, what if we inverted the characteristics of a philosophical zombie? Let us call such a creature an *inverse zombie*. An inverse zombie is *a creature that appears to be unconscious when in fact it is conscious*. Any conceptual investigation of a philosophical zombie's responses to external stimuli would be compatible with the behavior of a conscious being. But any investigation of an inverse zombie's responses (or lack thereof) to external stimuli would be compatible with the behavior of an unconscious being. The adage "appearances can be deceiving" applies in this context too. Whereas experience is entirely absent in the case of philosophical zombies, it is present in the case of inverse zombies. Characteristics of the unconscious *appearance* of an inverse zombie could be unresponsiveness to verbal commands, absence of spontaneous or evoked vocalization or speech, absence of spontaneous or evoked movement, and unresponsiveness to noxious stimulus. Like the philosophical zombie, the concept of the inverse zombie entails no

---

which I will not address here. For more on this issue, see David Chalmers, *The Conscious Mind* (Oxford: Oxford University Press, 1996) and David Chalmers, *The Character of Consciousness* (Oxford: Oxford University Press, 2010).

94. Though, strictly speaking, the above argument could be supported independent of philosophical zombie considerations.

95. Joe Levine, "Anti-Materialist Arguments and Influential Replies," in Velmans and Schneider, eds., *The Blackwell Companion to Consciousness*, 374.

logical contradiction and can therefore be considered both conceivable and possible. Unlike the philosophical zombie, however, inverse zombies are naturally probable and susceptible to empirical confirmation. An inverse zombie would have none of the behavioral characteristics and responses of a philosophical zombie, but would nevertheless be a subject of consciousness. Inverse zombies are not only conceivable; they actually exist: for example, individuals who experience "anesthesia awareness" fall into such a category. From an external observer perspective, these patients *appear* unconscious during general anesthesia. However, in 1 to 2 out of a 1000 cases, patients under general anesthesia may experience intraoperative events, and sometimes without any objective indices.[96] What application could an inverse zombie have in relation to our current discussion?

Since inverse zombies are real, any plausible theory of mind would have to be compatible with their existence. Recall the behaviorist theory of mind advocated by B. F. Skinner. Skinner claimed that, under the hypothesis of behaviorism, mental states are ultimately reducible to behavior: "We may take feeling to be *simply* responding to stimuli."[97] The usual philosophical criticisms posed to behaviorism are inspired by conceptual considerations alone and sometimes appeal to intuitions that behaviorists would find question-begging. However, the existence of an inverse zombie implicitly provides empirical evidence against behaviorism: an inverse zombie has feelings *without the possibility of behaviorally responding to stimuli*. Therefore, feeling is not simply responding to stimuli.

Finally, inverse zombies fly in the face of Dennett's heterophenomenology, an explanatory method which seeks to reduce first-person experiences to third-person *reports*.[98] Dennett even suggests that an appropriate way to test heterophenomenology is through experiments involving anesthetized animals.[99] How serendipitous. An inverse zombie presents a direct challenge to heterophenomenology. An inverse zombie has first-person experiences but

96. For the details, see George Mashour and Eric LaRock, "Inverse Zombies, Anesthesia Awareness, and the Hard Problem of Unconsciousness," *Consciousness and Cognition* 17 (2008), 1163–68. See also my "Philosophical Implications of Awareness during General Anesthesia," in *Consciousness, Awareness, and Anesthesia*, ed. George Mashour (New York: Cambridge University Press, 2010).

97. B. F. Skinner, "About Behaviorism," in J. Crumley, ed., *Problems in Mind* (Mountain View: Mayfield, 2000), 62 (emphasis added).

98. Daniel Dennett, *Sweet Dreams* (MIT, 2005), 144–50.

99. Daniel Dennett, "Who's on First? Heterophenomenology Explained," *Journal of Consciousness Studies* 10 (9) (2003), 19–30.

cannot report those experiences to others. For example, during some intraoperative events anesthetized patients experience painful feelings of being cut and cauterized, but cannot report those feelings to others. In her book, *Silenced Screams*, Jeanette Liska provides vivid testimony of what it's like to be in a state of anesthesia awareness and, at the same time, undergo the painful feelings of being cut and cauterized without the possibility of behaviorally responding:

> At that instant, the surgeon's electric knife, which cuts and cauterizes simultaneously, tore into my skin. It felt like a blowtorch. Lightning bolts of pain more intense than any pain I had ever experienced surged and ricocheted through my torso, finally exploding through the left side of my face. Drowning in an ocean of searing agony, I sensed the skein of my entire life unraveling, thread by thread. But I was the only one who heard my tortured screams—silent screams that reverberated again and again off the cold walls of my skull and into the black night of eternity.[100]

Even though there were no clinical indications of experience during general anesthesia, Liska experienced horrendous pain during her operation.[101] What lessons can be drawn? When any patient has first-person experiences during general anesthesia—without the possibility of reporting those experiences to others—we have an instance of an inverse zombie. Inverse zombies are not merely possible; their existence demonstrates that first-person feelings are not reducible to third-person reports and thus Dennett's heterophenomenology is false (or is most probably false) on empirical grounds.

In conclusion, phenomenal consciousness continues to resist the explanatory methodology of reductive physicalism (RP). Since the early pre-Socratics, RP has enjoyed over 2600 hundred years of reflection, formulation, and defense; yet RP still fails to explain experiencing subjects. In addition to presenting an empirical case against reductive functionalism about experience, I have argued mainly on empirical grounds that subjects and the phenomenal states they undergo are *not* "in fact the behavior of a vast assembly of nerve cells and their associated molecules."[102] Since the explanatory methodology of RP is

100. Jeanette Liska, *Silenced Screams: Surviving Anesthetic Awareness During Surgery* (Park Ridge: AANA Publishing, 2002), 14–15.

101. Shortly after her surgery, Liska described her painful experiences to her physicians but noted that various doubts were expressed about the possibility of awareness during general anesthesia. To lend credence to her testimony, Liska simply reminded them of detailed conversations that occurred during the surgical procedure (see Liska, *Silenced Screams*, 22–23).

102. Francis Crick, *The Astonishing Hypothesis*, 3.

logically and empirically unsatisfactory, perhaps we should consider adopting an explanatory methodology that accommodates subjective (or first-person) data and objective (or third-person) data. One such methodology is neurophenomenology, ably articulated by Francisco Varela and Evan Thompson: "The working hypothesis of neurophenomenology is that phenomenological data and cognitive scientific data can function as reciprocal constraints in the science of consciousness."[103] If we take subjective (or first-person) data as truly fundamental (i.e., irreducible to anything simpler in the physical world), then we can begin to develop a theory that accommodates the reality of ourselves as experiencing subjects.[104] Even though the above empirical results run deeply against RP, and thus to its simple third-person explanatory methodology, they fit very neatly within the methodology of neurophenomenology and empirically informed brands of dualism, such as emergent dualism (and possibly even certain formulations of nonreductive physicalism, such as the constitution view).[105] Over thirty years ago David Armstrong acknowledged that new problems and new lines of evidence could "come to light that will force science to reconsider the physico-chemical view of man."[106] Since that level-headed acknowledgment, substantial empirically based problems for reductive physicalism have been discovered; hence the explanatory gaps for reductive physicalism have only widened over time *through scientific progress*. Which is to say: recent progress in neuroscience has made it possible for scientists and philosophers to resist RP not merely on logical grounds but, to use a timely phrase by Armstrong, "for reasons of scientific detail."[107] Insofar as we seek to proportion our belief to the evidence, RP about experiencing subjects is unwarranted.

103. Varela and Thompson, "Neural Synchrony and the Unity of Mind" in *The Unity of Consciousness: Binding, Integration, and Dissociation*, ed. Axel Cleeremans (Oxford: Oxford University Press, 2003), 267.

104. For a compelling argument along these lines, see David Chalmers, *The Conscious Mind*; see also Dean Zimmerman, "From Experience to Experiencer," 168–96.

105. For more on the feasibility of this methodology, see David Chalmers, *The Character of Consciousness*, 50–51. See also my empirically motivated brand of emergent dualism in "Cognition and Consciousness," and my "From Biological Naturalism to Emergent Subject Dualism." For a formulation of the constitution view that accommodates first-person data and which is positioned to take third-person data seriously, see Lynne Rudder Baker, *Persons and Bodies* (Cambridge: Cambridge University Press, 2001).

106. Armstrong, "Nature of Mind," 137.

107. Armstrong, "Nature of Mind," 137.

CHAPTER 14

Explaining Consciousness

Kevin Corcoran and Kevin Sharpe

In his "Neuroscience and the Hard Problem of Consciousness," Eric LaRock argues on largely empirical grounds that the existence of phenomenal consciousness presents a formidable challenge to reductive versions of physicalism. As LaRock puts it, "The problem of phenomenal consciousness is truly a hard problem because it is not clear that a subjective individual point of view could ever be accounted for in terms of objective, physical structures and functions alone." Insofar as reductive physicalism is committed to there being a complete explanation of phenomenal consciousness and the subjective (first-person) point of view solely in terms of physical structures and functions, reductive physicalism looks to be a failed approach to consciousness.

What we propose to do here is to examine what sort of "account" or "explanation" about human persons that materialists, like ourselves, are committed to giving. It's only after we've done this that we'll be in a position to evaluate the explanatory prospects of materialism. As there are different sorts of explanations, there will be different ways to explain consciousness. That materialism is incapable of providing a certain type of explanation of consciousness counts against materialism only if materialism is committed to the view that an explanation of consciousness must be an explanation of that type. As we see it, LaRock is right in holding that certain kinds of explanations of consciousness are bound to fail and we agree that this failure opens up a certain kind of explanatory gap between the physical and functional, and the phenomenal. While a variety of reductive explanations of consciousness fail, we maintain that consciousness is susceptible to a kind of nonreductive explanation that's quite congenial to taking subjective data as fundamental and supports the broadly explanatory case for materialism that we put forward in our paper.

Even though one of us (Sharpe) is sympathetic to reductive physicalism, we'll speak here as though we agree on the irreducibility of phenomenal consciousness and a first-person point of view. Our reason for doing so is quite simple: our primary interest lies in defending *materialism*, which we take to be the view that human persons are *wholly physical substances*, and we think that some versions of materialism are exceptionally well placed to preserve the ineliminable and irreducible subjective, first-person point of view that LaRock argues for. We argue here that materialists need not be worried, even if the explanatory failures of reductive physicalism are conceded. We begin with a brief discussion of how we're using the terms "materialism" and "physicalism" in this reply. We then examine different ways in which consciousness may be physically (or functionally) explained. We conclude by discussing the prospects of materialist theories of human persons that take phenomenal consciousness and the first-person subjectivity it presupposes as fundamental and irreducible. The upshot is that the metaphysical and empirical considerations LaRock puts forward do not favor subject dualism over materialism, an upshot that LaRock may well be amenable to.[1] As he says, "Even though the above empirical results run deeply against [reductive physicalism], and thus to its simple third-person explanatory methodology, they fit very neatly within the methodology of neurophenomenology and empirically informed brands of dualism, such as emergent dualism (*and possibly even certain formulations of nonreductive physicalism, such as the constitution view*)" (our emphasis).

Physicalism and Materialism

While often used interchangeably, we want here to distinguish between materialism and physicalism. We are taking materialism to be a claim about the metaphysical composition of human persons. We're taking physicalism to be a claim about the nature of mentality. As we've already indicated, we take materialism to be the view that human persons are wholly physical entities, exhaustively composed of physical particles (the sorts of things it is the job of physicists to investigate) and, as such, human persons are neither identical to immaterial souls nor do they have them as parts. We take physicalism, on the other hand, to be the view that one's compositional nature *exhausts her entire nature*. In other words, according to physicalism (as understood here) there

1. By "subject dualism" we simply mean any theory according to which the subject of thought and consciousness either is, or has as a part, a nonphysical soul.

are no human person facts over and above compositional and related structural facts. Once a human person's compositional nature is fixed, every other fact about her (including all mental facts) is entirely fixed, without remainder. While physicalism—as a claim about the mind—comes in many varieties, we follow LaRock in focusing on reductive physicalism, which he describes as the view that phenomenal consciousness (and subjectivity in general) is entirely physical; that is, all facts about phenomenal consciousness are physical facts. On this view, phenomenal consciousness and first-person subjectivity are reducible, without remainder, to "facts about structure and function." LaRock cites Crick as a paradigm reductivist: "your joys and your sorrows, your memories and your ambitions . . . are in fact no more than the behavior of a vast assembly of nerve cells and their associated molecules."[2]

Most of LaRock's chapter is devoted to a highly detailed criticism of reductive physicalism as an approach to human consciousness, but he has relatively little to say about *materialism* as an approach to human persons (or the subject of human consciousness). On those brief occasions that LaRock does mention human subjects, they are run together with claims regarding consciousness. For example, in his conclusion he states, "I have argued mainly on empirical grounds that subjects and the phenomenal states they undergo are *not* 'in fact the behavior of a vast assembly of nerve cells and their associated molecules.'" But the arguments he offers in support of this exclusively concern the explanatory failures (and hence failure *tout court*) of reductive physicalism. To get a conclusion concerning *persons* or *subjects* from premises regarding *consciousness* and *subjectivity*, LaRock has to assume that materialism (or at least most garden variety versions of materialism) is committed to the reductive physicalism he objects to—otherwise the claim regarding subjects of consciousness would be a *non sequitur*. As we'll discuss in the last section of this reply, we reject this assumption. Materialism, or at least the minimal kind of materialism we defended in our paper—is neutral with respect to reductive physicalism. Before discussing this in more detail, we first turn to the issue of explanation.

Accounting For, Saying Why, and Explanation: The Issue of Reduction

The hard problem of consciousness is just the sheer fact of phenomenal consciousness itself. How is it that the complicated interaction of one hundred billion nerve cells and their several hundred trillion synaptic connections

2. Francis Crick, *The Astonishing Hypothesis* (New York: Charles Scribner's Sons, 1994), 3.

should be accompanied by *phenomenal experience*? How is it that something inherently subjective like a first-person perspective can be explained in terms of objective, physical mechanisms? How is it that our brains—a distributed assemblage of neurons and associated mechanisms—should give rise to a *singular, subjective experiencer*? There is absolutely nothing about the bio-chemical properties of human neural structures that even begins to suggest the accompanying presence of the qualitative character and subjectivity of phenomenal experiences. Nor is there anything about the bio-chemical properties of human neural structures to ground a reductive explanation of consciousness in terms of neural mechanisms and their bio-chemical properties, nothing that makes it intelligible how features of the latter sort are responsible for features of the former sort. Any such attempt is bound to leave out what's distinctive of phenomenal consciousness. We agree, therefore, with LaRock that functionalist and other reductive versions of physicalism that effectively eliminate phenomenal consciousness and reduce a first-person, subjective point of view to third-person, objective mechanisms are fatally flawed.

But what, exactly, should an account of, an explanation of, consciousness do? Ought it to say *how* phenomenal consciousness arises out of complex neural circuitry? Ought it to say why *those* features of external, physical objects get unified and tagged with *those phenomenal* markers? What is it to *explain* anyway? What is it to *give an account* of some phenomenon? The English word "explanation" enjoys great lexical plasticity in every day discourse. One might explain the meanings of words, how to brew Greek coffee, why the electricity went out in the neighborhood, or even the political context of the current Israeli-Palestinian madness. According to one understanding of what's involved in an explanation, there are two components of peculiarly *scientific* explanations, an *explanandum* (that which needs explaining) and an *explanans* (what does the explaining, or that which *accounts for* the *explanandum*). On one historically influential account, the *explanans* involves specifying a set of deterministic laws and initial conditions from which the *explanandum* is logically deduced or derived. The derivation of the *explanandum* from the *explanans* contributes to our understanding of why the *explanandum* occurred and makes its occurrence intelligible.

Another model of explanation, what LaRock calls "mechanistic explanation," proceeds by identifying the lower-level mechanism that explains the presence of a higher-level feature. When the lower-level mechanism successfully explains the presence of the higher-level feature *without remainder*, we can consider the higher-level feature reductively explained. LaRock illustrates this by citing Michael Tye:

> brittleness is caused by "the irregular alignment of crystals" and, as a result of this type of alignment, the forces that hold the crystals together are weak. That is why brittle pieces of glass shatter easily. (164)

The problem for reductive physicalism is that

> . . . it is difficult to see how any *objective* mechanism (by itself) could explain the *subjective* character of phenomenal states: even if we understood all of the fine-grained structures and chemical changes associated with the mechanisms of our brains, "we still seem to be left with something that cries out for further explanation, namely, why and how this collection of neural and/or chemical changes produces that subjective feeling, or any subjective feeling at all." (164)

The underlying assumption is that if there were in fact a complete explanation of consciousness in terms of the proposed reducing mechanism, there'd be no room for questions like "but how does this neural structure produce that subjective feeling?" For in the case of brittleness—a paradigm case of mechanistic explanation—the reducing mechanism closes off exactly this sort of question. Once we fully understand the nature of the lower-level reducing mechanism, e.g., irregular alignment of crystals and the resulting weak bonding relations, we have an intelligible link between the reducing mechanism and the reduced property and it is inconceivable that the higher-level property fails to be instantiated (given the reducing mechanism).

This *a priori* constraint on successful mechanistic explanations is most clearly stated by Levine (in his *Purple Haze: The Puzzle of Consciousness*), who focuses on a mechanistic explanation of why the boiling point of water is 212° at sea level:

> Given a sufficiently rich elaboration of the [chemical composition of water and the behavior of H_2O molecules when their average kinetic energy increases] it is inconceivable that H_2O should not boil at 212°F at sea level. . . .[3]

Since any neural mechanism can be conceived of in the absence of first-person phenomenal reality, it will never be the case that a complete understanding of a proposed reducing mechanism will render it inconceivable that a creature

3. Joseph Levine, *Purple Haze: The Puzzle of Conciousness* (Oxford: Oxford University Press, 2004), 79.

with the relevant neural structure fail to possess a first-person perspective and a capacity for phenomenal consciousness. As Levine put it:

> No matter how rich the neurophysiological story gets, it still seems quite coherent to imagine that all that should be going on without there being anything it's like to undergo the states in question.[4]

Thus, if a reductive explanation of consciousness requires closing the explanatory gap and closing that gap requires positing a mechanism that makes it inconceivable that the higher-level property be instantiated (given the proposed mechanism), then the explanatory gap is unclosable in principle. And assuming that reductive physicalism requires a reductive explanation of exactly the sort excluded by the explanatory gap, it follows that reductive physicalism is a failure.

However, whether subjectivity can be explained depends on what we mean by *explain*. We deny that it can be explained in ways analogous to the brittleness of glass and the boiling point of water at sea level; that is, *we deny that subjectivity is susceptible to a mechanistic explanation* that renders the instantiation of higher-level properties intelligible in terms of lower-level mechanisms. Yet we don't take this to imply that consciousness can't be explained. We think it can be explained, and indeed we've put forward an argument for materialism on the basis of this explanation. Even so we hold that the explanation is nonreductive.

Fundamentality and Nonreductive Explanation

Contrary to reductive physicalists, we take the first-person perspective and phenomenal consciousness as *fundamental*. That there is a first-person perspective and that phenomenal consciousness exists is, for us, indisputable and undeniable. There's absolutely no need to "naturalize" subjectivity and consciousness by reducing them to "scientifically respectable," i.e., purely objective, third person, phenomena. However, we believe that *how* objectively existing, third person observable phenomena such as the wetware and functioning of the human brain should produce such a phenomenon as a singular, *subjective* point of view not only has not yet been explained (contrary to some optimistic reductionists), but that its explanation may lay forever beyond our

4. Levine, *Purple Haze*, 79.

grasp. For it's plausible to believe that we are constitutionally incapable of ever providing an explanation of phenomenal consciousness in terms of neural structures and mechanisms, of saying just how *those* objectively existing elements—neurons and synapses, and networks of them—give rise to phenomenal consciousness and a singular subjective experiencer. If that's right, then reductive explanations of phenomenal consciousness in terms of neural circuitry and the like are bound to fail, in principle.

What we can expect the cognitive and neurosciences to do is to uncover the *mechanisms* and *structures* involved in various *facets* and *features* of phenomenal consciousness, but we should never expect such discoveries to explain either the sheer *existence* of phenomenal consciousness and a first-person perspective or what it is about these mechanisms that give rise to the features of subjectivity they do. While clearly there have been enormous gains and impressive strides over the past few decades when it comes to "explaining consciousness," we must be clear about what, exactly, we're explaining when we claim we're explaining consciousness. What we're doing is uncovering the neural mechanisms and structures implicated in specific facets and features of conscious experience. We can put it, if you like, in terms of uncovering the physical grounds of first-person, subjective experiences, but we're never saying *how these* physical grounds (i.e., mechanisms or structures) are paired with *those* particular phenomenal features of a conscious experience. That is to say, while the cognitive and neurosciences are making great gains in discovering the physical mechanisms that underlie our conscious mental lives, they are not providing experimental data that will close the "explanatory gap," despite what some optimists (practitioners of these sciences included) may claim.

While perhaps it's incumbent upon materialism to provide some kind of explanation of consciousness, we just argued that the kind of explanation required has no reductive implications and so it's not subject to the kind of "logical" explanatory objections LaRock raises to reductive physicalism. It's not subject to such criticisms because the kind of explanation we're interested in doesn't try to provide an explanatory link between consciousness and the physical mechanisms that underlie it that will make it intelligible why specific features of conscious experience are paired with particular mechanisms. In fact, the failure of such an explanatory link is exactly what we'd expect given the fundamental nature of consciousness and subjectivity.

But while a view like ours doesn't face the "logical" objections LaRock raises, it does face a version of the empirical challenge he raises for reductive physicalism. Given the kind of explanatory project we describe above, one which we think materialists can, and should, undertake, we're committed to a kind of pairing thesis: for every feature or aspect of phenomenal consciousness (or, more generally, first-person subjectivity), there's a physical mechanism with which that aspect of consciousness is paired. For example, in our paper we mention the role specialized visual processing areas play in visual perception (e.g., V4 is devoted to color perception and MT to perception of motion). As LaRock makes clear, the best evidence we have indicates that visual processing is distributed throughout many highly specialized visual subsystems, with each subsystem responsible for a different aspect of visual perception. But this gives rise to a binding challenge: how are the various aspects of visual perception—color, motion, shape, etc.—bound together into a single, unified conscious experience of an object with the features represented in the visual experience?[5] Since binding (and the associated unity of consciousness) is an undeniable aspect of our conscious experience, the pairing thesis implies that there is a physical binding mechanism. This is a problem for any view committed to the pairing thesis, because as LaRock argues in some detail, the most common binding hypotheses face seemingly intractable problems (e.g., he argues that the synchronization of neurons fails as a binding mechanism).

For the sake of argument we're willing to grant LaRock's objections to binding by synchronization, but what follows from this? Perhaps that there are aspects of our conscious experience for which there are currently no known mechanisms that account for those aspects. But what are we supposed to conclude from that? That it's likely there is no such mechanism? That seems premature and overly optimistic regarding the explanatory power of current neuroscience (if neuroscience can't currently explain it, then it's likely unexplainable). While neuroscience has seen an impressive amount of explanatory success in the past few decades, there is still a lot of undiscovered territory. Given the current state of the neuro and cognitive sciences, we shouldn't conclude from our present inability to discover the binding mechanisms that it's likely that there is no such binding mechanism. We may expect local failures of attempts to explain the unity of conscious experience, but this does not provide any reason to think that the failure is one of principle (as compared to say the failure of *a priori* functional reductions of consciousness which are failures in principle).

To sum up: there's a problem for materialism only if there is an in principle failure to discover a physical binding mechanism, and for all LaRock has

5. This is the "object feature binding problem" or the problem of explaining "objectual unity." LaRock raises other binding problems as well: "diachronic object unity" and "subject unity."

said that failure reflects the practical limitations of current neuroscientific explanations (or explanatory power) and is not an in principle limitation on neuroscientific explanations.

Conclusion: Materialism and Fundamental Consciousness

Finally, the question of the nature of the experiencer, the nature of the subject of experience, strikes us as a metaphysical question or puzzle and one that is not likely to be answered by any empirical science. Is the subject of experience *physical* or *non*-physical? We of course believe that the subject is physical. Is the subject identical with the organismic system as a whole, of which the brain is a part? At least one of us thinks not, as one of us believes that we are constituted by without being identical with our organism. But even here, this is no more than metaphysical speculation. What we are both agreed on is that there *is* phenomenal consciousness and that there *is* an ineliminable and irreducible first-person perspective to phenomenal consciousness.

Moreover, we don't see why or how dualism offers any advantages in this regard. No version of dualism seems any better situated to explain phenomenal consciousness or a first-person perspective, at providing a suitable explanation of how certain neural features and structures get paired with phenomenal data. In fact, the data LaRock puts forward not only doesn't support the existence of an immaterial soul, it fits just as naturally with certain non-reductive versions of materialism. In fact, since consciousness is explainable in the sense discussed above, and it's *that* type of explanation that supports materialism, not only does dualism fail to have an advantage, the advantage actually lies with materialism.

CHAPTER 15

From Non-Reductive Physicalism to Emergent Subject Dualism: A Rejoinder to Corcoran and Sharpe

Eric LaRock

In my "Neuroscience and the Hard Problem of Consciousness" (hereafter, NHPC, this volume), I argue primarily on neuroscientific grounds that reductive physicalism (RP), as an explanatory methodology, fails to provide theoretically satisfying answers to several target questions surrounding phenomenal consciousness. What is meant by phenomenal consciousness is essentially tied to a subjective individual point of view and not merely to the tincture of qualia; for every experience presupposes an experiencer (see Nagel 2012; Zimmerman 2011). For example, there is something it is like for a subject to feel joy, undergo chronic pain and nausea, touch a velvety surface, taste cinnamon, see a cardinal in flight, and hear Marty Freidman's melodious guitar sound while watching stars fall from the night sky.

Even though Corcoran and Sharpe plunk down a *physicalist promissory note* about phenomenal consciousness in their "Neuroscience and the Human Person," they suspend that note temporarily (in their reply to my NHPC) and "speak as though"[1] they are committed to irreducible phenomenal properties (or qualia). Why? In order to mount (what they take to be) a major challenge to my chapter, a challenge which revolves around the following consideration: even if reductive physicalism fails, there might be a species of physicalism that succeeds, namely, *non-reductive physicalism*.[2] Before addressing Corcoran and

1. See Corcoran and Sharpe's reply to my NHPC, titled "Explaining Consciousness" (hereafter EC, this volume). Unless otherwise stated, all quotations of Corcoran and Sharpe refer to their EC.

2. First, I don't disagree that there are irreducible phenomenal properties. Second, although I do not examine non-reductive physicalism in my NHPC, I will toward the end of this chapter, and I have elsewhere (e.g., see my 2013a).

Sharpe's major challenge, I begin by addressing some of their minor challenges (and/or misunderstandings).

Minor Challenges and Replies

Even though I spend very little time on the usual logically-based "explanatory gap" objections to RP, Corcoran and Sharpe spend considerable time developing a wider discussion of them in their reply to my NHPC—presumably, to point out the inherent limitations of such an *a priori* form of analysis against the backdrop of the inductive practices of neuroscience. This is not worrisome, however, for one could subtract my scant discussion of those logically-based "explanatory gap" objections, and yet it would not weaken the meat of my case one iota. That is because what is significant about my case is the *empirical evidence* I utilize to disconfirm the hypothesis of RP about phenomenal consciousness. Recall, I begin my case by showing that reductive functionalism (of the sort advocated by David Lewis and David Armstrong) fails to explain phenomenal consciousness *on empirical grounds*. For example, Lewis suggests that, under the hypothesis of reductive functionalism, it should be possible to reduce experience to abilities (i.e., functions), such as the ability to *recognize* objects. But recent evidence runs counter to this prediction: for example, subjects with associative agnosia disorder can no longer recognize objects, but can nonetheless visually experience them. David Armstrong also takes a reductive functionalist approach to phenomenal consciousness, in that he seeks to explain phenomenal consciousness in terms of a self-scanning mechanism in the brain (usually dubbed "selective attention" by neuroscientists). However, recent experimental data indicates that a subject's experience can emerge independent of the deployment of the mechanisms of selective attention (for details, see my 2012, and my NHPC, this volume; see also Koch and Tsuchiya 2007; Kosslyn and Koenig 1995; Treisman 2003).

After showing why reductive functionalism fails on empirical grounds, I then focus on a more specific target question related to phenomenal consciousness: *Is objectual unity explainable in neural terms alone?* Corcoran and Sharpe grant my empirically based objections to the binding by neuronal synchrony (BBS) hypothesis ("for the sake of argument"), and then advocate the idea that because neuroscience has shown that an object's distinctive features correlate (or "pair," to use their preferred lingo) with distributed (i.e., geographically separate) areas of the visual cortex, it follows that there is a physical binding mechanism: "Since binding (and the associated unity of consciousness) is an undeniable aspect of our conscious experience, the pairing thesis implies that there is a physical binding mechanism" (see Corcoran and Sharpe's EC, this volume). Notice, Corcoran and Sharpe do *not* actually explain how they were able to infer "that there is a physical binding mechanism" from the observation that an object's distinctive features correlate (or "pair") with distributed (i.e., geographically separate) areas of the visual cortex. Furthermore, they do not actually propose an alternative to the BBS hypothesis. They simply posit (independent of any actual evidence) that there is a physical binding mechanism. Not only does this implicitly beg the question, it also closes off other explanatory possibilities; thus, it is not surprising that Corcoran and Sharpe overlook a *multi-level* explanatory approach to objectual unity. Put rhetorically, why not suppose that a neuronal explanation is likely only part of the story (owing to a growing body of actual evidence) and thus could be *supplemented* with another ("higher") level of explanation, say, a psychological level; and that those two explanatory levels (notwithstanding further explanatory levels) could work mutually to provide a more theoretically satisfying account of objectual unity? Incidentally, the preceding consideration is not simply a logical exercise of making distinctions. I advocate a multi-level explanatory approach to objectual unity elsewhere (e.g., see my 2010a). It is also worth noting that, due to space constraints, I could not have possibly addressed every neuronal hypothesis of objectual unity; so I made the decision to focus on what has become the *dominantly defended* neuronal hypothesis of objectual unity, which is the BBS hypothesis. In fact, after I cite several important neuroscience papers that advocate the BBS hypothesis, I state: "For my purposes here, I focus my discussion on this dominantly proposed mechanism of binding" (see footnote 66 of my NHPC). I have, however, examined other purported neuronal hypotheses of objectual unity and have come to conclude that they, too, run aground due to important disconfirmations (e.g., see my 2006, 2007a, 2007b, 2008a, 2010a). Of course, even if Corcoran and Sharpe concede that we (currently) do not know how to explain objectual unity solely in neuronal terms, they could always plunk down another *physicalist promissory note* (and thus commit themselves to another philosophical stance without any actual evidence).

I then move on to a further target question related to phenomenal consciousness: *Is diachronic object unity explainable in neural terms alone?* After presenting evidence to the contrary,[3] I end the chapter by posing an empirical challenge to Dennett's *heterophenomenology*, a challenge which is based upon

3. For details, see my NHPC (this volume); see also my 2007a, 2008a, 2010a.

the actual (and not merely possible) existence of inverse zombies, subjects that appear to be unconscious *from a third-person point of view*, but are nonetheless phenomenally conscious of what's going on (both internally and externally) while undergoing a surgical procedure (for details, see Mashour and LaRock 2008, LaRock 2010b). What is significant about my case against Dennett's heterophenomenology (and RP in general) is the *empirical evidence* I utilize to disconfirm it.

Finally, the conclusion I draw (from the overall empirical case I present in my NHPC) is fundamentally about the explanatory failures of RP with respect to several target questions surrounding phenomenal consciousness. Accordingly, I do *not* draw the further negative ontological conclusion that *non-reductive* physicalism is false; nor do I draw the further positive ontological conclusion that substance dualism is true (or, to use Corcoran and Sharpe's terminology, that an "immaterial soul" exists, whatever they might mean by that phrase). In my NHPC, I thought it ambitious enough to show that reductive functionalism (of the sorts advocated by David Armstrong, David Lewis, and Daniel Dennett) and neurobiological reductionism (of the sorts advocated by Francis Crick and other recent neuroscientists) fail to provide theoretically satisfying answers to specific target questions surrounding phenomenal consciousness, owing to recent discoveries in neuroscience.[4] What broader lesson can be drawn here? Antireductionists about phenomenal consciousness no longer need to rely upon conceptually based arguments alone, but can build a case against RP that has a significant empirical foundation. In any case, I'm not in an epistemic position to foretell what neuroscience might explain in the future[5]—which is to say, I find Corcoran and Sharpe's slew of promissory notes incompatible with a basic ideal of science: namely, that we should proportion our beliefs to the *currently* available evidence (see also Lycan 2009, 2013). Scientists develop hypotheses against the backdrop of *currently* known

4. In the closing paragraph of my NHPC, I suggest that if the *explanatory methodology* of RP fails, then a natural alternative is a non-reductive approach to phenomenal consciousness. In this context, I merely mentioned the names of three non-reductive approaches that might be worth further examination, such as Varela and Thompson's (2003) neurophenomenological approach, Hasker's (1999) emergent dualist approach (see also LaRock 2010a, 2013a, 2013b; Lowe 2008; Zimmerman 2011), and Lynn Baker's constitution approach (e.g., see Baker 2000, 2001). Because my focus was on providing a neuroscientific appraisal of reductive physicalism in my NHPC, I did not address which of the aforementioned non-reductive approaches is theoretically preferable, but I have elsewhere (see my 2013a, 2013b; see also LaRock and Collins, "Saving Our Souls from Materialism," this volume).

5. Here, I'm not talking about the predictive power of a theory.

empirical data and they seek to confirm or disconfirm those hypotheses (see also Eccles 1993).

Major Challenge: Non-Reductive Physicalism?

Having addressed some of Corcoran and Sharpe's minor challenges, I take their major challenge to revolve around the following consideration: even if reductive physicalism fails, there might be a species of physicalism that succeeds, namely, *non-reductive physicalism* (NRP). While there might be disagreement about how to formulate a theoretically satisfying account of NRP, the view is usually taken to imply that intentional and cognitive properties are reducible; but that phenomenal properties (or qualia) are irreducible to the physical world (see Kim 2005). Advocates of NRP typically maintain that irreducible phenomenal properties *supervene* upon their respective subvenient physical realizers.[6]

While NRP has some merit about the irreducible ontology of phenomenal properties, I think it nonetheless falls short when it comes to certain questions about the unity of experience, such as subject unity (i.e., an account of the singularity intrinsic to every experience and how that singularity relates to the unity of experience across modalities of the brain).[7] Why? Presumably, under the hypothesis of NRP, the neural areas by which various kinds of phenomenal properties are realized correlate (or "pair") with activities in geographically different modalities of a brain. For example, a bee's buzzing *sound* correlates with neuronal activity in the auditory cortex while its yellow *color* correlates with neuronal activity in the visual cortex. Yet despite the spatial segregation of the bee's diverse phenomenal properties across my brain's modalities, I experience the bee as a unified object. Thus, making an appeal to phenomenal properties and their geographically distributed physical realizers (or "pairings") *per se* cannot be the complete story (for details, see my 2013a, 2013b). And it will not help Corcoran and Sharpe to appeal to their material composition view of

6. NRP (of a strong sort) usually implies that mental properties (including irreducible phenomenal properties) *entirely depend on, and are fully determined by, their respective physical processes.* Given some mental property *M* at t2, there is a physical process *P* at t2 that is necessarily sufficient for the instantiation of *M* at t2. The kind of necessity invoked here is typically understood as nomological necessity (see Kim 2000, 2006).

7. I also take issue with NRP's usual causal reductive stance regarding the issue of mental causation and have argued elsewhere that such a stance is unwarranted on evolutionary, logical, and neuroscientific grounds (see my 2013a, 2013b).

persons because the problems of vagueness and inelegance they face are legion (see LaRock and Collins, this volume; also see Unger 2006; Zimmerman 2011).

Scientists change their ontological outlook when the evidence pushes them to do so. Consider, for example, Maxwell and colleagues, who were pushed by the evidence to expand the ontology of physics beyond mere electromagnetic processes to include forces and fields (Chalmers 1995). Similarly, I propose that we expand the ontology of mind beyond the brain and irreducible phenomenal properties (or qualia) to include an irreducible subject, a singular entity in its own right, in order to provide a more elegant account of subject unity. This proposal coheres with the hypothesis of *emergent subject dualism*, or ESD (see my 2013a). According to ESD, once a brain achieves sufficient organization and activity, a subject is generated, holds an adverbial relation to its diverse phenomenal properties, and possesses causal power to influence the structures and functions of its brain. These core theoretical claims of ESD have been elaborated and supported on recent neuroscientific grounds elsewhere (e.g., see my 2010a, 2013a, 2013b).[8]

Due to space constraints, I will now (only very briefly) discuss how ESD provides an elegant fit to the data of experience about subject unity. Under the hypothesis of ESD, diverse phenomenal properties (e.g., seeing the *yellow* color and hearing the *buzzing* sound of a bee) belong to (or inhere in) a subject; and thus whenever a brain generates diverse phenomenal properties, it also generates a subject for the (adverbial) unification of those properties (for details, see LaRock 2010a, 2013a; also Zimmerman 2011). Analytic philosophers, who are also emergent dualists, are not alone on this score. For example, the Nobel prize-winning neuroscientist Sir John Eccles argued for a somewhat similar view decades ago: "the experienced unity comes, not from a neurophysiological synthesis, but from the proposed integrating character of the self-conscious mind" (1993, 362). In other words, on the adverbialist account I favor, when I see a yellow color and hear a buzzing sound, I *undergo* those diverse phenomenal properties as their common subject; and thus I am the phenomenal glue, as it were, that binds what would otherwise be geographically distributed phenomenal properties across my brain's modalities. Put simply, experience (of diverse phenomenal properties) is taken to be a "unitary state" of the subject that is not analyzable in terms of anything "over and above" the subject (see Jackson 1977, 59; see also my 2013a, 2013b; see also

8. For details about its testability in relation to subject-directed neuroplasticity, see my 2013a, 2013b; and about its simplicity, see LaRock and Collins, "Saving Our Souls from Materialism," this volume).

Chisholm 1969; Zimmerman 2010, 2011). The kind of unity discussed above should not be confused with a subject's capacity to recognize a difference between diverse kinds of phenomenal properties. For the very capacity to recognize a difference between diverse kinds of phenomenal properties already presupposes the singularity of the subject. As Dean Zimmerman observes, "If a single thinker can recognize the difference between sounds and colors, this thinker does not enjoy the ability to compare the two simply by having one part that does its seeing and another part that does its hearing, even if these parts are tightly bound together" (2011, 170).

Though I have only scraped the surface of ESD here, a few important theoretical implications follow: (a) an irreducible subject (a singular entity in its own right) makes an explanatory difference to the unity of experience; (b) an irreducible subject increases the combinatorial efficiency of information processing across modalities of its brain; and if (b) holds, then (c) follows: there is an increase in the survival value of any (modally diverse) brain that generates an irreducible subject (for details, see my 2013a, 2013b).

Primarily on empirical grounds, then, I conclude (1) that RP fails miserably to provide theoretically satisfying answers to several foundational target questions surrounding phenomenal consciousness, and (2) that it is theoretically preferable to go from non-reductive physicalism to emergent subject dualism.

REFERENCES

Baker, Lynne. *Persons and Bodies.* Cambridge: Cambridge University Press, 2000.

Baker, Lynne. "Materialism with a Human Face." In *Soul, Body and Survival*, edited by Kevin Corcoran. Ithaca: Cornell University Press, 2001.

Chalmers, David. "Facing Up to the Problem of Consciousness." *Journal of Consciousness Studies* 2 (1995), 200-219.

Chisholm, Roderick. "On the Observability of the Self." *Philosophy and Phenomenological Research* 30 (1969): 7-21.

Hasker, William. *The Emergent Self.* Ithaca: Cornell University Press, 1999.

Jackson, Frank. *Perception.* Cambridge, MA.: MIT Press, 1977.

Kim, Jaegwon. *Physicalism, Or Something Near Enough.* Princeton: Princeton University Press, 2005.

Koch, Christof, and Naotsugu Tsuchiya. "Attention and Consciousness: Two Distinct Brain Processes." *Trends in Cognitive Sciences* 11 (2007), 16-22.

Kosslyn, Stephen, and Olivier Koenig. *Wet Mind: The New Cognitive Neurosciences.* New York: The Free Press, 1995.

LaRock, Eric. "From Biological Naturalism to Emergent Subject Dualism." *Philosophia Christi* 15 (2013a), 97-118.

LaRock, Eric. "Aristotle and Agent-Directed Neuroplasticity." *International Philosophical Quarterly* 53 (2013b), 385-408.

LaRock, Eric. "An Empirical Case against Central State Materialism." *Philosophia Christi* 14 (2012), 409-428.

LaRock, Eric. "Cognition and Consciousness: Kantian Affinities with Contemporary Vision Research." *Kant-Studien* 101 (2010a), 445-464.

LaRock, Eric. "Philosophical Implications of Awareness during General Anesthesia." In *Consciousness, Awareness, and Anesthesia*. Cambridge: Cambridge University Press, 2010b, 233-251.

LaRock, Eric. "Is Consciousness Really a Brain Process?" *International Philosophical Quarterly* 48 (2008), 201-229.

LaRock, Eric. "Disambiguation, Binding, and the Unity of Visual Consciousness." *Theory and Psychology* 17 (2007a), 747-777.

LaRock, Eric. "Intrinsic Perspectives, Object Feature Binding, and Visual Consciousness." *Theory and Psychology* 17 (2007b), 799-809.

LaRock, Eric. "Why Neural Synchrony Fails to Explain the Unity of Visual Consciousness." *Behavior and Philosophy* 34 (2006), 39-58.

Lowe, E.J. *Personal Agency.* Oxford: Oxford University Press, 2008.

Lycan, William. "Giving Dualism Its Due." *Australasian Journal of Philosophy* 87 (2009), 551-563.

Lycan, William. "Is Property Dualism Better Off than Substance Dualism?" *Philosophical Studies* 164 (2013), 533-542.

Mashour, George, and Eric LaRock. "Inverse Zombies, Anesthesia Awareness, and the Hard Problem of Unconsciousness." *Consciousness and Cognition* 17 (2008), 1163-1168.

Nagel, Thomas. *Mind and Cosmos.* Oxford: Oxford University Press, 2012.

Popper, Karl, and John Eccles. *The Self and Its Brain.* London: Routledge, 1993.

Treisman, Anne. "Consciousness and Perceptual Binding." In *The Unity of Consciousness*, edited by Axel Cleeremans. Oxford: Oxford University Press, 2003, 95-113.

Unger, Peter. *All the Power in the World.* Oxford: Oxford University Press, 2006.

Van der Velde, Frank. "Binding and Consciousness from an Intrinsic Perspective." *Theory and Psychology* 17 (2007), 791-797.

Varela, F., and E. Thompson. "Neural Synchrony and the Unity of Mind." In *The Unity of Consciousness*, edited by Axel Cleeremans. Oxford: Oxford University Press, 2003, 266-287.

Zimmerman, Dean. "From Experience to Experiencer." In *The Soul Hypothesis*, edited by M. Baker and Stewart Goetz. London: Continuum Press, 2011, 168-196.

PART 3

Recent Debate in Theology about the Mind-Body Problem

CHAPTER 16

"Multidimensional Monism": A Constructive Theological Proposal for the Nature of Human Nature

Veli-Matti Kärkkäinen

Let me state as a way of introduction something which certainly is obvious but still is worth mentioning: there is currently a bewildering confusion about the nature of human nature not only among philosophers of mind and (those) neuroscientists (who think philosophically!) but also among Christian philosophers and theologians. On the one hand, common intuitions, universal religious teachings, and the mainstream of classical philosophy envision some kind of dualistic[1] account of humanity in which an important distinction is made between the physical and mental. On the other hand, among neuroscientists, philosophers of mind, and a large number of other scientists a monist-physicalist account has gained the upper hand.

When it comes to my own academic field, systematic (or constructive or doctrinal) theology, a couple of general observations are noteworthy. First, beginning from the mid-twentieth century or so, a definite shift has taken place away from traditional dualism towards a highly integrated, mutually conditioned account of the human person as a physical-mental totality. Second, unlike some Christian philosophers and biblical scholars, systematicians, however, have not yet engaged in any significant measure the dynamic interdisciplinary conversation among philosophers of mind, neuroscientists, and others. Indeed, at the moment of this writing I cannot think of one single major presentation of Christian doctrine of humanity written by a systematician which would contain a truly interdisciplinary dialogue.[2] What is most astonishing to me is

1. As is rightly noticed, a concept such as dualism has to be handled with great care and hence we should rather speak of dualisms (in plural).

2. This is of course not to deny the contributions of some systematicians, say Michael

the total omission of this kind of engagement in the recent massive two-volume theological anthropology by David Kelsey of Yale; in a theological discussion of more than one thousand pages, most everything else is investigated but not the contributions of philosophy of mind and brain sciences![3]

So, it is about time for systematic-constructive theologians to provide accounts of the nature of human nature. The plan of this essay is the following: I will first explain what kinds of underlying intuitions and assumptions lie behind my constructive proposal. Thereafter, I will engage in some detail the major contender to dualism(s) and physicalist monism in contemporary philosophy and theology, namely nonreductive physicalism. Although my own proposal owes to its insights, I also find it wanting in the final analysis. The rest of the essay following these two topics will be devoted to explaining and defending the program of "multidimensional monism."

Underlying Assumptions and Convictions

The constructive theological proposal of human nature developed and defended in this essay is funded by a number of convictions which I briefly mention here but do not have space to argue in much detail.[4]

First, I take it for granted that any contemporary theological account of human nature should acknowledge and endorse the current common knowledge of the integral connection between brain events and mental life. Intelligence, emotions, sociality, as well as behavioral patterns such as criminality or altruism can be linked very tightly to the neuronal basis. Notwithstanding complicated philosophical interpretations of neuroscientific results, there is

---

Welker of Heidelberg University, Germany and Niels Henrik Gregersen of Copenhagen University, Denmark who have discussed human nature in a widely interdisciplinary manner. What I am saying is that these contributions have not yet found their way to "normal" systematic theological presentations. In this regard, it is interesting that the two leading international constructive theologians who have published theological "summas," namely Wolfhart Pannenberg and Jürgen Moltmann have completely missed the interdisciplinary conversation about human nature although both of them for decades have interacted in doctrine of creation with natural sciences from cosmology to physics to quantum theory to evolutionary biology.

3. David H. Kelsey, *Eccentric Existence: A Theological Anthropology*, 2 vols. (Louisville: Westminster John Knox, 2009).

4. Detailed argumentation can be found in my *Creation and Humanity: A Constructive Christian Theology for the Pluralistic World*, vol. 3 (Grand Rapids: Eerdmans, 2015), chs. 12 and 13 particularly. The current essay is based on those materials, particularly ch. 12. Eerdmans has kindly granted rights for reproducing portions of the book.

no denying the tight link between the functioning of the brain and human behavior. Perhaps as a surprise to many comes the linkage between observed neural activity and exercise of spiritual and religious activities.[5]

Second, I claim that while the traditional body-soul dualism finds support in biblical terminology and theological tradition, it has been a great gain for theology to come to a new appreciation of the tight mutual relationship between the physical and mental. As Pannenberg notes, in light of current knowledge "we know conscious and self-conscious life only as bodily life . . . bodily functions condition all psychological experience. This is true even of self-consciousness."[6] I do not believe that this shift towards a unified, monistic, and holistic view is a result of an accommodation of theology to the demands of secular philosophy and sciences but rather the move is in alignment with earliest theological intuitions. Important early patristic thinkers defended the psychosomatic unity even when they of course continued distinguishing between body and soul (spirit). It can be argued that the rise in patristic and later Christian theology of body-soul dualism happened because theology capitulated before secular philosophy. Pannenberg goes so far as to claim that "[t]his process illustrates the acceptance by early Christian thinking of ideas that the Hellenistic culture of the age took for granted" and hence "is not an interpretation that has any essential place in Christian anthropology."[7] Consider that Pannenberg himself is not a monist or physicalist but rather represents an integral holistic property-dualist type of view. (For fairness' sake, it has to be added that even with the accommoda-

5. Groundbreaking interdisciplinary work is being done at the Institute for the Bio-Cultural Study of Religion founded by the neuroscientist Patrick McNamara and philosopher of religion Wesley J. Wildman; see the Web site for research and resources: http://www.ibcsr.org/. A massive collection of essays on evolutionary and neurological bases of religion, including neurotheology, as well as related issues, is the three-volume, *Where God and Science Meet: How Brain and Evolutionary Studies Alter Our Understanding of Religion, ed.* Patrick McNamara (Westport, Conn.: Praeger, 2006). (This whole work is available at http://m.friendfeed-media.com/a8cb89b353ba1c5245a32c16d8032aab7bfd0a72). For an insightful critique of neurotheology and neurology of religion, see Warren S. Brown, "The Brain, Religion, and Baseball: Comments on the Potential for a Neurology of Religious Experience," *Where God and Science Meet: How Brain and Evolutionary Studies Alter Our Understanding of Religion*, ed. McNamara, 2:229–44.

6. Wolfhart Pannenberg, *Systematic Theology*, Trans. by Geoffrey W. Bromiley, 3 vols (Grand Rapids: Eerdmans, 1991, 1994, 1998), 2: 181–82. Hereafter, *ST*; see also Joel B. Green, *Body, Soul, and Human Life: The Nature of Humanity in the Bible,* Studies in Theological Interpretation (Grand Rapids: Baker Academic; Carlisle: Paternoster, 2008), 16.

7. Pannenberg, *Systematic Theology* 2: 182; for "The Triumph of Dualism" in early theology, see Raymond Martin and John Barresi, *The Rise and Fall of Soul and Self: An Intellectual History of Personal Identity* (New York: Columbia University Press, 2006), 61–74.

tion, early theologians also critiqued some key aspects of pagan anthropology, including the immortality and preexistence of the soul, as well as its divinity.)

Third, I believe that even the mainstream biblical vision of human nature is not necessarily dualistic but advocates a holistic and integral view in which physicality plays a bigger role than tradition has claimed. By the middle of the twentieth century, or even before, both Old Testament and New Testament scholars had rediscovered the deeply holistic and integral account of humanity in the biblical canon.[8] Understandably this shift towards a (more) monistic conception was resisted by conservatives,[9] if not for other reasons than because it was first advocated by "liberals" (particularly R. Bultmann). Even Paul's view of human nature, once it had been saved from the overly Hellenistic with the acknowledgment of deep Hebrew influences, helped rediscover the category of the physical.[10] As a result, "a number of more recent, extensive studies have led to verdicts similarly supportive of Paul's essential wholism" and "emphasis on embodied life in this world and the next, while combating body-soul dualism."[11] The philosopher Nancey Murphy summarizes accurately the situation in the biblical scholarship on human nature:

> A survey of the literature of theology and biblical studies throughout the twentieth century, then, shows a gradual displacement of a dualistic account of the person, with its correlative emphasis on the afterlife conceived in terms of the immortality of the soul. First, there was the recognition of the holistic character of biblical conceptions of the person, often while still presupposing temporarily separable "parts." Later there developed a holistic *but also physicalist* account of the person, combined with an emphasis on bodily resurrection.[12]

8. Importantly, the Hebrew term *nephes* refers to the whole person rather than to mere "soul." The term occurs no less than about 800 times in the OT and has as its etymology the meaning of "throat" or "gullet"; hence, they denote human need (as a thirsty throat) and physicality; see further, Green, *Body, Soul, and Human Life*, 57. That said, the monist orientation of the OT does not rule out duality or plurality in its presentation of the human being, as even a casual reader notes.

9. An influential advocate of dualism has been the biblical study by the philosopher John W. Cooper, *Body, Soul, and Life Everlasting: Biblical Anthropology and the Monism-Dualism Debate*, 2nd ed. (Grand Rapids: Eerdmans, 2000), followed by other philosopher-theologians and even some conservative biblical scholars.

10. See John A. T. Robinson, *The Body: A Study in Pauline Theology* (London: SCM, 1952), 11.

11. Green, *Body, Soul, and Human Life*, 7–8.

12. Nancey Murphy, *Bodies and Souls, or Spirited Bodies?* (Cambridge: Cambridge University Press, 2006), 10.

To that summary statement, I would like to add an important observation from the pen of the prominent British biblical scholar James D. G. Dunn: "[W]hile Greek thought tended to regard the human being as made up of distinct parts, Hebraic thought saw the human more as a whole person existing on different dimensions. As we might say, it was more characteristically Greek to conceive of the human person 'partitively,' whereas it was more characteristically Hebrew to conceive of the human person 'aspectively.' "[13]

Fourth, it is clear to me that neither can the mental be reduced to the physical base nor can the causal power of the mental on physical be denied. Briefly put: I am against both reductionism and causal closure. It is absolutely fundamental to our concept of actions performed intentionally (as opposed to involuntarily) to assume mental causation.[14] A crucial issue for theologians is to defeat what the British neuropsychologist Donald McKay used to call "nothing-buttery,"[15] namely, the identity theory according to which all mental phenomena, whether intellectual, emotional, or moral, are but brain/neural states. Along with identity theory, I also reject other related theories of the mind-body relationship which eliminate mental causation, including psychophysical parallelism and epiphenomenalism.

Fifth, I believe that while behind traditional dualism(s) there are absolutely important intuitions and convictions which no authentic Christian theology cannot afford to leave behind, those intuitions can be maintained in certain types of monistic views as well. The key intuitions I have in mind include the following: that there is "more" to human life than just the material;[16] that there is something "more" than merely material processes that explain the uniqueness and dignity of human life; that affirming morality and an ethical base calls for "more" than material explanation;[17] and that there is hope for

13. James D. G. Dunn, *The Theology of the Apostle Paul* (Grand Rapids: Eerdmans, 1998), 54, quoted in Murphy, *Bodies and Souls*, 21.

14. My claim is not to deny that at the moment the causal interaction between the bodily and mental is one of the unresolved problems. We simply don't know currently as to "how reasons—our beliefs, desires, purposes, and plans—operate in a world of causes, and to exhibit the role of reasons in the *causal* explanation of human behavior." Fred Dretske, *Explaining Behavior: Reasons in a World of Causes*. Cambridge (Mass.: MIT Press, 1988), x.

15. Donald M. MacKay, *The Clock Work Image*. Downers Grove, (Ill.: InterVarsity Press, 1974), 21. See the now-classic argument in *A Materialist Theory of Mind*, ed. D. M. Armstrong, Rev. (London: Routledge, 1993 [1968]), for the view that mental states are nothing but brain states.

16. Keith Ward, *More Than Matter: Is Matter All We Really Are?* (Grand Rapids: Eerdmans, 2011).

17. E.g., Brandon L. Rickabaugh, "Responding to NT Wright's Rejection of the Soul:

life eternal and therefore, even at the moment of my personal death, I am not forgotten by God.

An appealing route to some prominent Christian philosophers, psychologists, and neuroscientists to negotiate between traditional dualism(s) and current moves towards physicalist monism is nonreductive physicalism. Would that be the way to go in light of the underlying convictions mentioned above? Let us take a closer look at nonreductive physicalism before proceeding on to the constructive proposal.

Nonreductive Physicalism: Promises and Liabilities

Whereas among neuroscientists the reductionist identity theory still seems to be the prominent view,[18] in Anglo-American philosophy of mind, nonreductive physicalism/materialism in its various versions seems to hold the dominant position.[19] The minimalist description of nonreductive physicalism simply is that in its attack on reductionism it considers the mental as an emergent novel property (or capacity or event) that "supervenes," that is, is dependent on the subvenient base, but that cannot be reduced to its base.[20]

How to defeat reductionism[21] is obviously the main agenda of nonreductive physicalists. Terminologically, an important distinction has to be made between "methodological reductionism," that is, "a research strategy of analyzing the thing to be studied into its parts," and "causal reductionism," "the view

A Defense of Substance Dualism," An Unpublished Presentation at the Society of Vineyard Scholars Conference, Minnesota, April 28, 2012.

(http://www.academia.edu/1966881/Responding_to_N._T._Wrights_Rejection_of_the_Soul_A_Defense_of_Substance_Dualism (6/10/2013); so also Moreland and Rae, *Body and Soul*)

18. For an important current defense of type identity, see *New Perspectives on Type Identity: The Mental and the Physical*, eds. Simone Gozzano, and Christopher S. Hill (Cambridge: Cambridge University Press, 2012).

19. John Bickle, "Multiple Realizability," *The Stanford Encyclopedia of Philosophy*, Spring 2013 edition, ed. Edward N. Zalta, http://plato.stanford.edu/archives/spr2013/entries/multiple-realizability/ (6/10/2013).

20. Many other more-or-less synonymous nomenclatures are used, including "[pluralistic] emergent monism," "constitutional monism," "open-system emergence" or "deep physicalism," "dual aspect monism," and "emergent dualism.") Most (but not all) of them are monist in a particular way, namely, *physically/materialistically* (while not denying the reality of the mental, including, in most cases, even religiosity).

21. An important current statement and defense of reductionism is Jaegwon Kim, *Physicalism, or Something Near Enough* (Princeton, N.J.: Princeton University Press, 2005), chap. 4.

that the behavior of the parts of a system . . . is determinative of the behavior of all higher-level entities" (also called "parts on whole" and "bottom up"), as well as "ontological reductionism," which claims that "higher-level entities are 'nothing but the sum of their parts.'" The last two are of course related, but regarding the latter, one needs to make yet another distinction. Whereas ontological reductionism claims that "as one goes up the hierarchy of levels, no new kinds of metaphysical 'ingredients' need to be added to produce higher-level entities from lower," for "reductive materialism," the higher-level processes are not only the function of the lower but they are not even "real." That is accurately called "reductive materialism." That is the target of all nonreductivists.[22]

A key resource for nonreductive physicalism is the use of the theory of emergence.[23] Emergence is the view that new structures, capacities, and processes will come to existence, that these cannot be reduced to the lower level, and that they can exercise a causal influence downwards. This means that the mental, most prominently, consciousness, is derived from the biological/physical basis but is not to be reduced to it and that it may have causal influence on the subvenient base.[24] The concept of "emergence," however, is a complicated matter. As a result, not any form of supervenience necessarily helps defeat the identity theory, as there are also reductionist interpretations thereof.[25] The one needed for an antireductionist program is one with the claim that there are a number of ways a particular supervenient property may be instantiated and that it is context specific (the principle of multiple realizability).[26] In other words, it has to be the case that mental properties (against the co-variation thesis) could change without the change in the base property due to contextual factors.[27] For example, a rich lady giving money to help a

22. See Nancey Murphy and Warren S. Brown, *Did My Neurons Make Me Do It? Philosophical and Neurobiological Perspectives on Moral Responsibility and Free Will* (Oxford: Oxford University Press, 2007), 57.

23. For a now classic essay, see Karl Popper, "Natural Selection and the Emergence of Mind," *Dialectica* 32 (1978): 339–55.

24. See Philip Clayton, *Mind and Emergence: From Quantum to Consciousness* (Oxford: Oxford University Press, 2004), vi.

25. For a reductionist version, see J. Kim, *Physicalism, or Something Near Enough*, 14; see further, Brian P. McLaughlin, "Varieties of Supervenience," in *Supervenience: New Essays*, eds. Elias E. Savellos and Ümit D. Yalçin (Cambridge: Cambridge University Press, 1995), 16–59.

26. The key scholars in the development of the concept have been Hilary Putnam and Jerry Fodor. See "The Nature of Mental States [1967]," in Hilary Putnam, *Mind, Language, and Reality: Philosophical Papers* (Cambridge: Cambridge University Press, 1975), 2:429–40; Jerry Fodor, "Special Sciences (Or: the Disunity of Science as a Working Hypothesis)," *Synthese* 27 (1974): 97–115.

27. See Murphy and Brown, *Did My Neurons Make Me Do It?*, 204.

poor man on the street corner can be a genuine token of generosity, while the same kind of gift by this married lady to her secret lover would not be. In other words, supervenient properties can be multiply realizable and therefore are not identity relations.[28]

If mental causation is to be affirmed, as nonreductive physicalists robustly do, then it means that there needs to be the possibility of the top-down (and whole-part) mental causation. That is not of course to deny bottom-up causation but to claim that that is not the only form. The most persistent critic of nonreductive physicalism, Jaegwon Kim, ironically makes the valid point as he claims that

> the emergentist and nonreductive physicalist are mental realists, and Mental Realism, via Alexander's dictum,[29] entails causal powers for mental properties . . . [as] mental properties, on both positions are irreducible net additions to the world. And this must mean . . . that mental properties bring with them *new causal powers, powers that no underlying physical-biological properties can deliver*. . . . To be real, Alexander has said, is to have causal powers; *to be real, new, and irreducible, therefore, must be to have new, irreducible causal powers.*[30]

Kim rightly concludes that apart from downward causation mental causation is not explicable. Because of this—and two related reasons, namely, rejection of causal overdetermination[31] and causal closure[32]—Kim rejects as incoherent the whole notion of nonreductive physicalism.[33] But doing so, as said,

28. Nancey Murphy, "Nonreductive Physicalism: Philosophical Issues," *Whatever Happened to the Soul? Scientific and Theological Portraits of Human Nature*, ed. Warren S. Brown, Nancey C. Murphy, and H. Newton Malony (Minneapolis: Fortress, 1998), 132–35. Hereafter, *WHS*.

29. That is, to speak of mental property (or any property for that matter) is to speak of causal efficacy (in other words: if mental events do not "do" anything, why speak of them at all!). It was formulated by Samuel Alexander, *Space, Time and Deity*, 2 vols (Toronto: Macmillan, 1920), 2:8.

30. Jaegwon Kim, *Supervenience and Mind: Selected Philosophical Essays* (Cambridge: Cambridge University Press, 1993), 350; see also Jaegwon Kim, "Making Sense of Emergence," *Philosophical Studies* 95 (1999): 5.

31. Jaegown Kim, "Non-Reductivist's Troubles with Mental Causation," *Mental Causation*, ed. John Heil and Alfred Mele (Oxford: Oxford University Press, 1995), 208.

32. Jaegown Kim, "Non-Reductivist's Troubles with Mental Causation," 209.

33. Jaegwon Kim, "The Myth of Nonreductive Materialism," *The Mind-Body Problem: A Guide to the Current Debate*, eds. Richard Warner and Tadeusz Szubka (Oxford: Blackwell,

he clarifies helpfully the main resources available and necessary for the antireductionist program.

Let us now consider the potential of a nonreductive physicalist proposal as set forth by some leading Christian scholars. There are lasting values in nonreductive physicalism that need to be carefully preserved. The foundational key value simply is the importance of physicality.[34] Beyond that, nonreductive physicalism is fairly successful in negotiating between the full embrace of the most recent scientific data concerning human behavior and the essentials of Christian (religious) intuitions. That said, it is not difficult to see the basic philosophical dilemma of nonreductive physicalism and that its claim for *physicality* as the ultimate base and explanation is its Achilles' heel: "say yes, and you seem to end up with a reductive physicalism; say no, and you aren't really a physicalist after all."[35]

In this context one cannot avoid facing the problem common to all physicalists, namely, that of the higher mental capacities, consciousness, including self-consciousness. Wittgenstein's challenges to materialists still call for a response: "The idea of a process in the head, in a completely enclosed space, makes thinking something occult."[36] One way to highlight the distinctive nature of mental life is to speak of "intentionality,"[37] that is, "aboutness," referring to something else. This aboutness-relationship is dramatically different from a causal relationship.[38] It is hard to contest what the philosopher of mind

1994), 242–60; J. Kim, "Non-Reductivist's Troubles," 208. Later in his evolving thinking Kim has come to grant the possibility and even need of a kind of mental causation—as long as the reductionist program is not thereby thwarted. Jaegwon Kim, *Physicalism, or Something Near Enough* (Princeton, N.J.: Princeton University Press, 2005), 9. He calls this view "conditional physical reductionism." *Physicalism, or Something Near Enough*, 5.

34. See Warren S. Brown, "Conclusion: Reconciling Scientific and Biblical Portraits of Human Nature," in *WHS*, 223.

35. Clayton, *Mind and Emergence*, 130. No wonder J. Kim considers nonreductive physicalism internally incoherent. See his *Mind in a Physical World: An Essay on the Mind-Body Problem and Mental Causation* (Cambridge, Mass.: MIT Press/Bradford, 2000).

36. Ludwig Wittgenstein, *Philosophical Grammar*, ed. R. Rhees, trans. A. Kenny (Berkeley and Los Angeles: University of California Press, 1974), §64. Similarly, idem, *Zettel*, ed. G. E. M. Anscombe and G. H. von Wright, trans. G. E. M. Anscombe (Berkeley and Los Angeles: University of California Press, 1967), §605.

37. For the groundbreaking work on intentionality we owe to the phenomenologist philosopher Edmund Husserl; see Spear, Andrew D. "Husserl on Intentionality and Intentional Content." In *Internet Encyclopedia of Philosophy: A Peer-Reviewed Academic Resource*, 2011, http://www.iep.utm.edu/huss-int/ (6/10/2013).

38. Philip Clayton, "Neuroscience, the Person, and God: An Emergentist Account," in *Neuroscience and the Person: Scientific Perspectives on Divine Action*, ed. Robert John Rus-

Jerry Fodor observed: "Nobody has the slightest idea how anything material could be conscious."[39] Titles such as *How Matter Becomes Imagination*[40]—even though written by senior neuroscientists, one of whom is a Nobel Laureate—simply promise too much. No human researcher can know, as Thomas Nagel so famously argued, "what it's like to be a bat."[41]

Furthermore, as surprising as it may sound, it seems to me that from a (natural) scientific perspective it is less than clear that physicalism is the right or even the best choice. It seems to many that current science is moving away from what "physical" (or material) used to mean. The physicist Arnold E. Sikkema notes that a key problem of nonreductive physicalism is "that it elevates the *composition* of entities as though what things are made of is of ultimate concern to a discussion of their ontology." As is well known, in the theory of relativity mass is nothing else but a form of energy (in relation to the speed of light); in quantum mechanics, treating subatomic entities as particles is complementary to regarding them as probability waves; and so forth.[42] The point here is that matter/physicality has become very elusive, virtually "non-material." And even if nonreductive physicalists would respond (as I guess they might) that the point of nonreductive physicalism is not on the composition, I think Sikkema's question calls for an answer.

The bottom line is this: what is matter/physicality? Is it totally different from the mental? If mental events, particularly consciousness, morality, and religiosity are but materially based processes, then the "matter" we speak of has little or nothing in common with our current scientific understanding! It may be, as the Jesuit scientist William Stoeger surmises, that the neuroscientific investigation pushes us to radically reconsider and change what "physical/material" and "non-physical/non-material" may mean.[43] In any case, as is well

---

sell, Nancey Murphy, Theo C. Meyering, and Michael A. Arbib (Vatican City and Berkeley, Calif.: Vatican Observatory and Center for Theology and the Natural Sciences, 1999), 191. Hereafter, *NP*.

39. Jerry Fodor, *Times Literary Supplement*, 3 July 1992, 5–7, quoted in Clayton, *Mind and Emergence*, 112.

40. Subtitle in Gerald Edelman and Giulio Tononi, *A Universe of Consciousness* (New York: Basic Books, 2000).

41. Clayton, *Mind and Emergence*, 111–12.

42. Arnold E. Sikkema, "A Physicist's Reformed Critique of Nonreductive Physicalism and Emergence," *Pro Rege* (June 2005): 23–24 (24).

Available at http://www.dordt.edu/publications/pro_rege/crcpi/119717.pdf (11/18/2012).

43. William R. Stoeger, SJ, "The Mind-Brain Problem, the Laws of Nature, and Constitutive Relationships," in *NP*, 132.

known, "matter" is not a well-defined scientific concept (whereas "mass" and "energy" are).[44] We even need a new vocabulary to speak of the mind and the mental. We probably cannot say the mental is "immaterial" or "non-physical" because that would cut off its deep integration with the brain (any more than we can say the mental is material). Would terms such as "trans-material/-physical" communicate that best?

The main point for my purposes is simply this: perhaps the premature jump onto the physicalist bandwagon by Christian scholars may not be as philosophically and scientifically advantageous as previously thought. There are also some urgent religious and theological reasons for continuing the quest. Beyond the obvious, that from the theological and religious point of view many would find it very difficult to think of ontology merely in terms of a staunch physicalist claim,[45] is the deeper claim that even for nonreductive physicalists who are not atheists, physicalism is only the penultimate option. All theistic traditions consider the Ultimate to be spirit/-ual; certainly that is case for all Abrahamic faiths. In this light, I feel sympathies for the philosopher-theologian Philip Clayton's preference for a "monism" that is not physicalist in itself although it takes physicality most seriously. He argues that we should not assume that the "entities postulated by physics complete the inventory of what exists" while insisting that "[r]eality is ultimately composed of one basic kind of stuff."[46] Rather, "recognizing the physical as one aspect among others will help develop a more fully orbed philosophy of science, recognizing the importance of the different methodologies of inquiry that rightfully play roles in the other scientific disciplines, rather than focusing on what some regard as the highly problematic ontology of the entities of mechanics due to their lying so far beyond imagination."[47] With these cautions and insights in mind, let us try our hand at a tentative constructive proposal for how to best understand the nature of human nature in light of theological, philosophical, and scientific contours.

44. William R. Stoeger, S.J, "The Mind-Brain Problem, the Laws of Nature, and Constitutive Relationships," in *NP*, 133–35; see also Michael Heller, "Adventures of the Concept of Mass and Matter." *Philosophy in Science* 3 (1988): 15–35.

45. Sikkema, "A Physicist's Reformed Critique of Nonreductive Physicalism and Emergence," 22.

46. Clayton, *Mind and Emergence*, 4.

47. Sikkema, "Physicist's Reformed Critique," 26.

"Multidimensional Monism": Towards a Holistic, Pluralistic, and Unified Account of Human Nature

I argue that human beings are "psychosomatic unities rather than dual beings composed of a spiritual soul housed within a material body."[48] Indeed, as Tom Wright reminds us, we should talk about "differentiated unity": "Paul and the other early Christian writers didn't reify their anthropological terms. Though Paul uses his language with remarkable consistency, he nowhere suggests that any of the key terms refers to a particular 'part' of the human being to be played off against any other. Each *denotes* the entire human being, while *connoting* some angle of vision on who that human is and what he or she is called to be."[49]

But isn't a proposal like that still dualist? Or to put it in another way: Are all notions of dualism to be carved out once and for all? I doubt it. It seems to me that all views which take the mental as real (existent) and which also therefore assume its causal efficacy, end up being property dualists of a sort. Certainly nonreductive physicalism is, similarly to emergent monism. It seems to me the Thomistic view, although it has by and large funded substance ontology,[50] can be tweaked to express the best intuitions of property dualism. What also comes to mind here is the physicist Roger Penrose's idea of the mental as "conscious substance"; it speaks of consciousness (which he also dares to call "soul") in a way that clearly belongs under property dualism.[51] Somewhat similarly, the philosopher of mind David Chalmers's idea of the "information states" in terms of "the double-aspect principle" which is based on the "observation that there is a direct isomorphism between certain phys-

48. John Polkinghorne, "Anthropology in an Evolutionary Context," in *God and Human Dignity*, eds. R. K. Soulen and L. Woodhead (Grand Rapids: Eerdmans, 2006), 93. Hereafter *GHD*.

49. N. T. Wright, "Mind, Spirit, Soul and Body: All for One and One for All; Reflections on Paul's Anthropology in his Complex Contexts," A paper presented at Society of Christian Philosophers Eastern Meeting (March 18, 2011); available at http://www.ntwrightpage.com/Wright_SCP_MindSpiritSoulBody.htm (11/26/2013).

50. Just consider this statement from *Summa Contra Gentiles* 2.69.2: "body and soul are not two actually existing substances; rather, the two of them together constitute one actually existing substance." Thomas Aquinas, *Summa Contra Gentiles*, eds. Joseph Kenny, O.P., various translators (New York: Hanover House, 1955–1957); available at http://dhspriory.org/thomas/ContraGentiles.htm.

51. Roger Penrose, *The Emperor's New Mind: Concerning Computers, Minds, and the Laws of Physics* (New York: Penguin Books, 1989)

ically embodied information spaces and certain *phenomenal* (or experiential) information spaces"[52] represents property dualism of some sort.[53]

In systematic theology, Moltmann's vision of "a *perichoretic* relationship of mutual interpenetration and differentiated unity"[54] and Pannenberg's "personal unity of body and soul"[55] speak the same language. The ethicist Niebuhr's associating the "self" with body but being reluctant to reduce self to the bodily reflects the same intuitions.[56] If I understand correctly "emergent dualism," it argues that once the mental emerges, it becomes a property on its own.[57] With all its deviations from classical Christian tradition, American process philosophy's monistic dipolarism represents yet another form of property dualism.[58] In sum: for every nonreductionist, the distinction, yet not separation, between the physical and mental is unavoidable in philosophical, theological, and scientific discussion.

Furthermore, I argue that the reality of mental life cannot be had without a (strong) theory of emergence, as explained above. It not only saves the mental but also helps establish its causal efficacy. This "radical kind of emergence"[59] holds robustly to the mind's downwards and whole-part causation. Strong emergence "is consistent with the neuroscientific data and the data with the constraints on brain functioning. At the same time, it has the merit

52. David J. Chalmers, "Facing Up to the Problem of Consciousness," *Journal of Consciousness Studies* 2, no. 3 (1995): 200–219; http://consc.net/papers/facing.html (1/24/2013).

53. David J. Chalmers, *The Conscious Mind: In Search of a Fundamental Theory* (New York: Oxford University Press, 1996), 305, cited in Ian Barbour, "Neuroscience, Artificial Intelligence, Human Nature," *Zygon* 34 no. 3 (Summer, 1999): 274. In response to Chalmers's proposal, see the rejoinders in *Explaining Consciousness: The Hard Problem*, ed. Jonathan Shear (Cambridge: A Bradford Book/MIT Press, 1999).

54. Jürgen Moltmann, *God in Creation: A New Theology of Creation and the Spirit of God*, trans. Margaret Kohl (Minneapolis: Fortress, 1993), 258–60 (259); he also speaks of the unity between body and soul in terms of covenant (260).

55. Main heading in Pannenberg, *ST* 2:181.

56. See Reinhold Niebuhr, *The Self and the Dramas of History* (New York: Scribner's, 1955), 26.

57. See William Hasker, *The Emergent Self* (Ithaca, N.Y.: Cornell University Press, 1999). Cf. the "integrative dualism" of Charles Taliaferro. See his *Consciousness and the Mind of God* (Cambridge: Cambridge University Press, 1994).

58. See further, Charles Hartshorne, "The Compound Individual," *Philosophical Essays for Alfred North Whitehead*, ed. F. S. C. Northrop (New York: Russell & Russell, 1967), 193–220; for a short discussion, see Barbour, "Neuroscience, Artificial Intelligence, Human Nature," 275–80.

59. Robert Van Gulick, "Reduction, Emergence and Other Recent Options on the Mind/Body Problem: A Philosophical Overview," *Journal of Consciousness Studies* 8, no. 1 (2001): 1–34.

of conceiving of mental activity in terms of mental causation, which accords well with our own experience of mental agency."[60] A good example here is how to best speak of human "personhood"; it can never be a matter of merely analyzing and investigating biological and physical processes. The physical explanation never captures "me," the person, *qua* person, but rather as an object of study.[61]

With the tight, in many ways indistinguishable, interdependency and communion between the physical and mental in mind, the British physicist-priest Polkinghorne suggests "dual-aspect" monism as a fitting concept to describe the holistic account of human nature. The emphasis on *monism* indicates that the classical metaphysical options of materialism, idealism, and Cartesian dualism are unsatisfactory in light of the current multilayered, complex, and dynamic understanding of reality, including human nature. Dual-aspect monism "acknowledge[s] the fundamental distinction between experience of the material and experience of the mental but which would neither impose on reality a sharp division into two unconnected kinds of substance nor deny the psychosomatic unity of human beings." A useful way for him to illustrate the nature of dual-aspect monism is quantum theory's idea of complementarity (superposition principle), which allows for two different/distinct states simultaneously. The main point about the *dual-aspect* nature is to argue that "there will be entities, such as stones, whose nature is located wholly at the material pole, and other entities, such as ourselves, who are 'amphibians,' participating in both kinds of polar experience," namely, mental and material.[62] Polkinghorne also reminds us of the obvious difference between the material and noetic/mental: whereas the former is "a world of process, characterized by temporality and becoming," the latter is "everlasting, in the sense that such truths just *are* and do not evolve." These two "worlds," however, are "complementary aspects of a larger created reality" and hence illustrate the duality that goes beyond material versus mental: "it must also embrace becoming/being and everlasting/temporal." Humanity belongs to both, and therefore, "a fully integrated metaphysics" is needed in which "the multiplicity of experience leads us to an account of considerable richness and subtlety."[63] The potential liability of the dual-aspect monism is that it may make the mental less than real

60. Clayton, *Mind and Emergence*, 139.

61. For comments, see the section titled "Person-Based Explanations and the Social Sciences" in Clayton, *Mind and Emergence*, 144–48.

62. John Polkinghorne, *Faith, Science and Understanding* (New Haven, Conn.: Yale University Press, 2000), 95–97 (95, 97).

63. Polkinghorne, *Faith, Science and Understanding*, 98.

and merely a matter of perspective or experience.[64] The dual-aspect monist, however, doesn't have to be liable to this weakness.

That is not yet the whole story. Both the basic intuition of the undifferentiated psychosomatic unity and dual-aspect monism imply more, as Clayton puts it: "We need multiple layers of explanatory accounts *because* the human person is a physical, biological, psychological, and (I believe also) spiritual reality, and because these aspects of its reality, though interdependent, are not mutually reducible." The term "ontological pluralism" may best describe this approach.[65] Moltmann's creative nomenclatures "spirit-body," "spirit-*Gestalt*," "spirit-soul," as complementary metaphors, echo this.[66] The German systematician Michael Welker warns us of the reductionism with regard to fixating on one particular aspect, either physicalist or mentalist. Whereas scientists fear the latter, humanists tend to fear the former. "There are simply too many anthropological insights and burning questions in social and cultural studies and in the natural sciences that cannot be hosted by this model." Not only the sciences but also biblical theology point to multidimensionality.[67] Prophetically, one may want to say, already decades ago in Paul Tillich's theology, multidimensionality came to the fore—the inorganic, organic, psychic, and spiritual as the fundamental dimensions of the human.[68] Similarly, the practical theologian Don S. Browning has for years developed a robust theology of the multidimensionality of human nature (with a view to discerning moral goods and values).[69]

Is my proposal then something similar to "neutral monism"?[70] Not only because that nomenclature carries a philosophical history that I do not want to identify myself with but also because in the final analysis it leaves so much

64. This is clearly the case in Max Velmans, "Making Sense of Causal Interactions between Consciousness and Brain," *Journal of Consciousness Studies* 9, no. 11 (2002): 75.

65. Clayton, *Mind and Emergence*, 148.

66. Moltmann, *God in Creation*, 262–64.

67. Michael Welker, "Theological Anthropology versus Anthropological Reductionism," in *GHD*, 319; so also Barbour, "Neuroscience, Artificial Intelligence, and Human Nature."

68. Paul Tillich, *Systematic Theology* (Chicago: University Press of Chicago, 1951), 3:22–23. Hereafter, *ST.*

69. D. Browning [his *A Fundamental Practical Theology* (Minneapolis: Fortress, 1991), 94–109, 139–70] lists the dimensions into which there is no need to go in detail here. For a short statement, see his "Human Dignity, Human Complexity, and Human Goods." In *GHD*, 299–316.

70. For a useful discussion with sources, see Leopold Stubenberg, "Neutral Monism," in *The Stanford Encyclopedia of Philosophy* (Spring 2010 edition), ed. Edward N. Zalta; http://plato.stanford.edu/archives/spr2010/entries/neutral-monism/ (6/10/2013).

unexplained (such as, how do we then have the multiplicity of features and properties we have?), I find Clayton's "emergentist monism"[71] quite a comfortable label. It may also be named "property pluralism."[72] Ted Peters's "emergent holism" would also fit the bill.[73]

But why not physical monism? Above I have expressed my reservations about nonreductive physicalism and will not repeat them here. While I greatly appreciate Jaegwon Kim's honesty when, as a staunch physicalist, he admits, "Physicalism is not the whole truth, but it is the truth near enough,"[74] I also think any authentic physicalism ultimately leads to "ontological physicalism," according to which all there is, is physical[75]—and that I do not take as a credible option. Unlike some theistic naturalists (W. Wildman, among others), I am convinced that only *non*theistic materialist naturalism can stay content with physicalism all the way. The reason is simply this: strictly speaking, ontological physicalism can only be penultimate for a theist. Hence, it seems to me that multidimensional monism, as argued in this project, fits better the key belief in Christian faith (and I guess, other theisms as well) of the complex unity of the finite world as God's creation. While exhibiting various properties as a result of rich creative divine work, the notion of the "unity of nature," as distinct from the infinity of the Creator God (who is Spirit), tells us all creatures share a common nature (however complex and multidimensional that may be).[76]

More precisely: What does theology have at stake in this debate on ontology? Clayton rightly notes that "[i]f one holds that all mental phenomena are only expressions of physical causes or are themselves, at root, physical events, then one has (at least tacitly) advanced a theory of the human person that is pervasively physical. It then becomes extremely unclear (to put it gently) why, *from the perspective of one's own theory of the human person*, a God would have to be introduced at all (except perhaps as a useful fiction)."[77] Now, that does not of course mean that a Christian physicalist couldn't introduce God. But the point is that a truly physical *anthropological* account does not make

71. That is also the view of Arthur Peacocke, "The Sound of Sheer Silence: How does God Communicate with Humanity," in *NP*, 219.

72. Clayton, Philip Clayton, "Neuroscience, the Person, and God: An Emergentist Account," in *NP*, 212; Roger W. Sperry means something similar in his *Science and Moral Priority: Merging Mind, Brain, and Human Values* (New York: Columbia University Press, 1983).

73. T. Peters, Ted Peters,. "Resurrection of the Very Embodied Soul?" in *NP*, 305.

74. J. Kim, *Physicalism, or Something Near Enough*, 6.

75. J. Kim, *Physicalism, or Something Near Enough*, 150.

76. See also Clayton, "Neuroscience, the Person, and God," 209–10.

77. Clayton, "Neuroscience, the Person, and God," 204.

it any easier than any other version of human nature; God has to be introduced "from outside," after all. Clayton lays out the options well: "If a theologian espouses physicalism, she may be forging an alliance with the majority worldview within the neurosciences, but she may also be giving up the most interesting rapprochement between theology and the sciences of the person just as she approaches that debate's most decisive issue." (Similarly, of course, traditional dualism may easily stall the dialogue with sciences.[78]) Perhaps, then, even in terms of dialogue (although theological convictions can never be primarily based on their usefulness), the best way for theology is to insist on the necessity but insufficiency of physical explanation.

When viewed from a historical perspective, not only the *opening* but also the full endorsement of nonmaterialist, in other words, idealist ontology has been the dominant position among Christians and other theists (both mono- and polytheists). The late American Reformed theologian Paul K. Jewett expresses succinctly this sentiment: "To be materially conditioned as conscious selves is not to be materially constituted as such."[79] Not only idealist philosophers such as Kant, Fichte, Hegel, Schelling, and numerous others,[80] but virtually all such thinkers from antiquity to recent times have been idealists of a sort; similarly most cultures in the Global South, particularly in Africa;[81] so also are the *advaita* (nondualistic) schools of Indian philosophy); and so forth. This suggestive listing alone would justify keeping the door open to nonphysicalist monism. It seems to me that Christian theology would do well to be cautious in going full-blown into physicalism because "we are in great danger of phrasing the discussion in such a way that the deepest and most significant issues of human existence simply never appear on the screen."[82]

The British philosopher-theologian Keith Ward has recently suggested another version of dual-aspect theory that he names "dual-aspect idealism" and situates between Cartesian dualism and physicalisms of all sorts (while

78. Clayton, "Neuroscience, the Person, and God," 204.

79. Paul King Jewett, *Who We Are: Our Dignity as Human; A Neo-Evangelical Theology* (Grand Rapids: Eerdmans, 1996), 9 (italics removed).

80. For an important discussion from the perspective of anthropology, see Martin and Barresi, *Rise and Fall of Soul and Self*, 185–90.

81. See Joe M. Kapolyo, *The Human Condition: Christian Perspectives through African Eye* (Downers Grove, Ill.: InterVarsity Press, 2005); John S. Mbiti, *Concepts of God in Africa*, 2nd ed. (Nairobi, Kenya: Acton Publishers, 2012 [1970]).

82. Philip Hefner, "Imago Dei: The Possibility and Necessity of the Human Person," in *The Human Person in Science and Theology*, ed. Niels Henrik Gregersen, Willem B. Drees, and Ulf Görman (Edinburgh: T. & T. Clark, 2000), 81.

taking physicalism very seriously). A student of Gilbert Ryle, who coined the term "ghost in the machine" ridiculing Descartes's dualism and turn to the inner self, Ward rightly contends that because "mind and consciousness are different from, something over and above, molecules and matter . . . they are not at all ghostly."[83] Indeed, he reminds us how radically different idealism is from the physicalism/materialism of contemporary naturalism, in its claim that "the material world . . . exists as an environment created by a primordial mind in which finite minds can exist in mutual self-expression and interaction. . . . It totally reverses the modern myth that minds are by-products of a purely material evolutionary process, completely determined by physical events in their bodies and brains."[84] At the same time, he also reminds us how vastly different contemporary materialism is through the lens of force fields, quantum theory, and string theory.[85] Now, as mentioned, Ward is not drawn to dualism *per se*; instead, he represents a property dualism of a sort.

What process philosophy is calling the "inner" life of the physical, Polkinghorne names dual-aspect monism, and the Oxford philosopher Horace Romano Harré, dual-side theories (of monism), all point in the same direction. While not idealist thinkers *per se*, they do think that even "material" processes somehow are not completely void of some kind of teleology and that the universe is more like an organism rather than a machine.[86] Ward refers to the human embryo: as much as current science eschews any notions of vitalism or (Aristotelian) teleology, we expect it to become an adult person, a highly complicated obviously purposeful process.[87]

The minimalist statement about human nature, going back to the beginning of this section, is then psychosomatic pluralistic unity. The nomenclature "pluralistic unity" also points to the need to dare to "confuse" and go beyond established categories (while holding to the best insights of each) such as idealism, physicalism, and monism.[88] Multidimensional monism is one such emerging proposal for continuing discussion and critique. With the shift away from traditional substance dualism (notwithstanding property dualism of some sort), the question arises whether to continue using the term *soul* at all.

83. K. Ward, *More Than Matter*, 10.
84. K. Ward, *More Than Matter*, 57.
85. K. Ward, *More Than Matter*, chap. 2.
86. K. Ward, *More Than Matter*, 81–83 (81).
87. K. Ward, *More Than Matter*, 83–84 (84).
88. See K. Ward, *More Than Matter*, 102–3.

Among the current advocates of nondualist accounts of human nature, including Christian nonreductive physicalists, the term *soul* has become a virtual anathema. By implication, it also happens often that all uses of that term, even if it is not used in the substance dualistic context, are deemed suspicious. While that attitude is understandable, constructive theologians should also exercise some critical faculties here. I do not consider it wise, let alone necessary, to leave behind the ancient term of *soul*, even if traditional dualism is let go. The reasons to continue using the term *soul* are the following: First, similarly to so many other terms whose meaning has changed, the theologians' task is to help the faithful to grasp its redefinition. Just consider the term *creation*. As much as its meaning has changed after the embrace by theology of the contemporary natural sciences' view of the evolvement of the cosmos, its deepest intuitions have stayed intact. (That said, theologians also must be careful not to change the term's meaning at their own wish as often happened in classical liberalism when, say, the whole possibility of Jesus' bodily resurrection was categorically denied.) Second, the term *soul* is so widely and frequently used in the biblical canon—and consequently, everywhere in Christian tradition—that its dismissal seems to be totally unfounded and counterproductive as it may cause the rejection of the proposal itself without further investigation. Third, there is also the interfaith consideration: although different religious traditions may mean different things when using the term, the cancellation in Christian tradition would not only look awkward and confusing to others but also seriously hinder dialogue. Fourth, blaming the use of *soul* (because of its close connection with substance dualism) for all kinds of ills in Christian life, say an anti-body attitude or isolationist spirituality or escapist eschatology, misses the main point, which is that most any conception of human nature may foster negative or positive spiritualities or orientations of religious life (just differently).

The late American Reformed theologian Ray S. Anderson offers useful guidelines for the systematic use of the term *soul*. Although my own constructive proposal of human nature does not exactly match his, these guidelines serve well regarding the term. First, *soul* does not denote a "substance or entity residing in the body" but rather the "whole person, especially the inner core of human personal life as created and upheld by God" (to which should be added that no less are body and other aspects of the multidimensional human being also upheld by God). Second, the terms *body*, *soul*, and *spirit* are not analytic distinctions but rather functional and overlapping with each other. Third, even though Christians have a firm hope for life eternal in the resurrected body as the gift of God, soul—no more than anything else in the human being—is not immortal by nature.[89] Fourth, as a result, rather than saying that the human person "has a soul," it is better to say that the "person is soul."[90]

Regardless of the terminological choice, all deviations from traditional dualism face the important questions of how to speak of an afterlife and continuation of personal identity. Although full discussion belongs to Christian eschatology, short notes are in order here.

So, how to think of afterlife in the post-Cartesian-dualism world? In other words, does it mean that leaving behind traditional talk about the soul and its disembodied existence means leaving behind the idea of life everlasting? No, it does not. Christian tradition never affirmed the immortality of the soul (as in Platonic philosophy) nor that only one part of the human person will be saved for eternity. In fact, in early theology, notwithstanding terminological (and at times, material) inconsistency, the divinity of the soul and, hence, its intrinsic capacity to survive beyond death was rightly rejected and replaced by belief in eternal life as the gift of God.[91] Furthermore, the hope for the resurrection was established for the whole person, not only for the soul.[92]

What about the continuity of personal identity? This has to be looked at from two complementary perspectives. Theologically speaking, guaranteeing the identity is the task of God, not ours.[93] Scientifically and philosophically speaking, identity is a task belonging to the human person, lasting all of one's life, embedded in growth and development in all areas, including personal development and social context. Embodied memory serves here an important role.[94] Whereas in this life, there is always the form of a timely sequence with its broken moments, when God's eternity comes to swallow the finite life, that "will represent the *totality* of our earthly existence."[95]

Polkinghorne correctly notes that in itself the soul's "role as the carrier of human identity is almost as problematic within life as it is beyond death." The continuity cannot be a matter of material continuity since atoms are in

89. Ray Anderson, *On Being Human* (Pasadena: Fuller Seminary Press, 1982), 182–83 (182). See Murray J. Harris, *Raised Immortal: Resurrection and Immortality in the New Testament* (Grand Rapids: Eerdmans, 1983), 237.

90. Anderson, *On Being Human*, 186.

91. Pannenberg, *ST* 3:571.

92. See T. Peters, "Resurrection of the Very Embodied Soul?" 322–25.

93. T. Peters, "Resurrection of the Very Embodied Soul?" 316.

94. Pannenberg, *ST* 3:562; for the importance of memory, see Augustine, *Confessions*, 10.17.

95. Pannenberg, *ST* 3:561; see also T. Peters, "Resurrection of the Very Embodied Soul?," 324.

constant flux through wear and tear. Perhaps the best way to speak of the continuity of identity is in terms of "the almost infinitely complex, information-bearing pattern in which the matter of the body is organized at any one time. This surely is the meaning of the soul."[96] Based on the foundational Christian teaching of the human being as the image of God, we have to say that "[w]hat gives us an identity that does not die is not our nature, but a personal relationship with God."[97] Embodied, the soul does not carry in itself the powers of natural immortality. "As far as science can tell the story, the pattern that is a person will dissolve with that person's death and decay."[98] This proposal seems to correspond to contemporary scientific understandings of information or the way complex systems could be understood—and all living beings are systems of some kind.[99] Aquinas's hylomorphic account of human nature is also based on these intuitions.

Now, seen from the theological point of view, this does not, however, mean that therefore when the person dies, that is all there is. Utilizing the concept of information, it can be stated that what the older soul theory rightly intuited was that "the faithful God will remember the pattern that is me and re-embody it in the eschatological act of resurrection." I couldn't agree more with Polkinghorne, who continues: "In making this assertion, I want to affirm the intrinsically embodied character of human being, without supposing that the flesh and blood of this world represents the only possible form that embodiment might take."[100] While I understand why Christian nonreductive physicalists—with justification—underline the importance of death's finality to combat the obvious misconception in which the soul were to possess natural powers of immortality and its independence, I also find the "gap" theory—that is, between my personal death and the final resurrection there is "nothing of me"—problematic from the systematic theological point of view. Not that I have any doubts whatsoever concerning the capacity of the Creator to re-create *ex nihilo* the resurrected per-

96. Polkinghorne, "Anthropology in an Evolutionary Context," 98; see also his "Eschatology: Some Questions and Some Insights from Science," in *The End of the World and the Ends of God: Science and Theology on Eschatology*, ed. Michael Welker and John Polkinghorne (Harrisburg, Pa.: Trinity Press International, 2000), 38–41.

97. John Zizioulas, "The Doctrine of the Holy Trinity: The Significance of the Cappadocian Contribution," in *The Trinity Today*, ed. Christoph Schwöbel (Edinburgh: T. & T. Clark, 1996), 58.

98. Polkinghorne, "Anthropology in an Evolutionary Context," 99.

99. John Polkinghorne, *The God of Hope and the End of the World* (New Haven, Conn./London: Yale University Press, 2002), chap. 9.

100. Polkinghorne, "Anthropology in an Evolutionary Context," 99–100.

son who has faced physical death (that belief is no more difficult than believing that in the first place the person was given the gift of life). Nor do I think that positing a "soul" is needed to guarantee continuity between this life and the life to come, because, simply put, making the soul the locus of continuity doesn't really explain much in the first place! My reservations lie elsewhere, namely, in the complex and mutually conditioned continuity vs. discontinuity relationship between life on Earth and life in the resurrected body as well as between my own personal eternal destiny vs. that of the whole cosmos. If the gap theory is followed, both of these themes, crucial to a systematic theological negotiation of eschatological consummation, may be frustrated.

In Lieu of Conclusions: Remaining Tasks and Questions

Calling this short writing an "essay" has been intentional. Its etymological roots (in Latin and old French) go back to ideas of "attempt," "trial," or "testing." These terms accurately express my intention here. I have attempted tentatively to imagine a credible systematic/constructive theological account of the nature of human nature in critical and sympathetic dialogue with neurosciences, philosophy of mind, and the best of theological traditions, past and current. Even when distinguishing my proposal from others, I am not thereby denying deep indebtedness to their insights.

A suggestive, tentative *essai* does not lead easily into hardcore conclusions! I would rather like to highlight some pertinent tasks for continuing collaboration:

The question of the biblical teaching on human nature is still without final clarification. While I feel sympathetic to some biblical scholars' view that in the first place the Bible is not seeking to instruct us in anthropology, I also believe that we need more work in clarifying particularly the meaning (to contemporary theology) of the apparent "phenomenological" dualism—or dualist rhetoric—of the Bible, particularly of the New Testament. Is it merely a matter of an ancient way of speaking?

Having mentioned that my own discipline, namely systematic (doctrinal) theology, is a late-comer to the kind of interdisciplinary conversation in theological anthropology common in some other doctrinal loci, particularly the doctrine of creation, I wonder, what is the reason for it? Is it because there is a default assumption that these kinds of questions of theological anthropology are best handled in the philosophy department? Or is there unwillingness among the systematicians to seek for collaboration?

Concerning the nature of monism I am suggesting, namely neither strictly speaking physicalist nor (necessarily, at least penultimately) idealist, I am looking forward to much interdisciplinary investigation concerning the meaning of those very concepts, namely "matter" and "mental." What if—as looks probable in light of where the natural sciences' accounts of the cosmos are going—the divide between the physical and mental becomes obsolete (at least in some sense); would that re-orient the theological talk about the nature of human nature? We also need continuing reflection on how the "mental" posited of humanity may be related to the "mental" in the whole cosmos.

BIBLIOGRAPHY

Alexander, Samuel. *Space, Time and Deity.* 2 vols. Toronto: Macmillan, 1920.

Anderson, Ray. *On Being Human.* Pasadena: Fuller Seminary Press, 1982.

Aquinas, Thomas. *Summa Contra Gentiles.* Edited by Joseph Kenny, O.P., various translators. New York: Hanover House, 1955–1957. http://dhspriory.org/thomas/ContraGentiles.htm.

Armstrong, D. M. *A Materialist Theory of Mind.* Rev. ed. London: Routledge, 1993 [1968].

Barbour, Ian. "Neuroscience, Artificial Intelligence, Human Nature." *Zygon* 34, no. 3 (Summer, 1999): 361–98.

Bickle, John. "Multiple Realizability." In *The Stanford Encyclopedia of Philosophy.* Spring 2013 edition. Edited by Edward N. Zalta. http://plato.stanford.edu/archives/spr2013/entries/multiple-realizability/ (6/10/2013).

Brown, Warren S. "Conclusion: Reconciling Scientific and Biblical Portraits of Human Nature." In *Whatever Happened to the Soul? Scientific and Theological Portraits of Human Nature,* edited by Warren S. Brown, Nancey C. Murphy, and H. Newton Malony, 213–28. Minneapolis: Fortress, 1998.

Browning, Don S. *A Fundamental Practical Theology.* Minneapolis: Fortress, 1991.

Chalmers, David J. "Facing Up to the Problem of Consciousness." *Journal of Consciousness Studies* 2, no. 3 (1995): 200–219. http://consc.net/papers/facing.html (1/24/2013).

———. *The Conscious Mind: In Search of a Fundamental Theory.* New York: Oxford University Press, 1996.

Clayton, Philip. "Neuroscience, the Person, and God: An Emergentist Account." In *Neuroscience and the Person: Scientific Perspectives on Divine Action,* edited by Robert John Russell, Nancey Murphy, Theo C. Meyering, and Michael A. Arbib, 181–214. Vatican City and Berkeley, Calif.: Vatican Observatory and Center for Theology and the Natural Sciences, 1999.

———. *Mind and Emergence: From Quantum to Consciousness.* Oxford: Oxford University Press, 2004.

Cooper, John W. *Body, Soul, and Life Everlasting: Biblical Anthropology and the Monism-Dualism Debate*. 2nd ed. Grand Rapids: Eerdmans, 2000.

Dretske, Fred. *Explaining Behavior: Reasons in a World of Causes*. Cambridge, Mass.: MIT Press, 1988.

Dunn, James D. G. *The Theology of the Apostle Paul*. Grand Rapids: Eerdmans, 1998.

Edelman, Gerald, and Giulio Tononi. *A Universe of Consciousness*. New York: Basic Books, 2000.

Fodor, Jerry. "Special Sciences (Or: the Disunity of Science as a Working Hypothesis)." *Syntheses* 27 (1974): 97–115.

Gozzano, Simone, and Christopher S. Hill, eds. *New Perspectives on Type Identity: The Mental and the Physical*. Cambridge: Cambridge University Press, 2012.

Green, Joel B. *Body, Soul, and Human Life: The Nature of Humanity in the Bible*. Studies in Theological Interpretation. Grand Rapids: Baker Academic; Carlisle: Paternoster, 2008.

Gulick, Robert Van. "Reduction, Emergence and Other Recent Options on the Mind/Body Problem: A Philosophical Overview." *Journal of Consciousness Studies* 8, no. 1 (2001): 1–34.

Harris, Murray J. *Raised Immortal: Resurrection and Immortality in the New Testament*. Grand Rapids: Eerdmans, 1983.

Hartshorne, Charles. "The Compound Individual." In *Philosophical Essays for Alfred North Whitehead*, edited by F. S. C. Northrop. New York: Russell & Russell, 1967.

Hasker, William. *The Emergent Self*. Ithaca, N.Y.: Cornell University Press, 1999.

Hefner, Philip. "Imago Dei: The Possibility and Necessity of the Human Person." In *The Human Person in Science and Theology*, edited by Niels Henrik Gregersen, Willem B. Drees, and Ulf Görman, 73–94. Edinburgh: T. & T. Clark, 2000.

Heller, Michael. "Adventures of the Concept of Mass and Matter." *Philosophy in Science* 3 (1988): 15–35.

Jewett, Paul King, with Marguerite Shuster. *Who We Are: Our Dignity as Human; A Neo-Evangelical Theology*. Grand Rapids: Eerdmans, 1996.

Kapolyo, Joe M. *The Human Condition: Christian Perspectives through African Eyes*. Downers Grove, Ill.: InterVarsity Press, 2005.

Kim, Jaegwon. *Physicalism, or Something Near Enough*. Princeton, N.J.: Princeton University Press, 2005.

———. *Supervenience and Mind: Selected Philosophical Essays*. Cambridge: Cambridge University Press, 1993.

———. "Making Sense of Emergence." *Philosophical Studies* 95 (1999): 3–36.

———. "The Non-Reductivist's Troubles with Mental Causation." In *Mental Causation*, edited by John Heil and Alfred Mele, 189–210. Oxford: Oxford University Press, 1995.

———. "The Myth of Nonreductive Materialism." In *The Mind-Body Problem: A Guide to the Current Debate*, edited by Richard Warner and Tadeusz Szubka, 242–60. Oxford: Blackwell, 1994.

———. *Mind in a Physical World: An Essay on the Mind-Body Problem and Mental Causation.* Cambridge, Mass.: MIT Press/Bradford, 2000.

MacKay, Donald M. *The Clock Work Image.* Downers Grove, Ill.: InterVarsity Press, 1974.

Martin, Raymond, and John Barresi. *The Rise and Fall of Soul and Self: An Intellectual History of Personal Identity.* New York: Columbia University Press, 2006.

Mbiti, John S. *Concepts of God in Africa.* 2nd ed. Nairobi, Kenya: Acton Publishers, 2012 [1970].

McLaughlin, Brian P. "Varieties of Supervenience." In *Supervenience: New Essays*, edited by Elias E. Savellos and Ümit D. Yalçin, 16–59. Cambridge: Cambridge University Press, 1995.

McNamara, Patrick. *Where God and Science Meet: How Brain and Evolutionary Studies Alter Our Understanding of Religion.* Vol. 1: *Evolution, Genes, and the Religious Experience*; Vol. 2: *The Neurology of Religious Experience*; Vol. 3: *The Psychology of Religious Experience.* Westport, Conn.: Praeger, 2006. (This whole work is available at http://m.friendfeedmedia.com/a8cb89b353ba1c5245a32c16d8032aab7bfd0a72.)

Moltmann, Jürgen. *God in Creation: A New Theology of Creation and the Spirit of God.* Translated by Margaret Kohl. Minneapolis: Fortress, 1993.

Murphy, Nancey. "Nonreductive Physicalism: Philosophical Issues." In *Whatever Happened to the Soul? Scientific and Theological Portraits of Human Nature,* edited by Warren S. Brown, Nancey C. Murphy, and H. Newton Malony, 127–48. Theology and the Sciences. Minneapolis: Fortress, 1998.

———. *Bodies and Souls, or Spirited Bodies?* Cambridge: Cambridge University Press, 2006.

Murphy, Nancey, and Warren S. Brown, *Did My Neurons Make Me Do It? Philosophical and Neurobiological Perspectives on Moral Responsibility and Free Will.* Oxford: Oxford University Press. 2007.

Niebuhr, Reinhold. *The Self and the Dramas of History.* New York: Scribner's, 1955.

Pannenberg, Wolfhart. *Systematic Theology.* Translated by Geoffrey W. Bromiley. 3 vols. Grand Rapids: Eerdmans, 1991, 1994, 1998.

Peacocke, Arthur. "The Sound of Sheer Silence: How does God Communicate with Humanity?" In *Neuroscience and the Person: Scientific Perspectives on Divine Action,* edited by Robert John Russell, Nancey Murphy, Theo C. Meyering, and Michael A. Arbib, 215–47. Vatican City and Berkeley, Calif.: Vatican Observatory and Center for Theology and the Natural Sciences, 1999.

Penrose, Roger. *The Emperor's New Mind: Concerning Computers, Minds, and the Laws of Physics.* New York: Penguin Books, 1989.

Peters, Ted. "Resurrection of the Very Embodied Soul?" In *Neuroscience and the Person: Scientific Perspectives on Divine Action,* edited by Robert John Russell, Nancey Murphy, Theo C. Meyering, and Michael A. Arbib, 305–26. Vatican City and Berkeley, Calif.: Vatican Observatory and Center for Theology and the Natural Sciences, 1999.

Polkinghorne, John. "Anthropology in an Evolutionary Context." In *God and Human*

Dignity, edited by R. K. Soulen and L. Woodhead, 89–103. Grand Rapids: Eerdmans, 2006.

———. *Faith, Science and Understanding*. New Haven, Conn.: Yale University Press, 2000.

———. "Eschatology: Some Questions and Some Insights from Science." In *The End of the World and the Ends of God: Science and Theology on Eschatology*, edited by Michael Welker and John Polkinghorne, 29–41. Harrisburg, Pa.: Trinity Press International, 2000.

———. *The God of Hope and the End of the World*. New Haven, Conn./London: Yale University Press, 2002.

Popper, Karl. "Natural Selection and the Emergence of Mind." *Dialectica* 32 (1978): 339–55.

Putnam, Hilary. "The Nature of Mental States [1967]." In Hilary Putnam, *Mind, Language, and Reality: Philosophical Papers*, 2:429–40. Cambridge: Cambridge University Press, 1975.

Rickabaugh, Brandon L. "Responding to NT Wright's Rejection of the Soul: A Defense of Substance Dualism." An Unpublished Presentation at the Society of Vineyard Scholars, Minnesota, April 28, 2012. http://www.academia.edu/1966881/Responding_to_N._T._Wrights_Rejection_of_the_Soul_A_Defense_of_Substance_Dualism (6/10/2013).

Robinson, John A. T. *The Body: A Study in Pauline Theology*. London: SCM, 1952.

Shear, Jonathan, ed. *Explaining Consciousness: The Hard Problem*. Cambridge: A Bradford Book/MIT Press, 1999.

Sikkema, Arnold E. "A Physicist's Reformed Critique of Nonreductive Physicalism and Emergence." *Pro Rege* (June 2005): 20–32. http://www.dordt.edu/publications/pro_rege/crcpi/119717.pdf (11/18/2012).

Spear, Andrew D. "Husserl on Intentionality and Intentional Content." In *Internet Encyclopedia of Philosopy: A Peer-Reviewed Academic Resource*, 2011, http://www.iep.utm.edu/huss-int/ (6/10/2013).

Sperry, Roger W. *Science and Moral Priority: Merging Mind, Brain, and Human Values*. New York: Columbia University Press, 1983.

Stoeger, William R., S.J. "The Mind-Brain Problem, the Laws of Nature, and Constitutive Relationships." In *Neuroscience and the Person: Scientific Perspectives on Divine Action*, edited by Robert John Russell, Nancey Murphy, Theo C. Meyering, and Michael A. Arbib, 129–46. Vatican City and Berkeley, Calif.: Vatican Observatory and Center for Theology and the Natural Sciences, 1999.

Stubenberg, Leopold. "Neutral Monism." In *The Stanford Encyclopedia of Philosophy* (Spring 2010 edition), edited by Edward N. Zalta. http://plato.stanford.edu/archives/spr2010/entries/neutral-monism/ (6/10/2013).

Taliaferro, Charles. *Consciousness and the Mind of God*. Cambridge: Cambridge University Press, 1994.

Tillich, Paul. *Systematic Theology*. Vol. 3. Chicago: University of Chicago Press, 1951.

Velmans, Max. "Making Sense of Causal Interactions between Consciousness and Brain." *Journal of Consciousness Studies* 9, no. 11 (2002): 69–95.

Ward, Keith. *More Than Matter: Is Matter All We Really Are?* Grand Rapids: Eerdmans, 2011.

Welker, Michael. "Theological Anthropology versus Anthropological Reductionism." In *God and Human Dignity,* edited by R. K. Soulen and L. Woodhead, 317–30. Grand Rapids: Eerdmans, 2006.

Wittgenstein, Ludwig. *Philosophical Grammar.* Edited by R. Rhees. Translated by A. Kenny. Berkeley and Los Angeles: University of California Press, 1974.

———. *Zettel.* Edited by G. E. M. Anscombe and G. H. von Wright. Translated by G. E. M. Anscombe. Berkeley and Los Angeles: University of California Press, 1967.

Wright, N. T. "Mind, Spirit, Soul and Body: All for One and One for All; Reflections on Paul's Anthropology in His Complex Contexts." Paper presented at Society of Christian Philosophers Eastern Meeting (March 18, 2011); available at http://www.ntwrightpage.com/Wright_SCP_MindSpiritSoulBody.htm (11/26/2013).

Zizioulas, John. "The Doctrine of the Holy Trinity: The Significance of the Cappadocian Contribution." In *The Trinity Today*, edited by Christoph Schwöbel. Edinburgh: T. & T. Clark, 1996.

CHAPTER 17

"Multidimensional Monist": A Response to Kärkkäinen

Stewart Goetz

I thank Professor Kärkkäinen for an interesting and challenging paper in support of the anthropological view that he calls "multidimensional monism." My response will largely be an explanation of why I remain unconvinced of the need to abandon soul-body substance dualism (dualism, for short).

I regard dualism as the intuitive starting point and, thereby, default position, when thinking about human nature. It is the view to be embraced unless there is some reason to jettison it. There is reason to think that Kärkkäinen agrees: "common intuitions, universal religious teachings, and the mainstream of classical philosophy envision some kind of dualistic account of humanity in which an important distinction is made between the physical and mental." While Kärkkäinen does not explicitly say that common intuitions, universal religious teachings, and mainstream classical philosophy envision *substance* dualism, he does go on to point out that "from the mid-twentieth century or so, a definite shift has taken place away from traditional dualism towards a highly integrated, mutually conditioned account of the human person as a physical-mental totality." "Traditional dualism" seems to stand in for "substance dualism." Further, Kärkkäinen acknowledges both that "traditional soul-body dualism finds support in biblical terminology and theological tradition" and that soul-body dualism became widely accepted "in patristic and later Christian theology."

Kärkkäinen maintains early Christian thought /the early church wrongly affirmed dualism because it "capitulated" to secular (Greek) philosophy. He favorably quotes Wolfhart Pannenberg's explanation of this believed misstep: "'[t]his process [of capitulation] illustrates the acceptance by early Christian thinking of ideas that the Hellenistic culture of the age took for granted' and hence 'is not an interpretation that has any essential place in Christian anthropology.'" At this point, I have two comments.

First, while it is true that the early church did make use of Hellenistic philosophy in articulating its anthropology, it is critical to remember that individuals like Plato philosophized about what Kärkkäinen calls "common intuitions." In other words, Plato articulated a more reflective conception of a belief affirmed by ordinary people. Contrary to what Kärkkäinen claims, it is most plausible to hold that early Christian theologians embraced dualism because, like him, they recognized dualism's roots in ordinary belief (common sense) and not because they were bamboozled by Hellenistic philosophy.

The early church's recognition of the need to connect with the anthropological thought of ordinary people is mirrored by Kärkkäinen's own cognizance of the contemporary church's need to connect with the anthropological thought of "the faithful":

> Among the current advocates of nondualist accounts of human nature, including Christian nonreductive physicalists, the term *soul* has become a virtual anathema. . . . While that attitude is understandable, constructive theologians should exercise some critical faculties here. I do not consider it wise, let alone necessary, to leave behind the ancient term *soul*, even if traditional dualism is let go. . . . [T]he theologian's task is to help the faithful to grasp its redefinition. . . . [T]he term *soul* is so widely and frequently used in the biblical canon—and consequently, everywhere in Christian tradition—that its dismissal seems to be totally unfounded and counterproductive as it may cause the rejection of the proposal itself without further investigation.

For what it is worth, my hunch is that the entrenched belief in dualism among the faithful, which Kärkkäinen maintains makes it advisable for theologians to continue to use the term *soul*, will prove far more difficult to uproot than he leads readers to believe. He seems to think that theologians can somehow finesse retaining talk about the soul in the presence of everyday folk while at the same time denying its existence as a substance or entity that is ontologically separate from its body. Here, I would like to issue a plea for honesty. Given that the *hoi polloi* do think of the soul as an entity that is distinct and separable from its physical body at death (if not before—how else do reports of out-of-body experiences make sense?), Kärkkäinen (and other monists) should not use the term *soul* with everyday people while failing to make clear that he has in mind something (e.g., functional mental capacities) other than what they do when they use, hear, or read the word.

Second, given the distinction between ordinary belief in and philosophical thought about the soul, it is important to understand that the Bible, because it is written for ordinary people, *presumes* or *assumes* dualism. It does not *teach* dualism. Here is Kärkkäinen: "The question of the biblical teaching on human nature is still without final clarification. While I feel sympathetic to some biblical scholars' view that in the first place the Bible is not seeking to instruct us in anthropology, I also believe that we need more work in clarifying particularly the meaning (to contemporary theology) of the apparent 'phenomenological' dualism—or dualistic rhetoric—of the Bible, particularly of the New Testament."

But why think such clarification is needed? Why not simply affirm that the phenomenological dualism or dualistic rhetoric of the New Testament reflects a genuine belief in the existence of the soul, where this belief is not taught but presupposed? As the experimental cognitive scientist Jesse Bering has recently argued, human beings are, at least initially, believers in dualism.[1] Similarly, the psychologist Nicholas Humphrey recognizes the human inclination to believe in dualism, and he cites others who deem this belief common:

> Thus, development psychologist Paul Bloom aptly describes human beings as "natural-born dualists." Anthropologist Alfred Gell writes: "It seems that ordinary human beings are "natural dualists," inclined more or less from day one, to believe in some kind of "ghost in the machine." . . . Neuropsychologist Paul Broks writes: "The separateness of body and mind is a primordial intuition. . . . Human beings are natural born soul makers, adept at extracting unobservable minds from the behaviour of observable bodies, including their own."[2]

Given that humans are natural believers in the soul's existence, it is completely understandable why the New Testament writers presupposed its existence and the early church did not need to get the idea of it from Hellenistic sources. Everyone already had the idea because belief in the soul is as universal as the air we breathe.

At this point, it is appropriate to ask about where in the New Testament we find evidence of belief in the soul's existence. For starters, consider what

1. Jesse Bering, "The Folk Psychology of Souls," *Behavioral and Brain Sciences* 29 (2006): 453–62.

2. Nicholas Humphrey, *Soul Dust* (Princeton: Princeton University Press, 2011), 195.

the apostle Paul says in 2 Corinthians 12:2–3: "I know a man in Christ Jesus who fourteen years ago was caught up to the third heaven—whether in the body or out of the body I do not know, God knows. And I know that this man was caught up into Paradise—whether in the body or out of the body I do not know, God knows."[3] The most natural/plausible reading of the text implies that Paul, like other ordinary human beings, simply presupposes a dualist soul-body distinction and it is his assumption of this distinction that informs and makes intelligible his comment about his journey to the third heaven and the possibility that it might have been made "out of his body." Paul conceptually captures this soul-body distinction here and elsewhere (cf. 2 Cor. 5:1–9) in terms of a self-body distinction, because it is part of common sense to equate the soul and the self (e.g., my soul (I) magnifies the Lord [Luke 1:46]).

Paul was a highly educated Pharisee. What about the less educated? We get a glimpse into their belief about the soul in various narrative contexts. For example, Jesus is reported as having cast out unclean spirits from people. If dualism were not the commonly accepted view, those who followed him would have found the idea of his casting out unclean spirits thoroughly perplexing, if not unintelligible. But they readily accepted it. There is also the issue of ghosts in the New Testament (as in the Hebrew Bible/Old Testament). When Jesus' disciples saw him walking on the sea, they thought he was a ghost (Matt. 14:26). And after the resurrection when he was in their midst, they thought they were seeing a spirit (Luke 24:37). Then, there is the incident with the appearance of Peter at the house of Mary, after he had been jailed by Herod. Those present insisted to a maid named Rhoda, who reported that Peter was at the door, that Peter himself could not be present but that it must be his angel (Acts 12:15). A particularly interesting passage is the story about Jesus asking his disciples about who people think he is. He is told that some think he is John the Baptist, others that he is Elijah, and others that he is Jeremiah or one of the prophets (Matt. 16:13–14). Even Herod, who had John the Baptist executed, wondered if Jesus was John (Matt. 14:2). Given that it is reasonable to assume that the Baptist's body could be easily located, it is thoroughly plausible to suppose that Herod and other ordinary people could have been thinking that Jesus was John's soul reembodied.

Some might be a bit uneasy with talk about ghosts and spirits. But they should not be, because this is just a way in which the *hoi polloi* express their belief in dualism. It takes philosophers like Plato to come along and start philosophizing about this common belief. Thus, what we must not do is think

3. All citations from the Bible are from the Revised Standard Version.

of dualism *per se* as theologians are prone to do—as a Greek, Platonic, quasi-Platonic, or Cartesian view. We must remember that there is a distinction between *generic* and *specific* dualism, where forms of the latter are Platonism (souls are immortal and survive death disembodied); Cartesianism (souls are not located in space); and Augustinianism/Thomism (souls are present in their entirety at all points in their physical bodies). A rejection of a specific dualism does not equate to a rejection of generic dualism.

I now turn to the issue of what Kärkkäinen thinks is wrong with dualism. I find it difficult to address this topic because I cannot find a clear statement of what he believes the problem is. At one point, he writes that "this shift [in theological circles] towards a unified, monistic, and holistic view is . . . in alignment with earliest theological intuitions." The difficulty here is that Kärkkäinen goes on to acknowledge that early patristic thinkers distinguished between and also defended the psychosomatic unity of body and soul. So how can contemporary theology's move toward a monistic anthropology be an alignment with earliest theological intuitions?

Perhaps we should look elsewhere for an explanation of contemporary theology's shift toward anthropological monism. Perhaps we should look to the influence of science. However, Kärkkäinen denies that "this shift . . . is a result of an accommodation of theology into the demands of secular philosophy and sciences." But while he denies any accommodation to science, he writes that "it has been a great gain for theology to come to a new appreciation of the tight mutual relationship between the physical and mental." "[T]here is no denying the tight link between the functioning of the brain and human behavior." "Intelligence, emotions, sociality, as well as behavioral patterns such as criminality or altruism can be linked very tightly to the neuronal basis." "[B]odily functions condition all psychological experience."

In light of these comments, it is hard not to believe that Kärkkäinen thinks knowledge of science is playing some role in influencing theology towards a monistic anthropology, even if the latter is not making an outright accommodation to the former. For example, he states how he thinks it is significant that:

> current science is moving away from what "physical" (or material) used to mean. . . . As is well known, in the theory of relativity mass is nothing else but a form of energy (in relation to the speed of light); in quantum mechanics, treating subatomic entities as particles is complementary to regarding them as probability waves; and so forth. The point here is that matter/physicality has become very elusive, virtually "non-material." . . . The bottom line is this: what is matter/physicality?

Given a commitment to monism and the "dematerialization" of matter by science, one might think that Kärkkäinen would be inclined toward embracing some form of idealism (the *philosophical* view that only souls and their ideas are real). While he acknowledges the possibility of "nonphysicalist monism" and "keeping the door open" to it, Kärkkäinen inclines towards what he terms "multidimensional monism" (MM), which maintains an ontological primacy of the physical from which the mental strongly emerges. Kärkkäinen approvingly cites Philip Clayton's insistence that strong emergence is consistent with the neuroscientific data and coheres well with our experience of mental agency. Given the strong emergence of the mental, MM ends up being a version of property dualism.

If it is not science that motivates an espousal of MM, what does? Kärkkäinen makes reference to "the basic intuition of the undifferentiated psychosomatic unity." The use of "undifferentiated" here seems to be important, because Kärkkäinen concedes that "the early patristic thinkers defended the psychosomatic unity even when they of course continued distinguishing between soul and body." So recognizing and endorsing psychosomatic unity is thoroughly compatible with embracing dualism. Perhaps, then, Kärkkäinen intends to affirm a basic intuition (one that is at odds with that of the *hoi polloi*) that a human being is a single entity with two fundamental kinds of properties (property dualism). If this is Kärkkäinen's view, then it might be the case that the disagreement between dualists and him about the nature of a human being ultimately boils down to a disagreement between fundamental intuitions. Confirmation of such a disagreement comes from another point that Kärkkäinen repeatedly makes about the irreducibility of mental causation/agency and a rejection of causal closure. Here it is important to remember that an affirmation of mental agency and rejection of causal closure is thoroughly compatible with dualism. Indeed, as a dualist I have written elsewhere in defense of the former and rejection of the latter.[4] Because nothing Kärkkäinen says about mental agency and causal closure is incompatible with dualism, maybe he concludes in favor of MM over dualism on the basis of a basic intuition.

What about personal survival of death? It is commonsensical to think that if I survive death, then something numerically identical with me persists

4. Stewart Goetz, "Making Things Happen: Souls in Action," in Mark C. Baker and Stewart Goetz, eds., *The Soul Hypothesis* (London: Continuum, 2011), 99–117; "Purposeful Explanation and Causal Gaps," *European Journal for Philosophy of Religion* 5 (2012): 141–55; and Stewart Goetz and Charles Taliaferro, *A Brief History of the Soul* (United Kingdom: Wiley-Blackwell, 2011), Chapters 5 and 6.

into the afterlife. Indeed, what could be more commonsensical than the view that if I survive, then indeed *I* survive. And if I am my soul, then we have a thoroughly plausible explanation of my survival of death: I survive death because my soul survives death. Dualists who are also Christian need not, as Kärkkäinen acknowledges, deny the bodily nature of the afterlife. They can affirm it by affirming that the numerically same *I*, a soul, receives not only a numerically distinct but also a different kind of body in the afterlife (flesh and blood cannot inherit the kingdom of God [1 Cor. 15:50]).

But what if there is no soul? Kärkkäinen approvingly cites the British physicist-priest John Polkinghorne and writes that he (Polkinghorne) "correctly notes that in itself the soul's 'role as the carrier of human identity is almost as problematic within life as it is beyond death.' The continuity cannot be a matter of material continuity since atoms are in constant flux through wear and tear." But it is because the body, and not the soul, is the subject of the constant in-and-out of atoms that it cannot be the locus of personal identity through time. And this is as true in this life as it would be in the afterlife. It is precisely because the soul is not composed of substantial parts (it is substantively simple) and is incapable of decomposition that it escapes the problem of change that afflicts the body. And the soul's being substantively simple does not entail that it is naturally immortal. Because it is a *created* substantive simple, it is metaphysically contingent and needs continuous preservation in existence by God who is metaphysically necessary.

According to Kärkkäinen (again citing Polkinghorne), "[u]tilizing the concept of information, . . . what the older soul theory rightly intuited was that 'the faithful God will remember the pattern that is me and re-embody it in the eschatological act of resurrection.'" But the soul theory did (does) not say that the faithful God will remember the informational pattern that is me and re-embody it. According to it, God will remember *me* (conserve me in existence) and re-embody *me*. If I were an informational pattern, would it not in principle be possible to re-embody multiple Stewart Goetzes? But there cannot be multiples of me. I am not a kind (type) of thing of which there can be many tokens (instantiations). I am a token of a type (rational soul). Kärkkäinen adds that "making the soul the locus of continuity doesn't really explain much in the first place." Well, if one believes in the ordinary sense of numerical sameness through time, I would humbly suggest that when it comes to the locus of continuity of the self, the soul explains just about everything.

CHAPTER 18

A Rejoinder to Goetz

Veli-Matti Kärkkäinen

Dr. Stewart Goetz has done a service with his gracious and strong critique of my *essai* on the nature of human nature. He helps me continue refining and clarifying the proposal-in-the-making although my own aim is more modest and humble than his. Differently from my honored respondent, I can't claim anything for my proposal similar to his claim, namely, that "the soul explains just about everything" (in this case, the "locus of continuity of the self," but more widely speaking, I take it) concerning the nature of human nature. Contemporary systematic theology—whose aim is to integrate biblical, theological, philosophical, and scientific (as well as, in my case, even religious) insights and contributions into a somewhat coherent view of human nature—operates with more tentative and humble explanations.

Only in one instance did Dr. Goetz seemingly misunderstand a key claim of my proposal—and I am sure it is because I have expressed my thoughts in a less than clear manner. Namely, he takes me as a materialist and wonders why I do not jump onto the idealist bandwagon. As a corrective, let me state that I do not argue that the mental (necessarily) derives from the physical—indeed, that is a central point of my "multidimensional" monism. Unlike nonreductive physicalism which believes that the material is the ultimate "bottom line" even for the highest mental capacities (even when, once emerged, they cannot be reduced back to the base), I leave open the question of the "base" from which the mental derives. Ultimately I argue—with all theists—that everything has its source in the spiritual because God is Spirit (John 4:26). Penultimately, I cannot say anything more than what I have said in my essay: that I do not believe that the "entities postulated by physics complete the inventory of what exists"[1] and that therefore a kind of "ontological pluralism" may be a fitting description. In the essay, I also called for a development of new language, new terminology to be able to speak of what the physical/material means and how that may relate to what we mean by "mental." That I speak favorably of emergence does not make me an ontological pluralist; I am just stating the point that in our evolving, evolutionary world for any capacity to come to existence, some kind of "emergence" has to take place.

Concerning whether I have succumbed to the temptation of letting the natural sciences rather than biblical revelation dictate the theological response to the question of human nature, I dare respectfully to disagree with Dr. Goetz's opinion. First of all, Christian theologians throughout history from Augustine to Aquinas and beyond have carefully investigated and gleaned from the best sources of current human knowledge. Indeed, Aquinas's attempt to think of human nature through the lens of a hylomorphic account of the soul as the form of the body was funded by Aristotelian philosophy as rediscovered by Muslim scholars. Whether Aquinas succeeded or not in his constructive proposal is a matter of debate; what is not, is his uncompromising commitment to divine revelation as the guiding light. Or think of this clear example: that Christian theology has made the shift from a six-day-driven literalist reading of the creation accounts of the Bible to embracing the (currently still dominant) Big Bang cosmology along with an evolutionary understanding of emergence of life and forms hardly constitutes a capitulation to secular forces.

When it comes the biblical intuitions about human nature, I fear I have to disagree strongly with my dialogue partner. Apart from the fact that I do not find the short biblical case studies provided in the response (of passages which have been extensively investigated by critical scholarship yielding diverse interpretive options) in any way unambiguously supporting substance dualism, the issue of what the biblical authors assumed and what they taught is quite complex. On the one hand, I of course agree with Dr. Goetz that biblical writers throughout the canon assume and employ dualistic(ally sounding) ways to describe human nature. However, that in itself hardly settles the issue of how we should think of the "composition" of the human being. Just take the example referred to above: that the Bible assumes everywhere the view of origins currently named the "young earth" theory is beyond dispute—along with Ptolemaic cosmology!—is of course not a reason to stick with that outdated view of the world. Analogically, the way biblical writers, in keeping with

1. Philip Clayton, *Mind and Emergence: From Quantum to Consciousness* (Oxford: Oxford University Press, 2004), 4.

their own times, speak of human nature should not be taken as *the* guide to how we currently understand the matter in light of hugely advanced scientific knowledge.

While I understand why my respondent seems to have a hard time affirming my continuing use of the term *soul* (which has become anathema to even Christian nonreductive physicalists), I also wish to help him better understand why I continue to use it. The term *soul* (and equivalents in everyday language such as *spirit*) is so deeply rooted in the Christian and wider spiritual/religious "language game"—and so prevalent in the biblical narrative—that there is absolutely no need or legitimate reason to drop it. On the other hand, as with terms such as *creation*, Christians need to be re-trained regarding its meaning. Analogically to the term *creation*, whose meaning has in many ways dramatically shifted because of contemporary physical cosmological knowledge but whose foundational theological meaning has remained intact (i.e., that creation is totally contingent on the Creator), *soul* can be used even with the demise of substance ontology. In this newly conceived meaning, the *soul* may denote either what it means (often) in the Old Testament, that is, "living human being" (as in Gen. 2:7; *nephesh*) or, more generally, the human being as the image of God destined for fellowship with God. I do not see why its linking with substance dualism would be necessary.

I find it surprising that Dr. Goetz was not interested in my careful engagement of nonreductive physicalism, which is an important way in contemporary philosophy (of mind), including Christian, to try to negotiate the nature of human nature after the discoveries of the integral relatedness of the physical, mental, social, emotional, and so forth. Although my assessment of nonreductive physicalism differs from the critique of substance dualists, I think Dr. Goetz and others could use some of that. Furthermore, I wonder why he only mentions in passing that, indeed, in many ways, my proposal is not as antagonistic to dualism in general; I myself argue that something like what is meant by property dualism results when reductionism is rejected and physicalism/materialism is not made the ultimate base of the mental (as in nonreductive physicalism). Property dualism—or, to be more precise in my case, "property pluralism"—simply says in this case that reality is "more" than matter and that even in its monism it cannot be contained within "one kind of stuff." (In closing, I hope that these descriptions, though slippery, are not read as contradictory statements but rather as attempts to transpose our insufficient terminology in order to encompass the utterly complex nature of what so far we call "physical" and "mental.")

CHAPTER 19

Whose Interpretation? Which Anthropology? Biblical Hermeneutics, Scientific Naturalism, and the Body-Soul Debate

John W. Cooper

Perhaps no doctrine is currently more hotly debated among Christian scholars than the unity of soul and body. Completely incompatible versions of monism and dualism are advanced by colleagues who believe the same Bible, worship together, and confess the same creeds. Some of us believe that human souls are specially created, whereas others hold that God originated them by evolution and generates them by gestation. Some look forward to fellowship with Christ between death and future resurrection, while others believe that we cease to exist until the resurrection, or that resurrection occurs immediately at death. Traditional Augustinian and Thomist dualisms still have advocates, but so do physicalism, emergentism, psychophysical monism, and idealism.[1] For current Christian academics—biblical scholars, theologians, philosophers, psychologists, and scientists—anthropology and eschatology are disputed doctrines rather than shared ecumenical affirmations.[2]

1. Augustine held to substance dualism—soul and body are two substances or entities conjoined. Aquinas held that humans are one substance constituted by two ingredients, a soul and the matter that it forms to be a living body. Currently Christians also endorse varieties of materialism or physicalism—the view that humans are physical/material beings whose souls and minds are generated by their bodies. But most materialists also affirm that mental and spiritual capacities are irreducible—they cannot be completely explained by physics and biology. Psychophysical monism holds that bodies and minds are aspects of something more basic. Idealists hold that humans are immaterial beings whose bodies manifest their presence in the physical universe.

2. Consider the widely diverse positions stated in *Faith and Philosophy* 12/4 (October 1995), on "Christian Philosophy and the Mind-Body Problem"; *Soul, Body, and Survival: Essays on the Metaphysics of Human Persons*, ed. Kevin Corcoran (Cornell, 2001); and *In Search of the Soul: Four Views of the Mind-Body Problem*, ed. Joel B. Green and Stuart L. Palmer (InterVarsity, 2005). *Whatever Happened to the Soul? Scientific and Theological Portraits of Human*

One key reason is biblical hermeneutics. Assuming that Christian scholars intend our academic conclusions about the body-mind relation to be consistent with Scripture, it is obvious that we hold widely different views of what the Bible teaches about the human constitution and what happens after death.[3] We do not interpret Scripture by the same methods, reach the same conclusions about its doctrine, or relate it to scholarship in the same ways. So when appeal is made to "the biblical view of human nature" to support a particular concept of the body-soul relation, it is fair to wonder (with apologies to MacIntyre): Whose interpretation? Which anthropology?

One might assume that disputes about anthropology and eschatology have deep roots in Christian tradition. For centuries, the differences among Eastern Orthodox, Roman Catholic, and various Protestant biblical hermeneutics have generated disagreements on many doctrines and practices.[4] It would not be surprising if our views of the body-soul relation and the life to come were among them.

But just the opposite is true. Throughout church history there has been general ecumenical agreement about the divine inspiration and enduring truth of Scripture's teaching and a virtual consensus that the Bible from beginning to end presents a dualism-in-unity anthropology. All traditions affirm that God made the first human by conjoining earthly and spiritual ingredients (Gen. 2:7). All agree that Scripture teaches a two-stage view of the afterlife—disembodied existence followed by bodily resurrection—which implies a temporary separation of body and soul. This anthropology and eschatology remain the doctrine of the Eastern Orthodox, Roman Catholic, and most Protestant churches to the present. There is a consensus as old as Christianity that Scripture teaches the distinctness and temporary separation of the soul.

Nature, ed. Warren Brown, Nancey Murphy, and H. Newton Malony (Augsburg Fortress, 1998), is an anthology of essays by a biblical scholar, a theologian, a philosopher, a psychologist, and several natural scientists who reject dualism and favor non-reductive biophysical monism.

3. Recent books on eschatology and anthropology include Joseph Ratzinger, *Eschatology: Death and Eternal Life*, trans. Martin Waldstein (Catholic University of American, 1988); John W. Cooper, *Body, Soul and Life Everlasting: Biblical Anthropology and the Monism-Dualism Debate* (Eerdmans, 1989; Eerdmans and Apollos, 2000); Joel Green, *Body, Soul, and Human Life: The Nature of Humanity in the Bible* (Baker Academic, 2008); and N. T. Wright, *The Resurrection of the Son of God* (Fortress, 2003). Ratzinger and Cooper affirm an intermediate state between death and resurrection and the body-soul dichotomy it requires. Green endorses monism and resurrection but denies disembodiment. Wright defends two-stage eschatology and temporary body-soul dichotomy consistent with Jewish holism, not Platonic dualism.

4. *The Bible in the Churches: How Various Christians Interpret the Scriptures*, ed. Kenneth Hagen (Marquette University, 1994).

But since the Enlightenment a significant disagreement about Scripture and hermeneutics has opened the way for the current diversity of eschatologies and anthropologies. Deists and Christian rationalists progressively abandoned historic supernaturalism and adopted theistic naturalism as the basis for interpreting Scripture and formulating doctrine. Modern theistic naturalism holds that all of God's actions in the universe occur within and conform to the laws and states of affairs in nature as understood by science. By the late twentieth century, the scientific world-picture of a universe evolving since the Big Bang persuaded many Christians that theistic emergent physicalism is the true and proper framework for understanding human nature, biblical anthropology, and eschatology, if not all of Scripture and theology. At the same time, many other Christian academics reject scientific naturalism and emergent physicalism and affirm the historic position as they engage the mind-body problem.

This essay focuses in more detail on the complex role of biblical hermeneutics in the body-soul debate.[5] It addresses the three main operations involved in relating Scripture to current philosophical and scientific views of the body-soul relation: exegesis of specific texts, formulation of doctrine from the results of exegesis, and application of doctrine to current concepts. These operations are not merely sequential but dialogical—they affect each other. Exegesis yields doctrine, which is applied to current perspectives. But doctrine in turn shapes exegesis, and current application shapes doctrine and exegesis.

These matters are complex, and this essay can only begin to address them. My main purpose is to highlight important connections between hermeneutics and the body-soul question—reasons why Christians find other Christians' appeals to Scripture compelling or unpersuasive. I attempt to summarize all viewpoints fairly and briefly state my own conclusions. Disagreements about exegesis and doctrine arise even when people share the same biblical hermeneutics. But most disagreements on central doctrines result from different views of Scripture, how it should be read, and what it teaches us today. My

5. I intend my description of hermeneutics to be accurate and broadly representative of both historic and modern approaches to Scripture. I have consulted Manfred Oeming, *Contemporary Biblical Hermeneutics*, trans J. Vette (Ashgate, 2006); Grant Osborne, *The Hermeneutical Spiral: A Comprehensive Introduction to Biblical Interpretation* (IVP Academic, 1991, 2004); William Klein, Craig Blomberg, and Robert Hubbard, Jr., *Introduction to Biblical Interpretation*, revised and updated (Thomas Nelson, 1993, 2004); David Jasper, *A Short Introduction to Hermeneutics* (Westminster John Knox, 2004); Werner Jeanrond, *Theological Hermeneutics: Development and Significance* (Crossroad, 1991); and Daniel Treier, *Introducing Theological Interpretation of Scripture: Recovering a Christian Practice* (Baker Academic, 2008).

thesis is that one's position on biblical anthropology and eschatology largely depends on one's attitude toward scientific naturalism, which currently implies evolutionary materialism or emergent physicalism—the view that the human soul has gradually evolved or emerged from matter.

Before proceeding, let me clarify my terminology and state my position. As I use the terms, *body* and *soul* and *monism* and *dualism* do not always have precise theological or philosophical meanings. They are primarily ordinary-language expressions of common-sense realism. Used in this generic, non-technical way, these terms express the religious and worldview beliefs of pre-scientific animists, Muslim clerics, atheists, and lay Christians, as well as the sophisticated versions of monism and dualism proposed by academics.[6]

The terms *monism* and *dualism* address not only whether body and soul are one or two constituents of human nature, but also whether the soul or person can survive death. The soul is the locus of personal identity, subjectivity, and agency. *Dualism* implies that soul and body are sufficiently distinct so that the former can exist without the latter, perhaps only by the supernatural action of God. *Monism* implies that soul and body are so closely related that the former cannot exist without the latter.[7] *Holism* implies the functional integration of soul and body. It is claimed by most dualists and monists and is the prerogative of neither.

My view is a version of the historic Christian interpretation of Scripture, to which I am committed unless rationally compelled to concede that it must be revised. As I read it, the Bible emphasizes the primary unity and integration of body, soul, and spirit in creation, redemption, and the life to come, whereas disintegration and separation result from sin and death. Although created for everlasting life, human persons are not naturally disembodied and may not be constitutionally immortal. Nevertheless, God supernaturally sustains souls (persons) in existence between death and bodily resurrection. I label this

6. Kevin Vanhoozer, "The Semantics of Biblical Literature: Truth and Scripture's Diverse Literary Forms," in *Hermeneutics, Authority, and Canon*, ed. D. Carson and J. Woodbridge (Zondervan, 1986), argues that the truth of Scripture is expressed in worldview ideas rather than precise propositions of academic theology or philosophy. The distinction between ordinary and academic language is important for the body-soul debate. Some suppose that if Scripture does not teach a philosophical position, then it has nothing to say about the issue. Nancey Murphy writes, "the New Testament authors are not intending to teach *anything* about humans' metaphysical composition." She claims freedom to endorse non-reductive physicalism and to deny the intermediate state; *Bodies and Souls*, 21–23.

7. Strictly speaking, this claim is true for materialism and psychophysical monism, not idealist monism. Idealists can affirm disembodied existence but do not give the body the same metaphysical importance as the soul.

view *dualistic holism* to emphasize that the unity of body and soul, not their separation, is basic in Scripture.[8]

Exegesis: Determining the Meaning of Biblical Texts about Body and Soul

There is broad agreement that biblical hermeneutics involves three interrelated operations: exegesis, formulation of doctrine, and application; or in other words, the interpretation of specific texts, determination of the teaching of Scripture as a whole, and engagement of biblical teaching with current faith and life. Even if hermeneutics is limited to exegesis, as some claim, Christians must still formulate and apply doctrine, so we must consider all three tasks in any case. In addition, we must take account of the mutual relations among exegesis, doctrine, and current application.

The first stage in understanding Scripture is *exegesis*—determining as best we can what the original text meant. Exegesis involves three inseparable aspects of the text—its linguistic, literary, and historical dimensions. Linguistic analysis considers the vocabulary, grammar, semantics, and syntax of the original language.[9] Literary analysis considers the genre of the text—historical narrative, poetry, law, wisdom, prophecy, letters, and others—and whether particular expressions are literal or figurative and what the figures mean.[10] Historical analysis considers a text's religious-cultural context and its links to other parts of the biblical canon.[11] These studies often yield a reasonably clear idea of a text's original meaning, at least in general. Consider the following examples of texts that are relevant to anthropology and eschatology.

Genesis 2:7 (NIV) states that "the Lord God formed the man from the dust of the ground and breathed into his nostrils the breath of life, and the man became a living being." Dualists have claimed this verse because it refers

8. Cooper, *Body, Soul* (2000), xxvii-xxviii, and "The Current Body-Soul Debate: A Case for Dualistic Holism," *SBJT* 13.2 (2009): 32–50. The 1989 edition of *Body, Soul* endorses *holistic dualism*, which makes the distinction rather than the unity basic.

9. See Osborne, *Hermeneutical Spiral,* "Part 1, General Hermeneutics." He includes historical analysis as part of linguistic analysis.

10. See Osborne, *Hermeneutical Spiral,* "Part 2, Genre Analysis."

11. See Osborne, *Hermeneutical Spiral,* "Ch. 5, Historical and Cultural Backgrounds." Historical analysis may also try to reconstruct the formation of the text from earlier sources, but this effort is often speculative and contributes little to understanding the text as it appears in the biblical canon.

to two basic ingredients, one material and the other immaterial. Monists have claimed it because it says that the man is one being, a living soul (*nephesh chayah*), not the conjunction of a body and a soul.

Careful exegesis complicates scoring the debate. The text narrates primordial history using a number of figurative elements and literary devices. It engages and challenges the heno-theistic-animistic worldviews of the ancient near east.[12] The man—*ha adam*—is formed from the soil—*adamah*—to till the soil in the garden. He becomes a *nephesh chayah*—a living soul (not a soul in a body)—when God breathes *neshama*—the power of human life—directly into the nose of his formed body. *Neshama* is a neither a power inherent in the soil nor an immaterial entity. It is an invisible life force that Mesopotamian religions regarded as divine or pro-generated by fertility gods (such as Baal and Asherah). Genesis 2 challenges this belief by proclaiming that Yahweh, the covenant God of Israel, made the first human directly. The man is not divine or quasi-divine. But based on Genesis 1, Genesis 2 implies that human *neshama* includes the distinctive abilities that image God. It is not merely the power of life shared by other creatures. In the Old Testament worldview, humans have the capacity to know and interact with God like angels and spiritual beings ("gods"), a capacity not shared by other creatures in earth, sky, and sea. Humans are both earthy and spiritual beings (Psalm 8). Thus Genesis 2:7 does make realistic worldview claims about God and the human constitution even though it is not written in clear conceptual language.

But does it favor a philosophical theory of body and soul? The input of two basic ingredients seems to rule out all kinds of monism—material, ideal, and psychophysical—because monism posits just one basic ingredient. Some kinds of monism attempt to preserve the duality by claiming that the generated aspect is irreducible or ontologically emergent. But in Genesis, God neither elicits the powers of human existence from the earth nor condenses the body from the human spirit. So materialism and idealism do not fit. Psychophysical monism comes closer because it affirms that humans are single beings with two correlative (but not basic) aspects. Dualism is scarcely more adequate. The two ingredients are not a material body and a spiritual soul conjoined, but a non-living body infused with a power. The Thomist view is *prima facie* promising because it asserts that a human is a single being or substance consisting of two ingredients. But it holds that the soul is the individual subsistent form and animating power of the body, whereas in Genesis 2:7 the body is formed by God, and *neshama* is a power that is individuated only when infused into

12. John Walton, *Ancient Near Eastern Thought and the Old Testament* (Baker Academic 2006), Ch. 9, "Understanding the Past—Human Origins and Role."

it. A dualism of material and immaterial ingredients from which God constitutes one complex psychosomatic being would be the closest fit (provided postmortem personal existence is possible). In sum, this text does not directly validate any standard philosophical position, although some are closer than others. But no doctrine is validated by a single text. We must move through the hermeneutical process to discern how Genesis 2:7 contributes to the anthropology of Scripture as a whole, and then relate the biblical perspective to the philosophical theories of the body-soul relation.

A second example of linguistic-literary-historical exegesis considers the Old Testament references to *sheol* or *hades* (Septuagint), the place of the dead.[13] If all of these texts are merely figurative references to physical death or the grave, then they provide no evidence for existence after death. But if some of them are realistic references, then they do indicate belief in postmortem existence of some sort, perhaps between death and the resurrection envisioned in Isaiah 26, Ezekiel 37, and Daniel 12. The Old Testament prohibitions against consulting the dead (Lev. 19:31, Deut. 18:11, Isa. 8:19) and the historical narrative of Saul's encounter with the deceased Samuel (1 Sam. 28) are clear evidence of belief that self-identical individuals do exist after death. Even if inactive or unconscious, their mere existence beyond physical death entails a dichotomy of the living person—a dualism of some sort. The dead are ghosts—ethereal remains of bodily humans—whose existence is insubstantial and powerless presumably because they no longer consist of the dust of the ground and *neshama* or *ruach* from which God made them. In addition to the biblical texts, historical evidence from other ancient near-eastern religions indicates widespread realism about the afterlife and a variety of non-philosophical body-soul dichotomies and body-soul-spirit trichotomies.[14] Greek beliefs about shades in Hades were not unique.

A final example of exegesis considers Paul's anthropological terms, which include *soul, spirit, mind, will, heart, body,* and *flesh.*[15] His vocabulary is complex, variable, and not easy to categorize. Consider his blessing: "your whole spirit, soul, and body" (1 Thess. 4:23). Monists claim that these terms refer to in-

13. Alan Bernstein, *The Formation of Hell: Death and Retribution in the Ancient and Early Christian Worlds* (Cornell, 1996), Part Two: "The Afterlife in Ancient Judaism," Ch. 5, "The Spirits of the Dead."

14. Cf. John Taylor, *Death and the Afterlife in Ancient Egypt* (Univ. of Chicago, 2001); the Egyptians were trichotomists who believed in an intermediate state and the resurrection of mummified bodies. Israelites knew the Egyptian beliefs. See also John Walton, Ch. 14, "Pondering the Future on Earth and After Death"; and Wright, *Resurrection*, Ch. 2, "Shadows, Souls, and Where They Go: Life Beyond Death in Ancient Paganism."

15. G. E. Ladd, *A Theology of the New Testament*, Ch. 33, "The Pauline Psychology."

separable aspects of the whole person, trichotomists say they refer to three constitutive parts, and dualists correlate *soul* and *spirit* in distinction from *body*. In fact there is insufficient evidence to vindicate any of these views. Occasionally Paul refers to parts or capacities that can sometimes function independently, as when he speaks of charismatic prayer using his *spirit* but not his *mind* (1 Cor. 14:14). Sometimes *flesh* and *spirit* do not refer to parts or aspects of persons but to our spiritual dispositions or orientations toward or against God—the old sinful nature against the new nature renewed in the image of Christ (Eph. 4:22–24). Interestingly, when Paul speaks of possible out-of-body experience (2 Cor. 12:2–4) and death (Phil. 1:20–24; 2 Cor. 5:1–10), he distinguishes *himself* from his body and flesh, using first-person pronouns rather than *soul* or *spirit*. This implies a common sense ego-body or person-body distinction rather than a soul-body or spirit-flesh distinction. All considered, Paul's anthropological terminology refers both to dimensions of the whole person and to distinct, separable aspects.[16] His anthropology is holistic and integrated but not monistic. It reflects his teachers, the Pharisees, rather than Greek philosophy.[17]

These examples illustrate the complexities of exegesis and the difficulty of validating one interpretation over competitors, much less one philosophical position. However, complexity does not open the door to subjective or arbitrary readings, however plausible or ingenious. An interpretation is valid only if it can account for all the linguistic, literary, and historical features of the text as adequately as any other proposal. Exegeses cannot be tested as rigorously as scientific hypotheses. But they can be as strong or weak as other historical and literary interpretations. For some texts, one reading is clearly more reasonable than others. For others, more than one may be tenable, and competent scholars who share the same methods, data, and view of Scripture can reasonably disagree.[18] Furthermore, it is important to distinguish between

16. James Dunn, *Theology of the Apostle Paul* (Eerdmans, 1998), 54, denies that Paul allowed for any dichotomy. But he presumes that Paul is a monist and does not fully consider all the relevant texts.

17. In Acts 23:6–8 Luke explicitly links Paul's affirmation of the resurrection and the existence of spirits [of the dead] with the teaching of the Pharisees. See Wright, *Resurrection*, 190–200, on the anthropology and eschatology of the Pharisees. The debate goes on. Joel Green, *Body, Soul, and Human Life*, 170–78, claims that Paul is a monist. George Van Kooten, *Paul's Anthropology in Context: The Image of God, Assimilation to God, and Tripartite Man in Ancient Judaism, Ancient Philosophy and Early Christianity* (Mohr Siebeck, 2008), argues that Paul synthesizes Jewish and Platonic anthropology.

18. E. D. Hirsch, Jr., *Validity in Interpretation* (New Haven/London: Yale University Press, 1967), is a classic discussion of criteria, including the author's intended meaning; see also the discussion of validation in Klein, Blomberg, and Hubbard, 201ff.

major and minor, central and peripheral, and general and specific exegetical issues. It is possible to agree on one without the other. Commentators might agree, for example, that Old Testament writers believed in existence beyond death without agreeing on the details or sources.

Exegesis is further complicated by its relation to doctrinal formation and current application—the other phases of hermeneutics. There are legitimate ways for doctrine and application to shape exegesis, as indicated in subsequent sections. But commentators sometimes interpret texts using assumptions that are inappropriate and yield faulty exegesis.

Anthropological word studies provide ready examples. Many pre-modern commentators, convinced that dualism is biblical doctrine, interpreted all occurrences of *body, soul*, and *spirit* dualistically even when not exegetically warranted.[19] Some modern scholars make the same sort of mistake in favor of monism.[20] Problematic linguistic theories are another common reason for faulty exegesis.[21]

But the abuses of exegesis do not invalidate its use. Scholars regularly identify and correct problematic assumptions and methods by pointing out how they unjustifiably limit, expand, or otherwise misconstrue the linguistic, literary, and historical data of texts. Sound exegesis is possible and regularly achieved even though it is neither certain nor infallible. It is fundamental to determining biblical doctrine, the next task of hermeneutics.

Doctrinal, Theological, or Canonical Interpretation of Anthropology and Eschatology

Biblical word studies combine exegeses of particular texts into generalizations about Scripture as a whole. This process moves toward the second phase of

19. Even my theological ancestor John Calvin, an excellent exegete, was not immune. His *Commentary on Genesis* 2:7 concludes that man is a body and an immortal soul, which is not what the text says or implies. Also *Institutes* I, xv.2, on the relation of body and soul, blends much sound exegesis with some unwarranted philosophical addenda.

20. An example of materialist exegesis is the exclusively physical-biological translation of *ruach* as breath or life-force and never as spirit, i.e. a non-physical being or power. This reductive translation ignores the facts that God is *ruach* (Isa. 31:3), and that *ruach* is sometimes a noun referring to angels and spirits (Judg. 9:23; 1 Sam. 16:14–16, 23; 1 Kings 22:21–24; 2 Kings 19:7; Job 4:15). Since spiritual powers manifest spiritual beings in animistic worldviews, human *ruach* may well have been considered substantive and not merely functional.

21. Osborne, *Hermeneutical Spiral*, 85–93, explains and illustrates nine modern semantic fallacies committed by biblical scholars, including the lexical, root, etymological, one-meaning, and false dilemma fallacies.

hermeneutics—doctrinal, theological, or canonical interpretation.[22] Its goal is to synthesize the teaching (not just the meaning) of all the texts and books of the Bible into a complete summary of biblical theology or basic Christian doctrine—what God wants the church of all ages to believe and practice. Thus theological interpretation affirms a general principle of sound reasoning—the conclusion must account for all the data.[23] The comprehensive summary of doctrine includes and organizes the cumulative teaching of Scripture on many specific topics, such as God, Jesus Christ, creation, sin, salvation, worship, social ethics, anthropology, and eschatology. What follows is a summary of traditional Christian theological hermeneutics in relation to anthropology and eschatology. The modern approach is different in crucial ways and is summarized in the next section.

The content of historic Christian doctrine follows from specific beliefs about Scripture. Although Eastern Orthodox, Roman Catholic, and confessional Protestant churches differ on the relation between Scripture and the church's interpretation of Scripture, they all hold that the Bible is the Word of God. God directed the formation and content of Scripture and continues to speak through it.[24] What God says is enduringly true, coherent, and authoritative in all that it teaches, so that biblical doctrine is full, rich, and detailed.[25] The Holy Spirit guided the human authors of Scripture to produce texts that are partial contributions to the comprehensive truth that God intends to communicate in canonical Scripture as a whole. It follows that individual authors

22. Osborne, *Hermeneutical Spiral,* Ch. 15, "Biblical Theology," and Ch. 16, "Systematic Theology"; Brevard Childs, "The Canon in Recent Biblical Studies: Reflections on an Era," Christopher Seitz, "The Canonical Approach and Theological Interpretation," and Anthony Thiselton, "Introduction: Canon, Community, and Theological Construction," in *Canon and Biblical Interpretation*, ed. Craig Bartholemew and Anthony Thiselton (Paternoster, Zondervan, 2006).

23. N. T. Wright's *Resurrection of the Son of God* is a masterful example of drawing eschatology and anthropology from a comprehensive exegesis of Scripture in its historical context.

24. Recent philosophical defenses of this view are Richard Swinburne, *Revelation: From Metaphor to Analogy* (Oxford, 1992, 2007), and Nicholas Wolterstorff, *Divine Discourse: Philosophical Reflections on the Claim that God Speaks* (Cambridge, 1995).

25. Website of the Greek Orthodox Archdiocese of America, Our Faith, "The Basic Sources of the Teachings of the Eastern Orthodox Church," http://www.goarch.org/ourfaith/ourfaith7064/, accessed 7/3/13; *Catechism of the Catholic Church*, Pt. I., Ch. 2, Art. 3, "Sacred Scripture"; *Belgic Confession*, Art. 3, "The Written Word of God," Art. 5, "The Authority of Scripture," and Art. 7, "The Sufficiency of Scripture." Most confessional Protestant churches do not deny the responsibility of the church to determine the right interpretation of Scripture. They regulate interpretation by adopting creeds and doctrinal standards, and by interpreting and applying Scripture on specific issues. But in principle Protestants subordinate the church to the final authority of Scripture rather than regard them as correlative.

express similar or compatible views, and that particular texts should therefore be interpreted so that their teaching is consistent with the canon (and sacred tradition) as a whole. Thus the Old Testament emphasis on law and the New Testament emphasis on grace are not contradictory but a redemptive development. The Preacher's resignation to the futility of life and confidence in God's providence in Romans 8 are complimentary, not antithetical, as are Paul and James on faith and works. All these differences are integral to the whole truth that God communicates in Scripture. The hermeneutical dialectic between text and canon aims at and has historically approximated a coherent synthesis of biblical doctrine that God intends humans to believe and practice.[26]

Applying this shared theological hermeneutics to anthropology and eschatology, the vast majority in Christian history, including the Anabaptists and Non-conformists who believe in "soul sleep," affirm what Wright calls a "two-stage view of life after life."[27] They also affirm the temporary separation of body and soul which it entails—an intermediate state between death and bodily resurrection.[28] This eschatology follows from all the exegetical data of Scripture taken together by the church since earliest times. Some biblical texts speak of death without mentioning an afterlife. Some envision immediate presence with God without mentioning the body or resurrection (e.g., 2 Cor. 5:6–9). Some refer to the souls or spirits of the dead (Acts 23:8; Heb. 12:24), and some of those indicate that they are conscious and active (Rev. 6:9–10). Some texts refer to resurrection but not when it occurs, while others specify the last day or the return of Christ (1 Thess. 4:16; 1 Cor. 15:51–52; John 11:24). These texts are not incompatible, competing accounts but parts of the whole divinely intended picture. Thus even if no text explicitly asserted the entire two stage view, it would logically follow because it is the only position that coherently includes what each and every text asserts. (The alternatives are immediate resurrection and non-existence between death and resurrection.) But the complete view is not a mere construct or inference. Jesus himself affirms and enacts both stages. He promised to be with the dying thief in Paradise on

26. The church's understanding of biblical doctrine can be enriched by further reflection on Scripture and adapted to new insights from history, philosophy, and science. But it does not fundamentally change.

27. See Wright, *Resurrection,* 199–206, 476–78.

28. See, for example, *Catechism of the Catholic Church* (1994), exposition of Articles 11 and 12 of the Apostles' Creed; website of the Greek Orthodox Archdiocese of America, Our Faith: "Death: The Threshold to Everlasting Life," http://www.goarch.org/ourfaith/ourfaith7076, accessed July 2013; *The Heidelberg Catechism*, Question/Answer 1 and 57 on the unity of body and soul in life, their separation at death, and their reunion at the resurrection.

Good Friday ("today"), and on Easter Sunday he rose bodily and appeared to his disciples (Luke 23:43; Luke 24). Thus Jesus actualized a disembodied intermediate state in Paradise and subsequent bodily resurrection, opening the way for us to follow (1 Cor. 15:20). This synthesis of all the relevant biblical texts is the ecumenical consensus.

Christians who profess the traditional view of Scripture and who nevertheless affirm monistic anthropology must, in the words of Nancey Murphy, "finesse or give up the doctrine of the intermediate state."[29] Bible scholars in this group seek to reinterpret the texts which apparently support dualism so that they are consistent with monism, rather than conceding that the texts do express dualism and dismissing them as anachronistic,[30] as Bultmann would.

A shared theological hermeneutics does not eliminate all disagreements about particular texts or their implications for biblical doctrine. But attention to the proper practice of shared hermeneutical principles can expose faulty arguments and doctrinal conclusions. I offer two examples from the body-soul debate.

First, because theological interpretation is comprehensive, it must take the measure and weight of all the relevant texts of Scripture. Selecting or working with only partial data is bad theology as well as poor scholarship. Dualists may not privilege texts about souls, spirits, and the afterlife. Monists may not ignore or marginalize them.[31] Furthermore, final conclusions must reflect all the exegetical data, not merely generalize from most of it. What is omitted could make a crucial difference. For example, it is indisputable that the Old Testament and Paul's letters emphasize the corporeality of human nature. But the emphasis on embodiment does not suggest monism if they also (infrequently) refer to the existent dead before the resurrection. Another violation of comprehensive theological interpretation is the common fallacy of false dilemma. This mistake would force us to choose either a disembodied soul or bodily resurrection, either Greek dualism or Hebrew monism, either a separable soul or body-soul integration, either death as non-existence or as trivial, either concern for the soul or for holistic ministry, and numerous others. But Scripture and the Christian tradition affirm both a disembodied soul and bodily resurrection, both the integral unity of body and soul and

29. Murphy, *Bodies and Souls, or Spirited Bodies?*, 23.

30. See, for example, Joel Green, *Body, Soul, and Human Life*, Ch. 2 and Ch. 5.

31. For example, Trenton Merricks, "The Resurrection of the Body and the Life Everlasting," in *Reason for the Hope Within*, ed. Michael Murray (Eerdmans, 1999), 261–86, argues that biblical anthropology is physicalist by appealing to numerous embodiment and resurrection texts but omitting all that support dualism.

their temporary separation. Proper hermeneutics demands sound reason and the whole truth.

A second example is development within the canon. Theological interpretation affirms progressive revelation when exegetically warranted. God revealed more in the New Testament than was clear in the Old Testament about the nature and destiny of humans, as well as the Trinity, the identity of the Messiah, and the way of salvation. The New Testament interprets and fulfills the Old Testament. The Old grounds and promises what the New reveals, but the Old is not the final word that defines and delimits the New. Thus even if Old Testament anthropology were monistic, it is backward to presume that Paul and the New Testament must therefore be monistic. A parallel mistake denies the Trinity because the Old Testament is monotheistic. In fact the Old Testament is not monistic, and the New Testament presents an anthropology and eschatology much like what the Pharisees and rabbis derived from their Hebrew Bible.[32] It is equally mistaken, as traditional Christians sometimes do, to read New Testament eschatology back into the Old Testament, as though Moses and David anticipated Heaven instead of *sheol*.

These examples illustrate that proper practice of theological hermeneutics can sort out bad arguments on both sides of the monism-dualism debate, even though it cannot resolve all disagreements. The examples also show that disagreements can result from inadequate practice of a shared hermeneutics. They do not always imply loyalty to competing hermeneutics.

Modern theological hermeneutics is significantly different than the historic approach to Scripture. I postpone presenting it until the second part of the next section because the difference arose historically mainly from the application of biblical doctrine to modern science.

Application: Biblical Anthropology and the Body-Soul Debate

Application is the third phase of hermeneutics. It uses biblical doctrine to evaluate and inform our lives and culture in the present. In this article, we apply Scripture by engaging current concepts of body and soul with biblical anthropology and eschatology.

The task of comparing biblical doctrine to scientific and philosophical concepts of the soul is a particular case of the general challenge of relating truth gained from Scripture to knowledge from experience and reason. Theo-

32. Wright, *Resurrection*, 475–79.

logians have labeled the two sources in various ways: the book of Scripture and the book of nature, supernatural and natural revelation, special and general revelation, revelation and reason, or more specifically, theology and science. For present purposes I use the term *revelation* for the teaching of Scripture, properly determined, and *reason* for the warranted conclusions of philosophy and science (without denying natural revelation and the rationality of Scripture).

The strategies for relating them are well known: Either revelation is the framework for interpreting and evaluating reason, or reason is the framework for interpreting and evaluating revelation, or they address different issues (compartmentalism), or they address the same issues in different ways (compatibilism), or they imply a third position with which both are compatible (harmonization). These strategies are not entirely exclusive because revelation and reason relate differently on different levels and different topics within a comprehensive synthesis of knowledge.

But for basic truth-claims that cannot be reconciled—whether about nature, history, morality, worldview, or God—there are only two basic strategies: Either the truth-content of revelation is the standard for judging the claims of reason, or the claims of reason are the standard for judging the truth-content of revelation. Simply put, historic theology and post-Enlightenment theology disagree about which one is the final standard, and this difference has major implications for biblical hermeneutics and Christian doctrine, including anthropology and eschatology. The doctrine of humanity, based on a plenary theological interpretation of Scripture, is the traditional standard for constructing philosophical anthropology and interpreting scientific studies of humanity. Modern theology typically uses current science and philosophical anthropology as standards for interpreting and appropriating Scripture. This difference is the key source of the current diversity among Christians over the biblical doctrine of human nature and the life to come.

Traditional Hermeneutics, Philosophy, and Science

We have noted the traditional ecumenical view of the inspiration, authority, and plenary truth-content of Scripture. This view of Scripture has led the ecumenical Christian tradition to conclude that God's action in creation and providence is both supernatural and natural, that creation has both spiritual and physical dimensions and creatures, and that humans are both spiritual and physical beings. The fathers and doctors of the church articulated this perspective—sometimes using modified ideas of Plato, Plotinus, and Aristotle and incorporating the science of their era—in their accounts of human composition. Augustine and Aquinas are preeminent examples. We may question whether their philosophical choices always represented Scripture accurately. But there is no question that they gave priority to supernatural revelation and theology as queen of the sciences. Orthodox Protestant theologians retained this order for relating biblical doctrine and other kinds of learning.

Modern science—Copernicus, Galileo, and Darwin—challenged both traditional science and biblical interpretation about the structure and history of the universe and humanity. Eventually—often with internal resistance and strife—most Christian traditions figured out how to accommodate and affirm modern science within a larger perspective, a framework that retains the essential beliefs about Scripture, supernatural theology, and the dualism-in-unity anthropology that they drew from Scripture. Most recently, Christian intellectuals have incorporated the science of human origins within the historic perspective, either as supernatural theistic evolution or progressive creation.[33] In sum, the ecumenical traditions have found reasonable ways of integrating modern science and biblical scholarship with the theological and metaphysical implications of their historic doctrine of divine revelation in Scripture and the worldview it expresses.

The ecumenical traditions altered their interpretations of Scripture to accommodate modern ideas only when rationally necessary, and they did not find it necessary to abandon the essentials of the traditional theological worldview. Their solutions typically relate science, philosophy, and theology as a hierarchy of disciplines addressing distinct but partially overlapping aspects of reality as disclosed in natural and supernatural revelation. Each discipline has its own domain and authority. But the foundational principles of science are philosophical (metaphysical and epistemological), and to some extent the relevant metaphysical and epistemological principles reflect or at

33. Supernatural theistic evolution holds that God supernaturally augmented biological evolution to create humans. See B. B. Warfield, "Calvin's Doctrine of Creation," *The Princeton Theological Review*, xiii (1915), 190–255, and John Paul II, "Message to the Pontifical Academy of Sciences: On Evolution" (1996), Catholic Information Network website, http://www.cin.org/jp2evolu.html. Progressive Creation and Intelligent Design affirm the scientific dating of the universe, the earth, and the fossil and geological records but not the paradigms of cosmic or biological macroevolution. They believe that God specially created new kinds of beings at various points in natural history and guided development within different kinds and levels of being. Progressive Creation's emphasis on specific divine acts that create distinct levels and kinds of beings fits the intention of Genesis 1–3 more fully than theistic evolution.

least are consistent with basic worldview beliefs. In this case these are Christian beliefs about God, the nature of things, and the human capacity to know them. Related in this way, science and philosophy can arrive at conclusions that are consistent with, if not actually conducive to, biblical claims about God's supernatural action, his special creation of humans with an immaterial ingredient, and disembodied personal existence. Science and philosophy can neither verify these claims of revelation nor rule them out.[34]

Modern Hermeneutics, Philosophy, and Science

Modern theology and biblical scholarship take distance from the traditional view of Scripture and its contents. During the Enlightenment, progressive Christians became convinced that theistic naturalism is more reasonable than traditional supernaturalism. Theistic naturalism, as held by the Deists and Spinoza, claims that God's presence and action in the world conform entirely to the natural order as understood by reason. Accordingly, critical biblical scholarship proceeds from the axiom of naturalism and its corollary, historicism, in its view of the origin and content of Scripture.[35] God reveals himself most explicitly in the history of religious experience.[36] The Bible is the cumulative result of oral and written religious expressions of the people of Israel and the early church. In general, the various books of Scripture express common core beliefs about God and his redemptive purposes. But they do so in terms of anachronistic, diverse, and sometimes incompatible views of nature, history, morality, the supernatural, and even of God.[37] Natural and historical

34. Ecumenical examples of comprehensive Christian perspectives are John Paul II's encyclical, *Fides et Ratio: On the Relationship Between Faith and Reason* (Vatican, 1998); Alvin Plantinga, *Warranted Christian Belief* (Oxford, 2000); J. P. Moreland and William Lane Craig, *Philosophical Foundations for a Christian Worldview* (Intervarsity, 2003); and Fr. Vladimir Shmaliy, "The Cosmology of the Cappadocian Fathers: A Contribution to Dialogue Between Science and Theology Today," *Faith and Philosophy* 22/5 (2005), 528–42.

35. C. Stephen Evans, *The Historical Christ and the Jesus of Faith: The Incarnational Narrative as History* (Oxford, 1996), for an elaboration and critique of the assumptions of critical biblical scholarship; also Alvin Plantinga, *Warranted Christian Belief*, Ch. 12, "Two (or More) Kinds of Scripture Scholarship"; Michael Legaspi, *The Death of Scripture and the Rise of Biblical Studies* (Oxford, 2010), Ch. 1.

36. Schleiermacher, Hegel, Schelling and their theological disciples elaborate this view of primary divine revelation.

37. Bultmann's famous incredulity toward the biblical worldview in "The New Testament and Mythology," *Kerygma and Myth* (1953; HarperCollins, 2000), is the most radical outcome

occurrences portrayed as supernatural, miraculous, or otherwise contrary to scientific knowledge of nature must be interpreted symbolically. As a result, modern theologians conclude that the enduring truth-content of Scripture is thinner, less specific, and more historically malleable than the traditional plenary view. In addition, many modern Christians hold that divine revelation in religious experience progresses beyond the biblical canon. Thus they claim that traditional theology distorts Scripture by arbitrarily harmonizing diverse perspectives, constructing an artificial consensus, and divinizing it as infallible final truth. Instead, modern theologians interpret Scripture, select tenable themes and ideas, and elaborate Christian doctrine in terms of what they regard as the best current perspective, whether idealism, romanticism, existentialism, a social liberation agenda, or a science-based worldview such as emergent physicalism.[38]

Theological anthropology and eschatology are part of this history.[39] Materialistic exegesis of the body-soul texts of Scripture was pioneered by Thomas Hobbes in the seventeenth century.[40] But until recently he had few followers. Dualistic and idealistic anthropologies remained prominent in philosophy into the twentieth century, and scientific naturalism was limited to the material realm. Thus nineteenth-century liberal theology, following Kant and Schleiermacher, could forgo a literal resurrection of the earthly body without denying personal immortality.[41] This position is reminiscent of Plato's radical dualism between the material and ideal dimensions of human existence. Cullmann's famous essay "Immortality of the Soul or Resurrection of the Dead?" was

---

of this view. Body-soul dualism, disembodied existence, and bodily resurrection are as outmoded as angels, miracles, and a literal return of Jesus.

38. Manfred Oeming, *Contemporary Biblical Hermeneutics: An Introduction*, trans. J. Vette (Ashgate, 2006), Part II, "The Plurality of Current Approaches to the Bible."

39. Jeffrey Burton Russell, *Paradise Mislaid: How We Lost Heaven—and How We Can Regain It* (Oxford, 2006), is an illuminating history of the impact of physicalism on Christian theology, anthropology, and eschatology.

40. Hobbes, *Leviathan*, Ch. 34, "Of the Significance of Spirit, Angel, and Inspiration in the Books of Holy Scripture," is materialistic exegesis and anthropology. He claims that souls, spirits, and angels are mental states of living humans that were mistakenly reified as distinct beings by traditional theology. He dismisses dualistic understandings of body, soul, and spirit as "pernicious Aristotelian nonsense." His arguments are quite current.

41. See Schleiermacher, *Christian Faith*, sec. 161, on the intermediate state and resurrection, and sec. 163, on eternal blessedness. He affirms eternal blessedness but is agnostic about the intermediate state and resurrection body because Scripture is unclear and all doctrinal constructions present insoluble problems. Kant argues for the immortality of the soul in *Critique of Practical Reason* and applies it to Christian eschatology in *Religion within the Bounds of Reason Alone*. Both men were major influences in liberal Protestant theology.

aimed primarily at this Platonic eschatology.[42] Monistic anthropology gradually gained traction among progressive Christians during the first half of the twentieth century as they accepted human evolution and scientific psychology, both of which viewed the soul as a function of the organism. But materialism remained difficult to integrate into the modern Christian worldview as long as it was associated with atheists such as Karl Marx and Bertrand Russell.

Christian materialism became tenable with the conjunction of two intellectual shifts during the mid-twentieth century. One is the return of mainline theology from Barth and Bultmann's stress on divine transcendence to post-Hegelian panentheism, which emphasizes the immanence of God in the cosmos and history.[43] The other is the conversion of science to Big Bang cosmology, which implies that the universe has been evolving ever since its beginning. Synthesized, these paradigms constitute a comprehensive worldview in which God has generated everything in the universe from primordial physical energy by entirely natural processes. If cosmic evolution is ontological—if it generates new and irreducible levels of being—then this perspective is aptly designated *theistic emergent monism*[44] or *theistic non-reductive physicalism*.[45] The human spirit, mind, soul, and body are natural transformations of physical energy.

This theological-scientific worldview is the framework from which many Christian academics currently approach biblical anthropology and eschatology. They believe that theistic emergent physicalism is the correct reading of the book of nature and the book of Scripture. They find that the biblical presentation of human nature is consistent with this perspective, emphasizing the earthliness, embodiment, integration, and mortality of this life, and anticipating bodily resurrection for the life to come. The few texts that support dualism—including special creation from distinct ingredients, and persons existing between death and resurrection—they treat as anachronisms, like

42. Oscar Cullmann, "Immortality of the Soul or Resurrection of the Dead?" in *Theologische Zeitschrift* (1956) and in *Immortality and Resurrection* (Macmillan, 1965) with essays by three other Harvard Ingersoll Lecturers.

43. Michael Brierly, "Naming a Quiet Revolution: The Panentheistic Turn in Modern Theology," *In Whom We Live and Move and Have Our Being: Panentheistic Reflections on God's Presence in a Scientific World*, ed. P. Clayton and A. Peacocke (Eerdmans, 2004); Cooper, *Panentheism: The Other God of the Philosophers—From Plato to the Present* (Baker, 2006). Teilhard, Whitehead, Tillich, Moltmann, Pannenberg, most liberation theologians, Peacocke, Polkinghorne, and Clayton are prominent contributors to this theological-philosophical-scientific perspective.

44. Arthur Peacock, *All That Is: A Naturalistic Faith for the Twenty-First Century*, ed. P. Clayton (Fortress, 2007), "Emergent Monism" and "Theistic Naturalism", 12–20.

45. Nancey Murphy, *Bodies and Souls, or Spirited Bodies?* 69–70.

the Bible's pre-scientific views of the solar system. Christians who take this approach conclude that biblical anthropology is much more compatible with monism than dualism. Because monism entails that humans cannot exist without bodies, they conclude that biblical eschatology implies either immediate resurrection[46] or non-existence (except in God's mind) until the future general resurrection.[47] A third hypothesis is that at death God splits the matter of the organism into a corpse and a person-sustaining body that endures until the resurrection—a noteworthy proposal consistent with two-stage eschatology.[48] In these ways, many Christians conclude that biblical anthropology and eschatology are consistent with theistic emergent physicalism.[49]

Conclusion: Let's Be Candid about Hermeneutics and Worldview

Whose interpretation? Which anthropology? These questions highlight the role of biblical hermeneutics as a major factor in the Christian debate about the body-soul or body-mind relation. The key hermeneutical issue is theistic naturalism construed in terms of evolutionary materialism or emergent physicalism, a worldview based on current science. One's attitude toward this worldview reliably predicts one's anthropology. Christians stand on both sides.

Many Christian scholars do not find sufficient reason in science and philosophy to affirm this worldview. Thus they do not think that science and philosophy defeat or undermine the historic interpretation of Scripture. They do not find this worldview adequate for the biblical doctrines of human origin, the image of God, the soul, and the life to come, or sufficient for a tenable philosophy of mind and moral agency. These scholars hold positions on the body-soul relation that are consistent with the historic Christian duality-in-

46. For example, John Hick, *Death and Eternal Life* (Westminster/John Knox 1994), Ch. 15, "The Resurrection of the Person;" and Wolfhart Pannneberg, *Systematic Theology*, Vol. 3 (Eerdmans 1998), Ch. 15, sec. 3, "The Kingdom of God and the End of Time."

47. For example, John Polkinghorne, *Science and Christian Belief: Theological Reflections of a Bottom-Up Thinker* (SPMK, 1994), "Eschatology"; and Trenton Merricks, "The Resurrection of the Body and the Life Everlasting," 261–86.

48. Kevin Corcoran, "Physical Persons and Postmortem Survival without Temporal Gaps," in *Soul, Body, and Survival: Essays on the Metaphysics of Human Persons*, ed. K. Corcoran (Cornell, 2001), 201–17; Timothy O'Connor and Jonathan Jacobs, "Emergent Individuals and the Resurrection," *European Journal for Philosophy of Religion* 2 (2010), 69–88.

49. It is noteworthy that both immediate resurrection and future resurrection after non-existence require God's supernatural action and an ontological person-body dichotomy after all.

unity position, either because they begin from it, or find that common sense, science, and philosophy support it, or both.

But many other Christians are convinced that science and philosophy do provide sufficient reason to affirm theistic emergent monism, to question traditional anthropology and eschatology, and to revise their interpretation of Scripture accordingly. Modern and postmodern Christians adopt this worldview as a comprehensive framework for hermeneutics and theology. Scholars who otherwise affirm historic confessional and evangelical Christianity adopt the perspective in more limited ways for metaphysics, anthropology, and eschatology.

In sum, Christians simply differ on whether there is sufficient reason—given everything we know from Scripture, science, and philosophy—to affirm, modify, or abandon historic Christian body-soul dualism. More basically, we disagree about the relative authority of Scripture, philosophy, and science as sources of truth about the human constitution.

I therefore encourage more hermeneutical clarity and transparency as we continue the dialogue. It is naïve or dishonest to quote Scripture or invoke "the biblical view of human nature" without putting our hermeneutical cards on the table. I call for more self-awareness and disclosure about our actual views of Scripture, methods of biblical interpretation, and the ways we relate them to our theoretical concepts of body and soul. Such candor could advance our discussions by locating common ground and distinguishing potentially resolvable differences from those that are beyond rational settlement.

I also urge hermeneutical transparency when we address non-professional audiences—especially students and lay Christians who are not familiar with the interpretive issues. It is as confusing and upsetting for traditional Christians to be told that the Bible is monistic and that Grandma isn't really in heaven with Jesus, as it is for modern Christians to hear that they must believe in immaterial souls and a literal return of Jesus from heaven. The body-soul question is much like the creation-evolution debate. Both are hermeneutically complex issues that have deeply spiritual significance for many people. None of us has the right to declare what Scripture teaches or what competent biblical scholarship has demonstrated without helping folks to ask the key questions: Whose interpretation? Which anthropology?[50]

50. I am grateful to Jason McMartin, Arvin Vos, and Thomas Crisp for insightful and helpful comments on previous versions of this paper.

CHAPTER 20

Whose Interpretation? Which Anthropology? Indeed: A Response to John W. Cooper

Brian Lugioyo

Ours is an exciting historical moment, where anthropological discussions, like these, are vital to the church's health. The discoveries of neuroscience and neurobiology have remarkably unveiled hidden aspects of the human life. With these discoveries the West's anthropology has been shifting to a more holistic, if not monist view. No doubt those who have interpreted Scripture's anthropology more holistically have seen an ally in these philosophical-scientific paradigms. Yet others have perceived this shift as an enemy to gospel truth. In this latter regard, John Cooper, in his essay promoting a dualistic reading of Scripture, suggests that Christian scholars who hold to monistic interpretations of Scripture predominantly do so on account of their prioritizing of science over the Bible. In other words, neuroscience has co-opted biblical exegesis. This is a serious claim; one I am glad to respond to.

Cooper's essay promotes a holistic dualism that is eschatologically orientated, emphasizing the immortality of the soul and arguing that this view is both historically ecumenical and scripturally established. His central argument is not necessarily that souls exist (in the body-soul debate), but that they exist in a disembodied form after death. This disembodied view is founded on the idea that the body lost its natural immortality after the fall, on account of its separation at death from the soul—which is sustained as immortal by God. This view, Cooper argues, is the anthropological view both of historic Christianity and in Scripture. He also posits that the reason for the body-soul debate in the last century is predominantly tied to the rejection of a historic supernatural hermeneutic that was replaced by a scientific one. For Cooper the immortality of the soul is a biblically revealed doctrine.

This brief essay, in response to Cooper's argument, is divided into three general sections. This first section deals with how we are to view theological anthropology throughout the life of the church, especially in light of Cooper's claim of a dualistic uniformity. The second section attempts to demonstrate how the biblical texts Cooper exegetes may more logically support a monistic position. And lastly, the third section will touch on why, leaving aside science, a monistic interpretation of Scripture is healthy for the church's ministry.

The Anthropology of the Church

To say that a doctrine is historic and ecumenical is to say not only that this doctrine has had a continuous presence throughout the life of the church, but also rhetorically to claim that it is indisputable, even foundational to the church's teachings. Both these claims tend to present, perhaps unwillingly, a monolithic view of the church's anthropological teachings, which obscures the contexts and emphases of the church's teaching in this area.

Cooper's claim that holistic dualism has been the historic position of the church is a sweeping generalization. A variety of anthropologies have been held throughout the life of the church, though dualistic varieties have been the most prevalent. Yet, dualisms are not all alike. Irenaeus's anthropology is different from Origen's, which is different from Augustine's, which is different from Thomas's, which is different from Cooper's. Though Cooper acknowledges differences, it would aid the discussion to clearly articulate the differences as well as the diverse contexts from which they arise. To posit a continuous ecumenical dualism is to minimize the widely divergent positions and their contexts, thus painting a uniformity that history cannot support. Cooper's assertion that dualism is the historic position of the church needs to be complexified.

That the body-soul debate is ancient is not in question. It is more ancient than Christianity itself. In the early church the debate arose in the context of defending the central anthropological teaching of the church, the resurrection of the body—a doctrine much maligned in the ancient world. Thus, in a setting that predominantly disparaged physical creation, especially the body, the fathers employed anthropological arguments and biblical exegesis that emphasized the physicality of human life against forms of Christian Gnosticism that exegetically argued for the radical priority of the immortal soul.[1] Within this early setting, anthropological orthodoxy was not tied to the immortality of

1. Elaine H. Pagels, "The Valentinian Claim to Esoteric Exegesis of Romans as Basis for Anthropological Theory," *Vigiliae Christianae* 26 (1972): 241–58.

the soul, but to the resurrection of the body. In some debates the fathers would even regard the image of God not as soulish (something modern dualists are wont to do, conflating Genesis 1 with Genesis 2), but as including a person's physicality. For example, against the Valentinian Gnostics, Iranaeus stated that

> . . . man, and not [merely] a part of man, was made in the likeness of God. Now the soul and the spirit are certainly a *part* of the man, but certainly not *the* man; for the perfect man consists in the commingling and the union of the soul receiving the spirit of the Father, and the admixture of that fleshly nature which was moulded after the image of God. (*Against Heresies* 5.6.1)

Repeatedly, heresies that elevated the nonmaterial soul and diminished the body have been rejected in the tradition. Ever since, the Christian tradition arguably has made the body the central component to ecumenical anthropology.

Cooper's presentation of the immortality of the soul as the defining element of a dualism that is historic and ecumenical diminishes the contexts of early anthropological discussions and misappropriates the importance of these discussions within history. It misappropriates the importance of this particular anthropological teaching by neglecting that there is a hierarchy of Christian anthropological teachings tied to the doctrine of creation and the resurrection of the body. The Apostles' creed and the Nicene creed do not speak of body and soul, even less of the immortality of the soul, but emphasize the resurrected body. In the formula from Chalcedon, soul and body are mentioned, not with regards to an immortal quality that outlasts death, but to convey Jesus's full humanity contra Apollinarius.

There is no unified or consistent anthropological dualism posited in the tradition when context is accounted for, particularly the conceptual categories that each age had at its disposal. As Cooper mentions, Augustine's anthropology is not Thomas's. Partially this is the case because Augustine uses the science of Neoplatonism. And Thomas's teachings on the vegetative, animal, and rational soul are due more to an exegesis of Aristotle than Paul. The differences in their anthropologies are tied not to exegesis, but to the science shaping their exegetical decisions. To say any less is to not understand this teaching in history. That they used the science of their age does not disparage their exegesis, but the hermeneutical spiral isn't easy to penetrate.

Additionally, to describe the absence of this discussion prior to the Enlightenment, as Cooper does, is to disregard how the commentators on Aristotle caused quite a stir in the 14th and 15th centuries. Various understandings of Aristotle led to differing views of the immortality of the soul, which would be discussed at the Fifth Lateran Council (1512–17). Up to this point, the church had no need for an ecumenical statement on the immortality of the soul, since the dominant science had not been questioned. But with the resurgence of Aristotle, some commentators discerned that Aristotle conveyed a view that the soul died with the body. On this basis as well as a deep concern with the church's teachings on purgatory, various Italian Evangelicals (including some Anabaptist groups) rejected the idea of the immortality of the soul and advocated a view commonly called psychopannychism (soul sleep).[2] This was the idea that when the body dies the soul waits unconsciously for the resurrection of the body (a view different from modern advocates of dualism). This led Pope Leo X to call a council where the philosophical and academic proofs for or against the immortality of the soul were to be rejected. Hence, the church said there, we do not get our anthropology from philosophy. As Eric Constant has shown, the Fifth Lateran Council did not condemn the idea of the mortality of the soul, but the philosophy that influenced this view, particularly Pietro Pomponazzi's view of "double truth."[3] The Italian Evangelical rejection of the immortality of the soul, George Hunston Williams argues, "may be considered the Italian counterpart of Germanic *solafideism* and Swiss predestinationism in contributing to the dismantlement of the medieval structures of sacramental grace."[4]

The anthropological debates and the diversity of their contexts are both fascinating and illuminating. These few discussions mentioned above predate the Enlightenment, so do the philosophical debates of Plato, Aristotle, Epicurus, and Zeno. I am weary of the claim that this body-soul debate is relatively new in the church and on account of the Enlightenment. What is seemingly new is the emphasis on the immortality of the soul against Christian anthropologies that prioritize the goodness of creation and centrality of the

2. See George H. Williams, *The Radical Reformation*, 3rd ed. (Kirksville, MO: Truman State University, 2000), 63–72. Here Williams states, "The magisterium insisted that each created soul, as the substantial form of the body, is capable of existing sentiently prior to the resurrection. This importation of natural theology into Catholic dogma was, in point of fact, much closer to Platonic philosophy than to the Bible. But the natural immortality of the soul had become so integral a part of the massive penitential and liturgical structure of Catholic moral theology that the philosophical threat to it moved Pope Leo X, in the first year of his pontificate, to condemn in 1513, at the eighth session of the Fifth Lateran Council, the philosophical proofs and disproofs of immortality in the universities and academic circles" (66).

3. Eric A. Constant, "A Reinterpretation of the Fifth Lateran Council Decree *Apostolici regiminis* (1513)," in *Sixteenth Century Journal* 23.2 (2002): 353–79.

4. Williams, *The Radical Reformation*, 70.

resurrection of the body exegetically.[5] When the early church fathers wrote on anthropological issues they emphasized the importance of the body and they challenged those who wanted to say too much in regard to the immortality of the soul. It obscures history to say that dualism is ecumenical when no council has affirmed it and when the key tenet of Christian anthropology has always been physically orientated whether dualistic or not.

Furthermore, the claim of ecumenical consensus, which Cooper uses as a criterion for the validity of a dualistic anthropology, should be elaborated on. Take for instance the Reformed doctrine of the spiritual presence that is neither historical nor ecumenical. The real presence of Christ's body in the Eucharist (a doctrine of the Eastern Orthodox, Roman Catholic, and various Protestant churches) shares an ecumenical consensus. Does this invalidate the Reformed doctrine? How does this criterion function in determining the validity of a doctrine in some areas and not others?

Cooper's use of the argument for a unified ecumenical tradition radically homogenizes a complex past. Rather than generalizing the tradition, we ought first to accurately illuminate the context of the various historical anthropological discussions, and second, to properly consider the weight of this body-soul discussion within the hierarchy of Christian truth. I believe that Cooper and I would agree on these points, our rhetoric aside.

Cooper's Exegesis

Establishing a theological anthropology from Scripture is difficult. The Scriptures do not provide a clear human blueprint. Scripture is predominantly concerned with God and humanity's relationship to God, and much less concerned with the constitutional makeup of persons.[6] Nevertheless, though the

5. On another, yet relevant, note it is curiously interesting that prior to the 19th century there was a historic and ecumenical practice of rejecting cremation, taking great care of dead bodies, and the building of cemeteries on account of the church's ancient anthropological emphasis on the body. And yet during the middle of the 19th century, some churches, influenced by anthropological dualism, accepted the practice of burning dead bodies, rejecting the historic practice. Exploring this shift in the church's care of dead bodies may be telling. See Diarmaid MacCulloch, *Christianity: The First Three Thousand Years* (New York: Viking, 2010), 160, 1013; and Robert Louis Wilkens, *The First Thousand Years: A Global History of Christianity* (New Haven, CT: Yale University Press, 2012), 47–56, 156.

6. See Joel Green, *Body, Soul, and Human Life: The Nature of Humanity in the Bible* (Grand Rapids: Baker Academic, 2008), 3. Here Green reminds us that ". . . the Bible is about God, first and foremost, and only derivatively about us. Study of the human person in the

Bible may not emphasize our makeup as a priority, it does provide important clues about what it means to be human, as Cooper affirms.

Cooper briefly provides three exegetical examples where one might discern a scriptural anthropology. The first two exegetical cases surround the first chapters of Genesis and the concept of *sheol*; the last one looks at Paul's language. As Cooper himself acknowledges, there are no clear-cut conclusions.

There exists in modern biblical scholarship a general consensus that the anthropology of the Bible is predominantly monistic, particularly in the Old Testament.[7] Even Robert Gundry, one of North America's most meticulous exegetes and an advocate for holistic dualism, states that "in the OT body and soul do not contrast. Man is an animated body rather than an incarnated soul. The breath which God breathed into molded clay at the creation represents the principle of life; and the soul that resulted is the human person as a whole. Thus man does not have a body; he is a body—a psychophysical unity."[8] Even dualists contest Cooper's exegetical conclusions on Genesis, as he well knows.

More specifically, the linguistic, literary, and historical analysis he provides seems sloppy. His linguistic analysis of *neshama* as an anthropological "ingredient" is semantically difficult to justify. This term's central idea is tied to the concept of life and vitality that are a gift given from God, which is related to other Hebrew nouns tied to life and breath, including *nephesh*, *ruach*, *chayyim*,

---

Bible—that is, a biblical—theological anthropology or, more simply, a biblical anthropology—is thus a derivative inquiry. It is secondary." See also, Nancey Murphy, *Bodies and Souls, or Spirited Bodies?* (New York: Cambridge University Press, 2006), 22.

7. Various reference books in contemporary Biblical Studies provide a monist anthropology; for example, the *Anchor Bible Dictionary*, *Theological Dictionary of the Old Testament*, etc. See also Brevard S. Childs, *Old Testament Theology in Canonical Perspective* (Philadelphia: Fortress, 1985), 199; Walter Bruegemann, *Theology of the Old Testament: Testimony, Dispute, Advocacy* (Minneapolis: Fortress Press, 1997), 450–54; Theo Heckel, "Body and Soul in Saint Paul," in *Psyche and Soma: Physicians and Metaphysicians on the Mind-Body Problem from Antiquity to Enlightenment*, ed. by John P. Wright and Paul Potter (Oxford: Clarendon, 2000), 117–31; Udo Schnell, *The Human Condition: Anthropology in the Teachings of Jesus, Paul, and John* (Minneapolis: Fortress, 1996); Paul Jewett, *Paul's Anthropological Terms: A Study of Their Use in Conflict Settings* (Leiden: Brill, 1971); N. T. Wright, *The New Testament and the People of God* (Minneapolis: Fortress, 1992), 252–56; and Joel Green, *Body, Soul, and Human Life*.

8. Robert Gundry, *Sōma in Biblical Theology: With Emphasis on Pauline Anthropology* (Grand Rapids: Academie Books Zondervan Publishing House, 1987), 118–19. It is also worth noting that in another essay, Gundry states that "The Bible does not teach a natural immortality (much less a preexistence) of the soul" ("The Essential Physicality of Jesus' Resurrection according to the NT," in *The Old Is Better: New Testament Essays in Support of Traditional Interpretations* [Tübingen: Mohr Siebeck, 2005], 189).

and *leb*.[9] His literary analysis conflates the significant literary differences of Genesis 1 and Genesis 2. And his historical analysis neglects the intimate creation stories of ancient Egyptian texts[10] and ignores the predominantly royal genre of Genesis 1 when tying the image of God with *neshama* in Genesis 2.[11]

In regard to his appeal to the concept of *sheol* as evidence for the immortality of the soul, again we are on precarious exegetical ground. Richard Bauckham after surveying the relevant Old Testament texts and various Second Temple texts concludes that

> Sheol is a kind of mythical version of the tomb, a place of darkness and silence, from which no one returns. This idea of the shades in Sheol is not belief in the survival of the spirit, the spiritual or mental part of a human being which goes on living when the body dies, as much Greek thought after Plato believed. The shades are not immaterial beings, but shadowy, ghostly versions of the living, bodily person, and they can hardly be said to live. They are dead, in a silent, dark, joyless—indeed, deathly—existence, cut off from God, the source of all life.[12]

Ignoring the overwhelming evidence and advocating that a few of the many uses of *sheol* substantiate a post-mortem existence is difficult to conceive. Finding a verse or two to validate one's own position does not create a consistent biblical theme. This is poor exegesis, especially since every instance of the term

9. See T. C. Mitchell, "OT usage of neshama," in *Vetus Testamentum* 11 (1961): 177–87.

10. See the *Wisdom-book of Merikare* in James B. Pritchard, ed., *Ancient Near Eastern Texts Relating to the Old Testament* (Princeton, NJ: Princeton University Press, 1969), 417; and the *Coffin Texts Spells* in William W. Hallo, ed., *The Context of Scripture: Canonical Compositions from the Biblical World*, vol. 1 (Leiden: Brill, 1997), 13. See also John Walton, *Ancient Near Eastern Thought and the Old Testament* (Grand Rapids: Baker Academic, 2006), 205–6.

11. See J. Richard Middleton, *The Liberating Image: The* Imago Dei *in Genesis 1* (Grand Rapids: Brazos Press, 2005).

12. Richard Bauckham, "Life, Death, and the Afterlife in Second Temple Judaism," in *The Jewish World Around the New Testament* (Grand Rapids: Baker Academic, 2010), 245. In regard to the biblical view of death in general N. T. Wright states, "All is given up. That is part of what death is. To insist that we 'possess' an 'immortal part' (call it 'soul' or whatever) which cannot be touched by death might look suspiciously like the ontological equivalent of works-righteousness in its old-fashioned sense: something we possess which enables us to establish a claim on God, in this case a claim to 'survive.'" See N. T. Wright, "Mind, Spirit, Soul and Body: All for One and One for All: Reflections on Paul's Anthropology in His Complex Contexts," paper delivered March 18, 2011, for the Society of Christian Philosophers: Regional Meeting, Fordham University, <ntwrightpage.com/Wright_SCP_MindSpiritSoulBody.htm> (accessed online June 2, 2014).

sheol does not intend to explicitly articulate the immortality of the soul, but usually death, judgment, or despair. Careful exegesis of these *sheol* texts and their contexts often reveals monistic tendencies rather than dualistic ones.

The last biblical example Cooper presents is tied to Paul's anthropological language. Here one ought to consider the first-century cosmological and anthropological frameworks that Paul and other New Testament authors made use of. God did not provide Paul and others a complete anthropology. Interpreting texts where anthropological language is used can be aided by understanding the first-century anthropological options. In this regard, the work of Troels Engberg-Pedersen is helpful in illuminating Paul's philosophical backgrounds.[13] Engberg-Pedersen convincingly demonstrates the use of Stoic thought in Paul's use of the term "spirit," and as such sees Paul and his writings pushing against dualistic philosophies of the day by using Stoic ideas that posit a more monistic anthropology, which is also consistent with the Old Testament. This is but one of many monistic interpretations of Paul.

Establishing our doctrinal anthropologies from the exegesis of Scripture is critical, yet hard, work. It is doubly difficult in synthesizing or developing a plenary dualistic view of anthropology from Scripture. Cooper attempts to synthesize from various parts of the canon to demonstrate a rational dualist view—however, the exegetical consensus of the Old Testament, Paul,[14] Luke,[15] and John[16] seems to offer a reasonable pattern that is opposite to Cooper's own conclusion. It also should be clearly stated that exegetes who discover a monistic account in Scripture would not state that their monistic interpretations stem from a priority toward science or philosophy, but rather that the exegesis of the texts speak for themselves—particularly in regard to the passages Cooper uses as examples.

13. See Troels Engberg-Pedersen, *Cosmology & Self in the Apostle Paul: The Material Spirit* (Oxford: Oxford University Press, 2010) and *Paul and the Stoics* (Nashville: Westminster John Knox, 2000).

14. See N. T. Wright, *Paul and the Faithfulness of God* (Minneapolis: Fortress Press, 2013), 490–94; Theo Heckel, "Body and Soul in Saint Paul," in *Psyche and Soma: Physicians and Metaphysicians on the Mind-Body Problem from Antiquity to Enlightenment*, ed. by John P. Wright and Paul Potter (Oxford: Clarendon, 2000), 117–31; Udo Schnell, *The Human Condition: Anthropology in the Teachings of Jesus, Paul, and John* (Minneapolis: Fortress, 1996); Paul Jewett, *Paul's Anthropological Terms: A Study of Their Use in Conflict Settings* (Leiden: Brill, 1971).

15. See Green, *Body, Soul, and Human Life*.

16. See Schnell, *The Human Condition*.

A Ministerial Hermeneutic

Theology has always included exegetical rigor, but never apart from the ministry and life of the church. Doctrines do not arise from an anachronistic *sola Scriptura* principle; they arise in the worshiping life of the church. The doctrine of the Trinity can be argued exegetically, but it was the experience of worshiping Jesus as God that was the decisive argument. As such our doctrines are tied to our worship, not just to our reading of texts. To approach the text of Scripture as a scientific blueprint that will reveal the secret truth of what it means to be human is to mangle the text and to avoid the human bodies we minister to week in and week out.

Thus, the modern appeal to more monistic understandings of persons has not been solely tied to a theological naturalism or scriptural exegesis, as Cooper outlines, but also to ministerial considerations. As I have written elsewhere, a "healthy theological anthropology begins in the context of the church."[17] A *praxis* hermeneutic can be another primary influence on our theological anthropological conclusions.[18]

As Cooper knows, various practical objections have arisen in the last century toward anthropological dualism.[19] It is the contention by various exegetes, theologians, and ministers that a dualistic position has facilitated dehumanizing practices like slavery[20] and sexism.[21] Though these dehumanizing

17. See Brian Lugioyo, "Ministering to Bodies: Anthropological Views of Soma in the NT, Theology, and Neuroscience," in *Reconsidering the Relationship between Biblical and Systematic Theology in the New Testament: Essays by Theologians and New Testament Scholars*, edited by Benjamin Reynolds, Brian Lugioyo, and Kevin Vanhoozer (Tübingen: Mohr Siebeck, 2014), 213–37, 233.

18. See Ray S. Anderson, *The Shape of Practical Theology: Empowering Ministry with Theological Praxis* (Downers Grove, IL: IVP, 2001).

19. John Cooper, *Body, Soul, & Life Everlasting: Biblical Anthropology and the Monism-Dualism Debate* (Grand Rapids: Eerdmans, 1989), 26–32, 179–203. It should be noted that in defending dualism against the objections from various scholars, Cooper does not engage any of the arguments of his opponents, but rather in a general manner groups them into six general challenges.

20. See Stephen G. Post, "A Moral Case for Nonreductive Physicalism," in *Whatever Happened to the Soul?: Scientific and Theological Portraits of Human Nature*, ed. Nancey Murphy, Warren Brown, and H. Newton Malony (Minneapolis: Fortress, 1998), 204, and Theo Witvliet, *A Place in the Sun* (Maryknoll, NY: Orbis, 1985). Also, Willie James Jennings articulates this issue in *The Christian Imagination: Theology and the Origins of Race* (New Haven, CT: Yale University Press, 2011).

21. See Post, "A Moral Case," 205–9; James B. Nelson, *Between Two Gardens: Reflections on Sexuality and Religious Experience* (New York: Pilgrim Press, 1983); Elisabeth Schüssler

tendencies are not necessarily required by a dualistic anthropology, forms of Christian dualism (rejected by a number of modern Christian dualists) have often been used by Christians to warrant and justify these abusive practices. And this is just one reason why the monist position is more ecclesially attractive, since such dehumanizing perspectives no longer become available.

The danger of modern dualism, which is more frequently experienced within today's church, is tied to the gnostic-like priority given to the spiritual self over the bodily self. Warren Brown and Brad Strawn show how the dualist character of much contemporary Christianity, with its inward focus, has created a hyper-individualistic and interior faith. They write that the "inward focus on the soul, fostered by dualism, creates a strong magnet drawing modern religious perspectives almost inevitably toward Gnosticism."[22] A dualistic anthropology cannot but elevate the interior life above the exterior life of the body. When Cooper ties personality, subjectivity, and agency to the soul that survives the body, the soul cannot but be more highly valued than the physical body, which cannot survive death. As such, modern dualism, even when strongly unitive, tends to have within its DNA the tendency to prioritize the soul over the body. This is a biblical and theological problem.

The central aspect of a person (if there is one central aspect) is much more than an ontological substance that survives death. A theology of what a person is has to reckon primarily with the person in front of us, neither the soul behind her nor the eschatological soul detached from a decaying body. It is difficult to conceive how the modern dualistic view aids the Lord's ministry to persons. Our view of persons matters; how we view them determines how we will minister to them.[23]

Conclusion

The body-soul debate is lively. And there will be strong defenses on both sides, employing various criteria for validity. Currently, I am convinced that by carefully listening to God's Word, by honing in on the church's historic

---

Fiorenza, "Feminist Theology as a Critical Theology of Liberation," *Theological Studies* 36.4 (1975): 605–26; and Rosemary Radford Reuther, "Motherearth and the Megamachine," in *Womanspirit Rising: A Feminist Reader in Religion*, ed. Carol P. Christ and Judith Plaskow (San Francisco: Harper & Row, 1979), 44.

22. Warren S. Brown and Brad D. Strawn, *The Physical Nature of Christian Life: Neuroscience, Psychology, & the Church* (New York: Cambridge University Press, 2012), 23.

23. See Lugioyo, "Ministering to Bodies."

physical emphases, by wrestling with the recent scientific discoveries of God's creation, and by tenderly ministering to the living persons under our care, we can reasonably argue that a non-reductive physicalist or monistic position is the most reasonable option the church has.[24] Hence, I find no justifiable reason to postulate the immortality of the soul, except the fear of death. But, I am confident that God raises people from the dead regardless of whether their soul is immortal or not.

24. I find that the following monistic works, which posit personhood physically, relationally, and narratively, particularly compelling: Green, *Body, Soul, and Human Life;* Brown and Strawn, *The Physical Nature of Christian Life;* and Murphy, *Bodies and Souls.*

CHAPTER 21

OK, But Whose Misunderstanding? A Rejoinder to Brian Lugioyo

John W. Cooper

Indeed, Prof. Lugioyo and I not only have different interpretations of Scripture. We also have different understandings of my paper and the monism-dualism debate. His response involves inaccurate and misleading accounts of my position, makes unwarranted claims about monism, and perpetuates common caricatures of dualism. In the interest of better understanding, I will reiterate my position and point out some problems with Lugioyo's reply.

First let me note that he does not challenge the main thesis of the paper—my summary of the Christian tradition's view of Scripture and hermeneutics and the differences between historic and modern hermeneutics, eschatology, and anthropology. If silence indicates agreement, I welcome it. He focuses on my defense of dualism, which is secondary.

His one disagreement with my summary is whether Christian monism prioritizes science over Scripture. But I do not make that charge, and I do not claim that every monist Bible scholar uses science. Instead I blame monism for reading Scripture under the influence of scientific naturalism and physicalism—problematic philosophy—not sound science. I argue that the dominant academic worldview from which mainline biblical scholarship and theology operate is emergent physical naturalism. I note that Christian dualists, such as John Paul II, coherently affirm evolution, neuroscience, and empirical psychology. In fact empirical science does not support monism because the data of consciousness and the data of neurobiology are irreducibly different and can only be correlated. Both dualism and monism construct philosophical frameworks for the data, and the data under-determine both. So science does not favor monism, monists should not caricature dualism as a scientific anachronism, and Bible scholars should be wary of naturalism and physicalism.

Lugioyo confuses holism with monism and fallaciously claims the high ground of holism for monism. Monism is the metaphysical theory that humans consist entirely of one ingredient or substance. Holism emphasizes the existential unity and integration of body, soul, mind, and spirit, whatever their metaphysical nature. The challenge for dualism is explaining integration. The challenge for monism is explaining how one substance can be irreducibly physical, mental, and spiritual. I elaborate that most traditional Christian anthropology affirms *duality-in-unity* or *dualistic holism*. It is just as holistic as any kind of monism in theory and in practice.

Throughout his reply, Lugioyo misrepresents my position as *the immortality of the soul*. With the tradition, I do affirm personal existence between death and bodily resurrection—that is, *temporary disembodied existence* or *the intermediate state*. But his description ignores my emphasis on soul-body integration in creation, the resurrection, and the Christian life, my statement that body-soul separation is an unnatural consequence of the fall, as well as my expressed doubt that the soul is naturally immortal. Lugioyo defines my anthropology as a whole in terms of a part which he misconstrues. In addition, *immortality of the soul* leaves the false impression that I harbor other connotations of the term—inherent indestructibility, other-worldliness, and preferred disembodiment, like Plato, the Gnostics, and "modern dualism."

I stand by my "sweeping generalization" about ecumenical doctrine, which Lugioyo challenges in his response. I do provide the clear framework he finds lacking when I define monism and dualism in terms of generic "common sense" views of the afterlife and the body-soul relation, not in terms of theological-philosophical concepts of the immortality of the soul. From earliest times to the present, the vast majority in ecumenical Christianity have believed that Scripture teaches a two-stage eschatology of disembodied existence and future resurrection. The diverse anthropologies in the history of Christianity comport with this doctrine and are therefore dualistic. This generalization is validly derived from church history and the current doctrinal standards and liturgies of Orthodox, Roman Catholic, and Protestant churches.

Lugioyo's challenge focuses on the immortality of the soul, which is too narrow. The diverse and complex views of the body-soul relation that he mentions provide no evidence that the church or its doctors were open to monist anthropology or alternative eschatology. Most Anabaptists who affirmed soul sleep were not monists, as alleged, but dualists—the soul exists but is unconscious. If Lugioyo intends to suggest that the soul and the intermediate state were unimportant to the Patristics because they emphasized the body and the resurrection, then he commits the disjunctive fallacy, because they affirmed them all. True, the Creeds do not mention the soul or the intermediate state. But this silence is not an argument for insignificance. The Creeds don't mention hell either, and no one doubts its doctrinal standing. Nothing in this section undermines my summary of ecumenical anthropology and its modern competitors.

Lugioyo judges my treatment of Genesis 2:7 to be "sloppy." Even if it is, I claim that this text is not decisive for dualism or monism, and I do not base my anthropology on it. My position, following historic Christianity, rests heavily on Scripture's teaching that we exist between death and resurrection. With most current scholarship, I argue that the few Old Testament references to the resurrection and the dead in *sheol* were elaborated during Second Temple Judaism by the Pharisees and rabbis into a robust "two-stage" view of the afterlife. This eschatological framework was appropriated by Jesus and Paul in the New Testament. I will not repeat the exegesis. But if the relevant texts say what the vast majority of Christians have taken them to mean, then persons do exist apart from their earthly bodies, and some kind of dualism is entailed.

I find Lugioyo's response to be "sloppy." His quote from Badham about *sheol* actually confirms my position, which is post-mortem existence, not the immortality of the soul. The dead are "shades . . . in a silent, dark, deathly existence." Pedersen and most Old Testament scholars share this view of *sheol,* so they do not support monism as claimed. Mere subsistence entails dualism—Samuel and David are body-shaped ghosts without flesh, blood, and bones. With respect to the New Testament, Lugioyo diverts attention to Paul's philosophical background and completely avoids dealing with the classical texts for the intermediate state—Jesus' passage from death to resurrection, Paul's anticipation of absence from the body and presence with the Lord, and his identification with the eschatology and anthropology of the Pharisees. My paper even acknowledges monist attempts to account for the intermediate state. But Lugioyo provides no monistic exegesis or eschatology. Nothing in this section weakens my argument.

Concerning anthropology and praxis, let me explain why holistic dualism—without Lugioyo's caricatures—is a more solid basis for Christian life and ministry.

One caricature is dualism's alleged complicity with sexism and racism. There is no significant connection among monism, dualism, sexism, and racism. Lamentably, some dualists have claimed that their souls are superior to others. But many more have challenged sexism and racism because all human souls equally image God irrespective of physical differences. Is monism better?

If humans are bodies, then physical differences might have different values. The Nazis adopted Nietzsche's monism in support of their sexism and genocide. Does that implicate all kinds of monism? Lugioyo's insinuation poisons the well and imputes guilt by association.

A second caricature is his own "sweeping generalization"—the dreaded specter of "modern dualism" that has turned "much contemporary Christianity" toward "gnostic-like" spiritualism. I don't doubt that some Christians are introverted other-worldly dualists—maybe lots of them in circles familiar to Lugioyo, Brown, and Strawn. I've also heard rumors of the mythical Descartes, whose pernicious dualism has induced great masses of people to live as isolated, disembodied, apathetic egos. But I don't know of any significant modern Christian dualists who fit these descriptions. Does Calvin, Luther, Edwards, Wesley, Kuyper, Warfield, Billy Graham, Martin Luther King, Rick Warren, Dallas Willard, John Paul II, or Francis I? These leaders have promoted the whole Gospel, integral praxis, and holistic ministry. None thinks that "the central aspect of a person" is just "an ontological substance that survives death." "Modern dualism" is a straw man constructed to make monism look good by comparison.

A third caricature is Lugioyo's allegation that dualism is fatally flawed by a tendency to elevate the soul over the body—sooner or later, a difference leads to a separation. This claim is a non-sequitur that moves from *possible separation* to *a tendency to separate* to *almost inevitable separation*. It may be true for artifactual unions, such bricks and mortar or nuts and bolts. But it is not true of organic unity, such as bones and marrow or flesh and blood. Holistic dualists affirm the organic unity of body and soul. Furthermore, it is not always unbiblical to prioritize soul over body. Jesus recommends it (Matt. 10:28), and so does Paul (1 Tim. 4:8). If monism teaches that sex is as important as worship, or physical health is as valuable as spiritual health, then it is unbiblical. Not all good and necessary things are equally valuable or edifying. Finally, if it is fair to argue that dualism is genetically flawed, then monism deserves the same treatment. "Sauce for the goose . . ." It would be right to conclude that the conceptual DNA of non-reductive physicalism and emergent monism are inevitably reductionistic and deterministic. Likewise, if "modern dualism" is responsible for otherworldly Christianity, then "modern monism" is responsible for the worldliness of Christians and the "health and wealth gospel." No one in the monism-dualism debate should use such bad arguments.

I don't dispute that monism can be holistic. But it offers nothing to integral Christian praxis in personal life and mission in society and culture that faithful holistic dualists have not long practiced. What monists cannot self-consistently do is minister in some difficult circumstances. They cannot comfort the dying with the words of Jesus: "today you will be with me in Paradise." If they offer immediate resurrection, they contradict Scripture and either assume dualism—one person switching bodies—or posit two different body-persons. The only other option is non-existence until the resurrection. But that prospect will disappoint the vast majority of the faithful who anticipate being "absent from the body and present with the Lord" (2 Cor. 5:8). In the ethics of life and death, monism cannot regard early-stage embryos and the severely mentally impaired as persons because persons are defined in terms of higher brain functions. In ministry to physically handicapped, paralyzed, and sexually disoriented people, monists cannot help them distinguish themselves from their bodies. Clearly, denying the soul to promote integral Christian praxis gains nothing and undermines some crucial kinds of ministry.

Professor Lugioyo's reply reinforces my conviction that Christian holistic dualism is more faithful to Scripture and more reasonable than monism, especially the physicalism that he endorses. I hope that our exchange promotes mutual understanding of the monism-dualism debate so that it is not just a shouting match between different interpretations.

Contributors

Editors

THOMAS M. CRISP, Professor of Philosophy, Biola University

STEVEN L. PORTER, Professor of Theology and Philosophy, Talbot School of Theology and Rosemead School of Psychology

GREGG A. TEN ELSHOF, Professor of Philosophy, Biola University

Essayists

ROBIN COLLINS, Distinguished Professor of Philosophy, Messiah College

JOHN W. COOPER, Professor of Philosophical Theology, Calvin Theological Seminary

KEVIN CORCORAN, Professor of Philosophy, Calvin College

STEWART GOETZ, Professor of Philosophy, Ursinus College

WILLIAM HASKER, Emeritus Professor of Philosophy, Huntington University

VELI-MATTI KÄRKKÄINEN, Professor of Systematic Theology, Fuller Theological Seminary

ERIC LAROCK, Associate Professor of Philosophy, Oakland University

BRIAN LUGIOYO, Associate Professor of Theology and Ethics, Azusa Pacific University

J.P. Moreland, Distinguished Professor of Philosophy, Biola University

Timothy O'Connor, Professor of Philosophy, Indiana University

Jason D. Runyan, Associate Professor of Neuropsychology, Indiana Wesleyan University

Kevin Sharpe, Chairperson and Associate Professor of Philosophy, St. Cloud State University

Daniel Speak, Professor of Philosophy, Loyola Marymount University

Richard Swinburne, Emeritus Nolloth Professor of the Philosophy of the Christian Religion, Oxford University

Index